ZERO
REGRETS

ZERO REGRETS

BE GREATER THAN YESTERDAY

APOLO OHNO

WITH ALAN ABRAHAMSON

ATRIA BOOKS

NEW YORK LONDON TORONTO SYDNEY

ATRIA BOOKS

A Division of Simon & Schuster, Inc.
1230 Avenue of the Americas
New York, NY 10020

First Atria Books hardcover edition October 2010

ATRIA BOOKS and colophon are trademarks of Simon & Schuster, Inc.

For information about special discounts for bulk purchases, please contact
Simon & Schuster Special Sales at 1-866-506-1949 or business@simonandschuster.com.

The Simon & Schuster Speakers Bureau can bring authors to your live event.
For more information or to book an event contact the Simon & Schuster Speakers
Bureau at 1-866-248-3049 or visit our website at www.simonspeakers.com.

Note: Apolo Ohno used the training methods mentioned in this book under very careful,
intensive professional supervision.

Manufactured in the United States of America

10 9 8 7 6 5 4 3 2 1

Library of Congress Cataloging-in-Publication Data is available upon request.

ISBN 978-1-4516-0906-6
ISBN 978-1-4516-0908-0 (ebook)

To my father, Yuki.
My hero, best friend, coach, mentor, Dad.

PROLOGUE: TOWARD A EUPHORIC CLARITY

I am my father's son.

Because that is so, I am also very much my own man. My path in life is my own.

But it is because of my dad, Yuki, that I could find my way in the first instance and keep going at those moments when I faltered. And thus it is not the successes I have had—on and off the ice, at the Olympic Games and beyond—that I most appreciate.

It is the journey.

A journey I have undertaken in concert, if not always in perfect harmony, with my father and with the many others who have helped shape and guide me; a journey I have undertaken carrying this in my heart and my soul:

Zero regrets.

The late, great basketball coach John Wooden used to say, "Success is peace of mind which is a direct result of self-satisfaction in knowing you did your best to become the best you are capable of."

Zero regrets.

It's a philosophy not just about sport but also about life. School, business, academics, love—anything and everything.

Zero regrets.

Life is about making the most of it. While we can. Because we can.

It's complicated and yet not. You have to figure out who it is you want to be. Not what you want to be—who. There has to be a vision, a dream, a plan. Then you chase that with everything you've got. That means you have to put in the work, the practice, the training. There aren't any shortcuts. If you want something, you have to be 100 percent clear in how you plan to get it. You have to be relentless in your pursuit.

I didn't ever want to be complacent. I didn't want to think back about my day and think, *Yes, Apolo, that was good enough.* So this is what I would say to myself when I would lie down in bed at night: *Zero regrets.* I would think it, and I would even say it out loud to myself. This is what I would say to myself when I was hammering out miles on the treadmill: *No regrets.* Sometimes inside my head, sometimes out loud. This is what I would say when I was in the weight room: *Absolutely zero regrets.*

I knew to a certainty that if I pushed myself too hard on the treadmill, I would suffer the next day. Maybe I would be almost too tired on the ice. So I would say to myself, too: *Forget about tomorrow.* What if today were the last day of training you could be remembered for? What if this particular interval that I was doing on the treadmill right now—right now!—was the last one I would be remembered for? That's how I trained. That's how I approached it.

This path in the pursuit of victory within the Olympic Games was one that I took on occasion to the utmost extreme. This path was not mine alone; over the years, many people reached out and lent their expertise and their knowledge, eager to help me be my best. With a nod to such unbelievable support, I nonetheless decided to take a singular path in preparing for the 2010 Vancouver Games, one that was lonely, one that was hard, one that most would shy away from, one that came laden with unreal expectations. Simply put, I needed to keep myself in a bubble. I wanted to create a very simple environment in which only a few key people were around me most of the day and for weeks at a time. From this place, I was able to confront my insecurities. I could smile as I confronted fear, my confidence building in my ability to do what I was trying to accomplish.

In the past, I may have faltered, taken a misstep, taken a step back. For me, this time around, that was not an option. I was attempting to be stronger than I thought possible. Such strength did not come from my physical self; it started within the depths of my mind. That severe shift in your mental approach—the "shift of mechanism"—was so incredibly important in creating victory, regardless of whether I would end up standing on the podium or not. The path or road less traveled is often one that is filled with the most reward and joy. I lived—I live—for the moment.

When I am asked now to speak at businesses, when I speak to the chief executive officers of Fortune 500 companies, what's on the table is inspiration: how to get it, find it, keep it, to take that particular company to the next level. When I'm told, for instance, "We're looking to take our skill set to the next level," I like to say, "We all want something. Have you clearly outlined what it is? Do you have a clear understanding of how to direct your focus and get there?" It doesn't need to be a complete plan in every detail—but the more clear you are about exactly what you want and the better definition you have of what it's going to take to get to that point and beyond, the more likely those things are to come to fruition.

They say the more you think with particularity about things, the more you acknowledge the wanting of a specific thing, the more you articulate that out loud, then the more likely it is to come true. There is great truth in that. It takes a really clear understanding of how to reach a point and what it's going to take to get there.

Ultimately, you test yourself. It's race day. Or whatever the context: it's a test if you're at school, a big presentation if you're in the business world. Whatever that context, you put yourself to the test.

Winning does not always mean coming in first. Second or third, even fourth—they are wins, too, no matter what anyone says. Real victory is in arriving at the finish line with no regrets. You go all out. And then you accept the consequences.

That's what makes a champion—in sports, in business, in life, in your relationships with family and friends. You go with heart, with excitement and enthusiasm, with soul.

This is just some of what I have learned from my father—what he taught me and then what I have learned by and for myself. My father instilled in me passion, purpose, and pride. And, as well, dedication, discipline, and drive. I made those values mine. Along the way, I won eight Olympic medals. That makes me, they say, the most decorated American in Winter Games history.

———————

THAT HUMBLES ME.

It's especially humbling when you consider how it all started. My dad came to the United States with no money. He spoke no English. He had three cameras around his neck—one Canon and two Nikons—figuring that if times got really, really tough, he could sell them and have maybe enough money to eat. He made his way to Seattle. There he worked as a janitor, as a dishwasher. He thought he wanted to become an accountant and instead became a hairstylist. He raised me by himself. When I was young, he tried most of all just to keep me busy—swimming, singing, skating. Anything just to tire me out.

When I was eleven, we watched the 1994 Winter Olympics together on television. Those were the Olympics from Lillehammer, Norway, the Games most people remember for the Tonya-and-Nancy show. Not in our house. Short-track speed skating—now, that was cool. To me, the skaters looked like action superheroes.

I tried it. I liked it. My dad drove me around Seattle and the Pacific Northwest, to Vancouver. I got better. I got noticed. When I was just fourteen, I was invited to train with a junior national team developmental program all the way across the country in Lake Placid, New York. I didn't want to go. In fact, I didn't go. And then I did. Because my dad showed me what trust, what courage, and what love are all about. Here, he understood, was an extraordinary opportunity, and when opportunity like that comes around, you have to go for it.

Otherwise, what are you left looking at? Regret.

In Lake Placid, I got good—really good. It seemed like I was a lock for the 1998 Olympics. Except I bombed out. And then my dad showed me what it's like to have faith in someone. Genuine, profound, life-changing faith. Through one risky, extraordinary act, he gave me—and then I seized—a second chance.

This is how and where my journey really took off. From there, I have lived so much that has played out on the public stage—in three different Olympic Games, the chaotic silver and the gold that sparked so much controversy in Salt Lake City in 2002, the seemingly "perfect" race in Torino in 2006, the four-for-four medals count in Vancouver in 2010 that became three-for-four when I was disqualified in the 500-meter sprint just moments after it appeared I had won what would have been an eighth medal.

I have eight. That's short-track. No regrets.

In Salt Lake, for instance, coming around the final turn of the 1000 meters, it looked like the race was mine. I was ahead, sprinting for the finish line; here was my first Olympic medal, and it was going to be gold. But in a flash, that gold was gone, four of the five of us in the race down on the ice in what might be the most freakish short-track accident that has ever occurred or ever will occur. There was only one guy left upright, Steve Bradbury of Australia, who had been at least 30 meters behind the rest of the pack; while the rest of us were trying to pick ourselves up, he sailed through and across the line to win the gold medal.

Not for one second—not then, not now, and not ever—have I ever been anything but satisfied, completely satisfied, with that race and how it all turned out.

How is that possible? Because this race turned out just the way it obviously was supposed to happen. It didn't matter then and doesn't matter now that I might have been the fastest guy, the strongest guy, the best guy in that race. It didn't matter and doesn't matter that I got tripped up and that I went crashing into the pads on the side of the rink through no fault of my own. It wouldn't have solved anything to look around and wonder who had caused the crash and start playing the blame game.

The first thing to do was to get myself together and get across the line—to win silver.

I did that, got my blade across the line, won the silver medal.

The way I finished proves that nothing is ever over until it is, in fact, over. It turned out that I had sliced one of my thighs open in the crash. But it never occurred to me to do anything but get stitched up as fast as possible and get out to the podium so I could accept my silver medal with a genuine smile. The world was watching, kids especially were watching, and it is so important to handle yourself—no matter the situation—with class and with grace. It is more important to be a champion off the field than on; that's what resonates with me.

That night, and continuing over the years since, some people have said to me, "Do you feel bad you didn't win?" The answer, then and now, is no, I don't feel bad. I feel great. I went to the Winter Olympics; I represented my country, my team, and my family to the best of my ability. There were three medals, and I won one.

I won silver, and I was thrilled about it.

In thinking about this book, what I wanted it to be and what I wanted to express, I was clear that I did not—repeat, *not*—want it to be merely an autobiographical recount of those medals with a healthy dash of my winning turn on *Dancing with the Stars* thrown in for good measure. Nor did I want it to be about my personal life and, in particular, women I've dated or perhaps who wanted to date me.

I did not want to write a book out of some sense of self-indulgence, or perfectionism, or self-adoration. No. Instead, I simply wanted to make plain what I have learned along my path in the hope that my journey would encourage others to strive for what is needed, to reach for the unreachable, to recognize that everyone makes mistakes but the point is to bounce back stronger.

What I've accomplished, and how I got there—sure, those experiences matter.

But they matter not as evidence of what I have done. Instead, they matter as points of reference along the way, experiences that have helped mold and shape me on my personal journey to become who it is I am destined to be. They are signposts of obstacles encountered, challenges confronted, and lessons learned.

Every single one of us has a path to travel. Everything happens for a reason. This I believe. Not to sound preachy or religious, but I profoundly believe God has a plan for me.

I was blessed with certain gifts. Those gifts have put me in a position where I might inspire others I might touch along the way—and they, in turn, can help illuminate my path.

To those who thus might suggest that athletes, especially Olympic athletes, are not role models, I say: I see it differently. We all need something and someone to believe in. We need to work hard and dream big dreams and chase those dreams with abandon, with zero regrets.

CARRYING THE STRUGGLE

Nikos Kazantzakis, one of the greatest
Greek philosophers and writers of the twentieth
century, once offered a thought that
resonates so powerfully because it illuminates
an essential truth, not only about sports
but about life itself. He said:

"You should not ask if you will succeed or not.
That isn't what matters the most. The only thing
that matters is your struggle to carry it further.
God reckons that—the assault—to our account
and nothing else. Whether we win or lose is
His affair, not ours."

Indeed, we should not ask if we are going to
win or lose. That's not an answer we can know
beforehand. Instead, what if we frame the
question differently—to ask, what is our duty,
each of us, as an individual? The answer then
comes far more elegantly. It is, simply, to carry
the struggle forward—to do our very best in
everything and anything.

CHAPTER 1

I know almost nothing about my mother.

This is what I know: Her name is Jerrie Lee. She was adopted. She was several years younger than my dad when I was born. They split up when I was an infant.

That's pretty much it.

Because I was so young when my parents separated, I have no memories whatsoever of my mother. Zero. Not of her holding me. Not of her being there with me. Not of her kissing me. Nothing. It's a void, an empty space. Moreover, because my personality is the way it is—and, as well, I am who I am—I have no real desire to know her.

In Federal Way, Washington, the town near Seattle where I grew up, not many people had both a mother and a father. My situation, me and my dad, just seemed ordinary. I would go to friends' homes, where there were brothers and sisters, cousins and nephews, one parent, multiple grandparents—some combination. It was normal for me to have just a dad. I didn't think twice about it.

I admit to some bit of curiosity about her; I'm naturally interested in cultures and ethnicities, and yet I only know half my family. And my extended family is not at all big. There's my dad; his mom, who still lives in Japan; and his father, who passed away a few years ago.

Why, for instance, is my beard tinged red? Is it because of my mother's side?

My dad and I have talked about my mom only in bits and pieces. The only reason I even know what I do is because of a quick conversation he and I had several years ago.

I asked him, "What's my other half?"

He said, "I don't really know. I know your mom was adopted—but beyond that, I really don't know much."

I remember only a couple of photos of her, and those are pictures that were around when I was much younger.

One used to sit in my bedroom. It had been glued onto the side of one of those small wooden block cubes, maybe four inches by four inches. The picture showed her holding a baby me. It was clear in the picture that she was looking at me—but that's all that was clear, because her face was hidden in the shadows. I couldn't see her face. Pretty much all I could see is that she had long brown hair.

The other photo—again, you can't see her face. The picture was taken as sunset was coming, the sunlight hitting a window, and so there's not enough light in the picture to show her face. Besides, she was looking away.

That's it.

Those are my memories.

It's not weird and it's not selfish to say that I don't feel I have been shortchanged. My dad—he did it all.

————————

IT GIVES MY father great pleasure now when he is stopped wherever he—or we—go, and upon meeting him, someone says, "Thank you for raising Apolo."

My dad is an extraordinary man. He wants only the best for me. He leads by example on so many fronts. He is in some ways my best friend. He's my best teammate, my best coach, my top consultant. He's my biggest supporter and my biggest fan.

We work as a team. We are a team. It is incredible, actually—the whole story. Single dad raises Olympic medalist? And yet, because it's our story, because we have lived it together, it seems maybe as if it simply was meant to be.

Our story starts in Japan, where my dad was born and raised. His father's—my grandfather's—family had traditionally been farmers of some repute there. The family name, Ohno, breaks into two pieces, *Oh,* meaning "great," and *no* for "field." My grandmother's side, as we understand it, carries genuine samurai warrior blood in the line; her maiden name was Yasunaga.

When my father's father was a young man, he decided to get away from those fields. He went to Tokyo to study. He knew no one there—no family, no friends. What he had, however, was determination and belief in himself. Ultimately, my father's father—his name was Kokichi—would make his way all the way up to what is in Japan an important position indeed, vice president of a state university.

My father is the older of two brothers. As my grandfather was working his way up within the Japanese academy, my dad—like many an industrious, obedient, conforming Japanese son—was making good marks in school. It was made abundantly plain to my dad, and to everyone around him—his parents, his teachers, and his friends—that the path to success for a good Japanese boy held a most distinct outline: good grades in elementary school, good grades in middle school, good grades in high school, good grades in the university examinations, good grades in college itself—and then a job and job security for life.

The competition, as my dad remembers it, was just crazed, with every single kid in every single family cramming for whatever test was coming up next and then, as soon as that exam was over, cramming for the next one. A typical day would revolve around school, of course, but that was just the start, because then there was what you had to learn after school to get ready for some next batch of exams. By the time my dad was in middle school, in Iwate, a northern Japanese prefecture where my grandfather was working at the time, my dad was already thinking, *What is this all about? Why am I doing this?*

Dinner? There was time to eat?

Sleep? Who had time for sleep? My dad slept maybe five hours per night just to get ready for the entrance exam for high school.

Which, of course, he passed—only to end up essentially alone. My grandfather, who would be transferred between different prefectures every three to five years, got moved, but my dad, who had gotten into a school of the sort that sent its graduates to the top Japanese universities, wasn't about to go anywhere but right there. So there he was: fourteen, and fending for himself. He felt alone, and no wonder. He was living in a house that was not quite a dorm, not quite a boardinghouse, forced to make do in an environment in which most of the young men around him were typically older, many already in college.

He could handle that.

But this was what he could not deal with: in school, he would look around, and what did he see? Very little evidence anywhere of any sort of passion.

There seemed to be strangely little emotion of any kind around him in his school routine. Every day of class seemed just one more step on the march toward the all-consuming entrance exam for the Japanese version of an Ivy League–style university. Everyone around him seemed locked into what life had seemingly ordained.

My father, though, was not about to resign himself to anything.

If the Japanese establishment seemed to be programming its people a certain way—well, no system was going to force him into it or, for that matter, into anything. He began to feel bored, and then impatient, and then increasingly restless. *You know,* he finally thought to himself,

I ought to get out of Japan. Make my own personal exodus. Embark upon my own individual journey. I will, he vowed, *go to school. Just not this kind of school, in this kind of environment.*

Where to go?

Here was the entire world before him.

Here, near, was the Pacific Ocean, lapping at Japan. There, far, all the way over on the other side of the Pacific, the United States.

There.

My dad finished high school in Japan. And then he left, to find a new life.

————————

TO SAY THAT my grandparents were disappointed in my dad's choice would be an understatement. Their oldest son was doing—what? And going—where? To a country with which they had no meaningful connection of any sort?

To say that my dad thoroughly underestimated the challenge that lay ahead of him would also be putting it gently. He had no friends in the United States. He had no family. What if he got sick? What if something dumb happened? What if there were a horrible accident? What then?

"You're only eighteen," he was told. "Who are you kidding?"

My dad's response: "I'm going."

His response to the several objections that were raised, some of them exceedingly rational and commonsense: "Who cares?"

My dad was daring. He was resourceful. He had utter confidence in himself that somehow he would figure it out. Plus, his mind was made up, and once his mind was made up, there was no second-guessing. There was no room and no time to be scared or to entertain even a sliver of doubt. "I'll manage," he told his parents.

My dad's first stop in the United States, cameras around his neck: Portland, Oregon. He spoke almost no English.

Once in Portland, he decided he wanted to go to Seattle. The problem was, his English was so lame he couldn't even say "Seattle." He would say something like "Sheetle." He would ask for directions, and everyone would get all pensive and say, "What?" At the same time, my dad likes to say, there was a major difference between what he was expecting and what he was now finding in the United States. The protocol he had been used to in Japan, especially in public, of being appropriate, indeed proper—an entire world of rules and regulations that dictated who talked to whom and the ways certain people could talk to others who might occupy a different station in life—none of that seemed to matter on this side of the Pacific, even if you pronounced the name of the city "Sheetle." American culture was entirely different, and for the most part, the Americans he was meeting were incredibly down-to-earth folks, not only polite but also glad to try to help. It didn't matter if they didn't understand exactly what he was saying. Somehow they understood.

My dad set about learning English—not only to survive but also as a gesture of respect. While he was learning the language, he worked at any job he could get; he was a janitor, a busboy, a dishwasher, a newspaper deliveryman, you name it.

Nothing was beneath him.

Hard work was not, in any way, beneath him, either.

Yuki Ohno, janitor, reporting for the graveyard shift.

The overnight shifts are long gone, but still Dad gets up every day at three-thirty in the morning. Don't ask what you can do between three-thirty and six, when the sun is starting to peek over the horizon and stores start to open. But he's up. Every morning. No alarm. He just gets up. Dad has always been disciplined in this manner. His whole life, he has been a ridiculously hard worker. So even as he was washing floors and doing whatever else he needed to do to survive, he was also saying, "I have to go to school." All those graveyard shifts reinforced the essential notion that the way to a better job was, in fact, through school. Plus, he was smart; he wanted the intellectual challenge.

An accountant, Dad thought. *I'll become an accountant, a CPA.*

To this day, Dad has no idea why he thought he wanted to be an accountant. But that's what he thought, and here he learned another lesson: It is okay to try something and not have it work out, as long as you give it your all. There could be no shame in saying, "That's not for me," as long as you could say when you walked away from whatever it was, "I gave it everything I had."

Which is what happened as my dad encountered the intricacies of accounting. He thought one day, *I am just not cut out for this sort of numerical analysis, at least as a career. So now what?*

There was no time for feeling *woe is me,* no wallowing in self-doubt. Life favors those who make decisions and who take action—who do something. Even if whatever that is wouldn't seem to be the first thing on the obvious radar, given one's upbringing and experiences.

Like . . . being a hairstylist.

My father, in a pivot of quiet bravery, allowed himself to try something entirely new. He gave himself permission to make a 180-degree tack, to explore a different side of his personality, his artistic self. Mind you, this was not out of desperation. He had little money, but he was not driven by poverty. Instead, he was on a quest to find out who he truly was, what gifts in life he had been given, and how he could find fulfillment in expressing those gifts.

What Dad had discovered among the nerdy would-be accountants was that while numbers didn't do much for him, being around people did. And where did you find all kinds of people from every walk of life? At a hair salon.

Dad enrolled in cosmetology classes at Central Seattle Community College. This, it turned out, was his calling. Within a year, he won a haircutting contest, and this made for another moment of self-awakening. He was not only artistic, he was competitive.

In the early 1970s, Seattle had its own distinct fashion sense and style. Polyester, as my dad remembers, was everywhere. It seemed as if hardly anyone dressed up. If you were out for a night at the opera or a fine meal, even if you were wealthy, everyone was styling some serious polyester.

It was, after all, the 1970s.

So here came the anticoiffeur movement—the trend in hair very much a statement that represented a significant break with curlers and dryers, with the teased and set looks that had come before and had made a very different sort of statement. The trend now was to look as if you had spent no time affecting just the right look: to jump in the shower, towel your hair dry, shake it just so, and be ready to go. The secret to that trick: such a cut required extraordinary precision, because the cut itself gave the style its shape. This was a style that was simultaneously organic and geometric. It was both daring and obviously the product of undeniable artistry. It was practical and yet expressive. It was all of that, all at the same time, and for my dad, it was a revelation. He thought, *I've got to learn how to cut hair just like that.*

Vidal Sassoon was just then exploding onto the American scene. He was handsome and dashing, so debonair that he had a few years before married the actress Beverly Adams; she had played Cassandra in the movie *How to Stuff a Wild Bikini.* She'd also filled the recurring role of Lovey Kravezit in a series of Dean Martin movies. Dad went to London to study at one of the Sassoon schools.

When he came back to Seattle, suddenly Dad was a hot number. Everyone wanted him. He worked long hours; in addition to his work as a stylist, he did a lot of teaching and training. Make no mistake—Dad was big-time. Fashion shows. Catwalks. Travel to Europe. He was hanging with the beautiful people, and he helped make them even more beautiful.

How did all this happen? He was good, of course. But mostly, he was passionate about what he was doing. Everything else flowed from that.

With a partner, Dad opened his first shop. The décor included a rubber tree, with branches covering the walls and the ceiling—kind of a jungle theme, mixed with a marine effect thanks to an enormous chain the landlord hung from the wall, down which water trickled along the links.

It was its own distinct world, and Dad was at the center of it. In the store, an assistant would wash a client's hair; Dad, dressed in a suit—a suit!—would do the cutting; an assistant would then finish up with the blow-dry. It was frenetic and fun. In the evenings, of course, there might be more fun—parties of all sorts. It was, after all, the 1970s.

———————

I ARRIVED IN May 1982.

In those days, babies and new moms stayed in the hospital for two or three days. Even so, that wasn't enough time for me to get a name. When we left the hospital and went home, I was still solely Baby Ohno.

It's not that my dad hadn't been busy trying to decide what name to bestow upon me. He had been working at it with diligence. He had gone through all sorts of baby-naming books, but nothing jumped out at him. He had even started flipping through the dictionary. Still nothing.

As he was searching, it somehow came to him; even now, he still doesn't know how he put it all together. The *Ap,* as he tells it, is rooted in ancient Greek and means "steering away from." The *lo* means "look out, here he comes." The *o* in the middle serves as a bridge between the first and second parts.

Obviously, my father had big dreams for his very little boy. As I got older, as I grew to be a man, his hope was that I would literally fulfill the destiny he could foresee for me, that I would prove to be a leader and so much more, someone who would inspire those I touched to reach for their better selves.

Apolo: look out, here he comes, and there he goes—there. And all of you—you'll want to follow him.

That is what Dad not only wanted for me but also what he saw for me when I was just several days old.

To be clear: it's Apolo with one *l*. The name was designed to be unique. It's not "Apollo" with the double *l*, one of the most important Olympian deities, the god of light, sun, archery, music, poetry, and more. Nor, despite the fact that the Apollo missions were flying to the moon in my dad's first years in the United States, is it a takeoff on those spaceships.

One *l*. Apolo.

On top of which, Anton, my middle name, means "priceless."

My initials, A.A.O., deliberately evoked a Japanese expression that is more or less pronounced "ei-ei-oh," an ancient battle cry that soldiers would shout three times in a row to get amped up—a Japanese version of "rah, rah, rah!"

As for "priceless"—that's what it was when it dawned on Dad that, though he might be able to cut hair in his stylish suits, it was an entirely different thing to change diapers. The suits gave way quickly to more sensible clothes as he and my mom went their separate ways and he became completely and thoroughly responsible for me. All the parties that he used to be invited to—he wasn't hanging out with his guy friends at those parties anymore, either.

He was lonely. And, needless to say, terrified.

As a man, he had little confidence at first in his ability to assume the role of both parents. Biologically, he was, of course, not in the least bit female. Moreover, as the older son in a family of two boys, he had absorbed none of the thousands of quiet ways that a girl might learn from her mother how to be a mom herself one day.

Every time Dad would drop me off at a babysitter's or at some child-care facility, he worried. Was the facility reliable? Who was doing the actual sitting: a competent person or the television? Was the place clean—or at least clean enough?

I just don't know if I can continue, Dad would sometimes think to himself as he would drop me off. Every parent knows how wearying it can be, especially the very early years. Moreover, there was no question that he simply needed to keep making money to support the two of us; if someone wanted or needed a cut on a Saturday, he then needed to find someplace for me.

It's all just too scary, Dad would think. *This is a constant challenge.* Are we going to make it? Really?

There were times when his car was broken. He would take the bus to work, and that would be nearly an hour each way. And then he would have to arrange to come get me late, and then when he'd pick me up late, we'd go home, and it was so late and he would be so tired.

Are we going to make it? Really?

At the same time, with each passing day, each week, each month, his confidence grew. Of course, being a dad was the most challenging thing he had ever done, way more demanding even than showing up in a new country. But he never wavered. He had made up his mind that we were in this together, and once my father makes up his mind, that's that.

One very good thing about being a hairdresser: nearly all his clients were female. As soon as he started opening up to all these women about the situation, they would suggest this answer or that option. By simply acknowledging his fears and opening up about them, he suddenly had all this willing support.

As time passed, Dad came to understand another fundamental truth: if you stick with something and you keep doing it, you build more and more confidence. He also found he had within him an enormous well of empathy. Here were all these single moms in the same sort of boat he was, raising a child—or children—without the teamwork of being in a partnership. And thus, with each success, no matter how minor, he understood the wholly fulfilling joy that comes with raising a child. That kept him, and us, going.

Especially in those uh-oh moments, of which there were many, because I was an especially energetic and strong-willed little boy. Mostly, I remember running around like crazy and being as active as possible. This is the kind of kid I was: In Montessori school, when I was maybe three, I refused to come inside from recess in the middle of a driving rain. I climbed to the top of the monkey bars and sat there, arms crossed, refusing to come down. Why would I come down? I was King of the Hill. The teachers called my dad. He had to come to the school to coax me off my throne.

When I was five, Dad bought me a bicycle and a set of training wheels. He took the bike out of the trunk of the car and put it on the sidewalk; he turned away for just a moment to grab the training wheels, intending to attach them to the frame. Just that fast, I grabbed the bike, launched myself onto the seat, and took off—my first time on the bike. It wasn't elegant—I wobbled. But I did not fall.

I quickly learned about hills. On a bicycle, you could go fast downhill. It was exhilarating—once you learned how to control the bike, it seemed like you were flying.

Pretty soon, I was riding the bike everywhere. Or I was climbing trees. Or swimming; Dad enrolled me in swim school when I was six. Or skating; he took me to a local roller-skating rink on Thursdays starting when I was seven. Even singing; he put me in the local choir. Until my voice changed, I had a three-octave range. In school, he enrolled me in a program for gifted students.

This was the plan: keep Apolo busy. It ought to keep me out of trouble, Dad thought.

FOR A GOOD, long while—more or less until I was in middle school—Dad's plan worked just fine.

He worked. I went to school, did all those extracurricular things, and, along the way, turned into the classic latchkey kid. I learned how to cook—spaghetti, lasagna, chicken, burgers—and how to take care of myself. Dad and I even worked out how I should answer the door at our town house if a stranger showed up; we had a thorough emergency-procedure plan. By age eight or nine, I already saw myself as independent in the extreme—except for the one time I was alone at home watching some monster movie and got so freaked out I had to call Dad. The monster—I can still remember—had a huge vein pulsating in his forehead; it looked like his head was going to explode.

Dial, dial. Ring, ring.

"When," I demanded, "are you coming home?"

"What," Dad asked, "are you talking about?"

Dad typically worked six days a week. Sunday was our day together. No babysitters. Nobody but us two. Many, many times we would leave the house on Saturday evening and drive to what became our place along the Pacific shoreline in western Washington; we would spend Sunday there, turning around late, getting home in time for Dad to put me to bed so I could get up in the morning and get to school. It's where we would spend holidays and summer breaks, too: the Iron Springs Resort, in a little town called Copalis Beach.

If by "resort," they meant "luxury"—no. The cottages there were simple units with a kitchen, a living room, a bedroom or two, all with spectacular views. If by "resort," they meant "secluded"—for sure. Iron Springs is isolated to begin with; it's a long way from anywhere. Sometimes when we were there, it would seem as if no one else could possibly be around. The world in front of us was gray sand and the churning gray sea; around us, green forest and mountain streams.

One summer when we were there, it rained—a warm rain, gentle, as if it were Hawaii, not the Olympic Peninsula of Washington State. We were both drenched, soaked to the skin. Abruptly, the sky cleared; it was not just sunny, it was glorious. We found a piece of driftwood and ate the lunch Dad had packed. No one—and I mean no other person— was near. It was just us and gulls and bugs and sandpipers. We could hear the roar of the ocean, in and out. The wind shifted, and the salt air suddenly carried the sweet smell of wild strawberries. We found the berries and sampled them—delicious.

At Iron Springs, we would follow paths without knowing where they would lead. We used to hike up streams bathed in steam, the sun warming the shallow water. This was just my father and me, in wild and open nature, in all the seasons—winter, spring, summer, fall.

We would come home from those trips, and I would hold a seashell to my ear, and Dad would say, "Apolo, the ocean is calling you. Do you hear it?"

I did not hear anything like the ocean at the swimming pool when I was swimming lap after lap. But I nonetheless got to be a pretty good swimmer. When I was twelve, I was a state champion in the 100-meter breaststroke. I held club records in the breaststroke and the back-stroke. Dad dreamed of me going to Stanford University.

But I didn't really like swimming. Swimming is very, very difficult. I swam mostly to make Dad happy.

Skating—now that was different.

The moment I saw in-line skates—four wheels in a straight line, not the two-and-two of a quad skate—I wanted a pair. On in-line skates, you could really go fast. I quickly became not only very good but more, an age-group national champion and record holder.

I also acquired the nickname that would stick with me for years: Chunky.

It came about this way: At in-line practice, one of the other kids appointed himself chief nickname giver. He decided to call one kid

Chuck; the kid's real name was not Chuck. Chuck? Why Chuck? Who knows?

The nickname giver named another kid Worm. A third Miggy. Me—Chunky, which itself was short for Chunky A, the A for Apolo. Why Chunky? Because I ate like a horse. So Chunky I was, and Chunky I would be, and Chunky I still am to some old in-line friends, even a few short-trackers.

Though they hardly make the sports pages in your daily newspaper, they hold in-line competitions everywhere—Florida, North Carolina, Nebraska. We didn't fly. Typically, Dad drove us there, in a brown diesel Volkswagen Rabbit. He hated that car; to this day, he still hates it. It would overheat and then overheat some more.

I hated it, too; one day, I was sure, I would find myself in a car I would appreciate. This was not a vehicle to appreciate.

The nationals usually were held in Lincoln, Nebraska. On our way there once, in the middle of the Rocky Mountains, we got caught in a vicious blizzard. The snow was so intense you couldn't read the green directional signs by the interstate. We kept going because—what else were we going to do? End up in a ditch, maybe.

When, inevitably, we slid into the ditch, the snow was so deep and cushionlike it didn't feel like we were hitting anything. We just slid and then bounced like a ping-pong ball.

And then we were stuck.

I had fallen asleep in the back of the Rabbit. Up front, Dad worked to free the car. He tried rocking the car back and forth. That got us more stuck. A guy stopped and came up to the Rabbit; he tried to push it out; no go. The guy said the highway was going to be shut down but not to worry—he would call a tow truck. And then he left.

Dad had zero faith that a tow truck was going to come rescue us. It was him and me; we had gotten ourselves into the situation, and now we just had to keep working at it to get out. Back and forth he rocked, back and forth, back and forth—until finally the tires caught and we slid out onto the highway, backward.

The interstate was, in fact, closed. So we ended up taking back roads all the way from Denver to Lincoln, arriving at two or three in the morning. I was coughing. Dad was coughing. Along the way, we had seen a motel but had decided not to stay there to make sure I got to the race on time—which I did. Of course, I was so tired I didn't do well. But I remember still the excitement of the racing there and how I used to get so nervous. The "heat box"—a holding pen of sorts, where skaters wait for their races to be called—was little more than a bunch of chairs in the middle of the skate rings; I remember vividly sitting in those chairs and being so anxious. My stomach would flutter, and I felt for sure like I was going to throw up. My head was pounding. Emotionally, I was just going crazy. And then they'd call the race, and I felt instant relief.

At the line, I felt both calm and exhilarated simultaneously. It was great, the racing itself—pushing myself, trying to be the best.

PASSION

———

Passion is caring for something, loving something, dedicating a portion of yourself, your mind, your heart, and your soul—because you're passionate about it.

Passion is the spark for everything. By itself, passion is never enough. Just like talent is never enough. But it's your fire starter.

Without passion, you won't do something 100 percent. That's the bottom line.

And what's the point of doing something if you're not doing it 100 percent?

CHAPTER 2

Many still remember the Winter Olympics in 1994 for one of two very different things.

Those Games took place in Norway, in the hamlet of Lillehammer. Everyone who was there says they almost seemed like something out of a fairy tale, with athletes and fans happily mingling together at night on the main street of the little town.

Most of America remembers it for Tonya and Nancy—the on-the-ice climax to the long-running drama involving figure skaters Tonya Harding and Nancy Kerrigan. Tonya was from Portland, Oregon, just down the road from Seattle. But in the Ohno home, she and Nancy were bit players. These were the Games at which I first saw short-track speed skating.

It was like nothing I had ever seen before.

The track was short. The ice was slippery. The racers wore tight-fitting competition suits that made them look like superheroes. These guys leaned over at these impossible angles with what looked like blades or knives on their feet. They powered around in packs at speeds that reached 35 miles per hour. They crashed with some regularity. Sometimes the crashes were spectacular.

Short-track, as it turned out, was still relatively new that year to the Olympics. It had been a demonstration sport in 1988 at the Calgary Winter Games. It had formally become a medal sport for the first time in 1992 at the Games in Albertville, France.

Short-track started in Europe more than one hundred years ago. As early as 1906, skaters in the United States knew about it, and in the 1920s, crowds would pack Madison Square Garden to see it. For years and years, Canadians and Americans dominated the sport; then it caught on in the Far East, especially in China, Japan, and South Korea.

Pack-style speed skating had been seen before in the Winter Olympics, in 1932, when the Games were held in Lake Placid. Those races were held on the 400-meter oval that was then and is still today the norm for so-called long-track racing. That, though, was a one-off. In long-track, which has been part of the Olympic program since 1924, skaters race in pairs against the clock. The fastest time, in whatever pairing produces it, wins.

In short-track, you win by crossing the finish line first, no matter the time. You race four to six to a pack. Elimination heats lead to semifinals and finals. The track, set in a hockey-style rink, is only 111.12 meters around; the course is marked by rubber blocks in the corners. You're allowed to skate into the "infield," but you have to come back outside to go around the blocks. You're allowed to touch the ice with your hands.

In long-track, though you're paired with another athlete, you're essentially racing against the clock. That is, you're racing against yourself. There's nobody trying to pass you. There's nobody bumping you. There's nobody blocking you, pushing you, getting in your way. In short-track, you could race up to six other guys on the ice at the same time. You have to position yourself during the race at the right times. You hesitate, and you can go just that fast from first to last.

There's such a premium in short-track on strategy and on the mental game. In the longer events, for instance, the action starts off slow and picks up speed later, the jockeying early on aimed at staying behind. If that seems counterintuitive, it's also just plain smart. Being in front brings with it wind resistance, and dealing early in a long race with that resistance burns up energy you might well need on the final laps.

In short-track you need both endurance and speed, even if you're not taking part in the longer races. You have to advance through heats, quarterfinals, and semifinals just to get in position to win; that takes staying power.

"That," I said, watching the pack night after night on TV, "looks so cool."

Dad said, "Well, maybe then you ought to try it."

Three weeks later, I was on the ice. Just having fun.

I started at a public skate in Spanaway, Washington, near Olympia, at a rink being used by a short-track club. There was no coach there that day. Nothing of the sort.

Another early effort was at a rink in some industrial area around Seattle—I can't even remember where. Because crashes are so common in short-track, it's imperative that the boards marking the side of the rink be covered with protective padding; here the boards amounted to mattresses, and those mattresses covered maybe 20 percent—at most—of the boards. A couple of guys smashed into the boards that day; they quit right then and there.

I knew almost nothing about what I was doing or how I ought to be doing it. I only knew it was fun. You know the feeling of being on a roller coaster when you get whipped around? It was a little like that, except that you are controlling the speed and you're on one leg.

Fun.

From Federal Way down Interstate 5 to Eugene, Oregon, is about a five-hour drive. There was a short-track club there, and so Dad drove us down. I laced up my skates, excited because I had just gotten new blades. I stepped out onto the ice and pushed off, expecting to glide away—except there was no glide. What? All the other skaters on the ice were zipping by, their skates making a *whoosh-whoosh-whoosh* sound as they glided around, and I was mostly just pushing and sweating, confused and embarrassed. In the stands, Dad looked puzzled.

Another skater saw what was going on and stopped. He said, "You have to sharpen your skates."

"What? What do you mean?"

"When they're new," he said, "the edges are serrated. You sharpen them until the ridges are gone so you can glide."

"Oh."

Obviously, I knew next to nothing about my equipment.

Skate blades come in different lengths, I would learn, generally twelve to eighteen inches; as a general rule, the longer the blade is, the faster it is. Much later, my blades would run seventeen and a half inches long. Each blade is exquisitely sharp. It's interesting to compare a short-track blade with a hockey blade. The hockey blade has a built-in hollow; a short-track blade is flat, and you sharpen it with, naturally enough, a flat stone. When the blade is sharp, you can run your hand along it, and it feels like a knife—just a little thicker.

In short-track, you get to your outside edge for a second, if that, and then only in the straightaway. The turns are all inner edges; most short-trackers are on what's logically called the inner edge. Technically speaking, that means the blade has to have other certain, very specific, characteristics.

Think of the way the top of a knife runs straight, while the bottom holds a curve. It's much the same for a short-track blade. The arc at the bottom determines how much metal is actually in contact with the ice. If it's more rounded—the way a hockey skate is rounded—the blade is easier to turn; at the same time, you're always pushing because you don't feel you can glide. A flatter blade makes you feel like you're gliding strong; at the same time, it's harder to turn.

Now for another dimension: a short-track blade is bent. When you buy a blade, it's straight. It then has to be bent in an arc that mirrors the direction of the turn. That helps the metal grip the ice around turns. In the same way that the arc on the bottom of the blade is a sensitive thing, so, too, is the bend. Too much, and it seems like you're sticky because it feels like all the blade is on the ice, carving away. Not enough, and you get skaters saying, "I can't turn."

One other important feature about a short-track blade: it's placed off-center so that the left of the boot doesn't touch the ice when a skater leans into the turn.

A short-track boot laces higher up the ankle. Good ones are made from customized foot molds and with materials that are heavy enough to stabilize the foot and ankle around corners. Helmets are essential in short-track; knee, shin, and neck guards can be helpful. A skin suit that fits the body can reduce wind resistance. Needless to say, you need gloves for the ice but also to protect your hands from other blades. That's especially important when you're going around a curve, when your hand can go down on the ice to help maintain balance.

A world-class short-tracker can develop an intuitive feel for all that equipment. The boots: you lace them up and you do or you just don't like the way they feel, even if you can't quite say why that's so. The blades: you take that first push across the ice, and you immediately recognize that something's not quite right. It's not the boots, it's the blade. Or you take that first push, and it feels amazing. You can't say why that is, either; it just is the way it is.

That day in Eugene, I was the farthest thing from world class. I had no feel. But at least I knew, after I was told, to sharpen my blades. So I did, and that same day I raced. I still remember one of the others I skated against: a pretty girl, with a blond ponytail, a little older than me.

She would go by me, her hair blowing behind her; she might even have lapped me.

I might be a national in-line champion, but in short-track, I obviously was not very good.

Yet.

Dad and I started to drive up to Vancouver, just across the border in British Columbia. Short-track was a much bigger deal then in Canada than in the United States; there were any number of strong skaters in Vancouver I could watch and learn from, and there were more frequent competitions. Besides, it was for sure a shorter drive than to Eugene.

I loved everything about learning to skate and race in Vancouver. I was twelve, thirteen years old. I would learn from the Canadians, mimic them, take the feeling I saw on the ice and try to make that me. Really, I just loved it. The cool angles. The speed. The Canadians seemed like superhuman cartoon characters whipping around the ice. The whole thing looked fake. The power, strength, explosiveness, and strategy these guys were laying over: it just didn't look real.

And just the overall insanity of the thing, when you thought about it. It was unlike anything I had ever encountered.

While I was on the ice, Dad sat in the stands with his video camera, taping everything. He had taped swim meets for years, so this was natural for him. When we'd get back home, I'd watch the tapes, see what I was doing wrong and sometimes even right, watch the others—Bryce Holbech, Andrew Quinn, Philippe Tremblay, and the other Canadian boys would get down—and learn.

I started picking it up quickly. My skating began to feel smooth. And quiet. And fast.

As things went along, I became good friends with a lot of the Vancouver people. They were so welcoming, and I became known as "the kid from the States." I still had from my swim days one of those oversized swim coats; mine was red, white, and blue and was emblazoned with the words "Highline Swim Club." That was the coat I would wear in the heat box.

The Canadians gave me a lot of love, and in turn, I fell in love with Vancouver: the diversity of the people I would see on the streets, the food, even the weather. A lot like Seattle but just a little bit different. It seemed so far away and so close. It made for a departure, an escape from my normal life in Seattle. I could be somebody else, a different person, somebody whom nobody in my neighborhood back home knew. In Vancouver, I was just that kid from the States.

Back home, they didn't know me as a skater. I was just one of the homies.

————————

MAYBE SOME OF my friends back home had an inkling I was doing something. But they truly had no idea just what and genuinely did not care.

In-line, short-track, whatever.

Looking back, it's so abundantly clear now what an at-risk kid I was then. It's why, now, I seek out middle school audiences, as a way to give back, with me as Example A of how you can become who you want to be.

Dad's plan all along had been to jam my days with so much school, so many sports, so many activities that I'd be too tired to be tempted to do anything stupid. Unfortunately, that plan failed to take into account all that is adolescence. Or the strong will that was so keenly a part of me by fourteen, just as it was for my father when he was fourteen, and for his father before him.

The notion that I would get from Federal Way to Stanford? It started with such promise.

In grade school, I was put into a gifted-student program. My vocabulary was spectacular, in part because I had a superhigh reading level—I read at a twelfth-grade level when I was just in second grade—

and I had taken a speed-reading class, so I read voraciously. In this gifted-student program, we were challenged in ways that even now seem incredible. In third grade, for instance, we not only followed the stock market—we followed stock cycles and the periodization of stock market flux. Hedge fund manager? Financial analyst? High-powered lawyer or executive? Why not?

Academically, I was so ahead of the curve that, as I went along, I used to tutor kids much older than me, particularly in math and algebra and then geometry. Also, I could—when I wanted—focus with a laserlike intensity on whatever the subject might be. I can, I would learn when I got older, bring a focus with my eyes to a subject—any subject—that's maybe three times as detailed as what's normally done. I have the test results.

On the other hand, I was easily distractible. I am still easily distractible. My laptop, my cellular phone—they call to me even when I'm doing other things. A grade school teacher, Mrs. Watkinson, could barely handle me because I was so frequently distracted. I'm sorry I was so bad, Mrs. Watkinson.

I went through puberty early. It all started when I was just twelve.

On top of which, I had to endure the ups and downs that could happen only in those years. We came back to school once after vacation, and my skin had broken out so badly it looked like I had Skittles all over my forehead. I was sitting in history class—Pacific Northwest history—with my friend Gavin. A girl I liked—Angela, I still remember—sat down next to us. She looked over at me and said, "Oh my God, Apolo, what happened to your face?"

The shame. The embarrassment. The humiliation and mortification.

I put my head down, and it stayed down for the rest of that class. Our teacher noticed. He said, "Apolo, you're awfully quiet today."

What was there to say?

As interested as I was in girls, I was more interested just in hang-

ing out with my friends. Before seventh grade started, I had been as-
signed to all honors classes. I showed up only to find out that none of
my friends was in those classes. So I dropped out of the honors rota-
tion and went back to a "normal" schedule. After that, a kind way to
describe my approach to academics would be to say that I was going
through the motions. I didn't apply myself. I didn't feel any direction of
any sort. My dad would tell me, "Apolo, you've got to do your school-
work," but I would brush it off.

That fast, I had become not just defiant but superdefiant in dealing
with my dad. All I wanted to do was hang out with my friends. It was
all I wanted, all I cared about. After school and on weekends, when I
would hang out at their houses, I found out quickly that other parents
didn't seem nearly as exacting as my dad, nor were they as concerned
about ensuring their kids were held to a strict schedule. "Oh, Apolo,
why don't you just skip that practice and stay here? Or maybe we can
take you boys to the mall or somewhere?"

I also discovered that some of my friends had more stuff than
I did. If my dad had held off giving me a particular video game on
the grounds that I was too busy and, besides, we didn't really need
to spend his hard-earned dollars that way—well, here was that game
at So-and-So's house. Along with a lot of other games and other cool
stuff.

Just keeping me busy didn't work. I found space. And it wasn't all
that hard.

Again, all this happened fast. Going to school abruptly became
more about me setting up what was going to happen for the weekend
than anything that might happen while I was there. Now I showed up
on the campus of Saghalie Middle School, home of the Skyhawks, not
to learn, I was there just to kick it.

It says everything you need to know about Saghalie when you read,
as you can now on the school's website, of "another year of very few
High Level incidents (very safe campus)!" When I was there, it seemed

the place was covered in gang-related graffiti. To be clear, the school wasn't—isn't—bad. It just had some badass kids. Or at least kids who *thought* they were bad.

Those graffiti-covered walls and halls made what seemed like a perfect stage for break-dancing. At least it seemed that way to me. So I would dance. If you would have asked anyone back then, I was known in middle school as a kid who liked to entertain. I liked to make people laugh; I was very, very social. In the school cafeteria, there was the area where the black kids ate, the area for the white kids, the one for the Pacific Islanders, another for the Asians. I never picked sides. I hung around the Asian kids mostly, but I bounced around everywhere. I didn't care.

So this was my new routine: I went to school. I came home from school. I hung out with friends. I was on my own—Dad was at the salon—and I knew when he was supposed to come home.

In middle school, I started hanging out with a bunch of older guys, guys in their junior or senior year of high school, maybe even a little bit older. On what seemed like a daily basis, I would see fights happen. On weekends there was always some drama—more fights, it seemed. Dad never knew, because I was basically staying with friends. It seemed like I would hardly sleep from Friday to Monday; we were just hanging out.

In ninth grade, one of my friends was taken into custody. He was selling marijuana and ecstasy. He was a serious street pharmacist. A lot of my friends were like that. It was also in ninth grade that my dad knew for certain that the situation held considerable peril. He found out, for example, that a bunch of us had plans to blow up a school toilet. Why were we planning to do such a thing? I don't know.

Then came a ninth-grade dance. Me and my crew had rented two white limousines. Dad saw the limos, took in the kids who jumped out, and asked, naturally enough, "Who's paying for this?"

Nobody's parents were paying for it, was the answer. My friends had their own cash.

Because I had matured physically so early, these guys I was hanging around with were under the impression I was older, too—sixteen or seventeen. It's not as if anyone checked. One day Dad came home early; a bunch of these guys were at our house. Dad was furious. He said to these boys, "Look, I can't this instant find all your moms and dads and confront them. But unless that's what you want me to do, you have to get out right now and not come back, ever."

Dad was becoming seriously stressed about me. What was I doing? Sports, and the success I was having in short-track—Dad quietly hoped that would be enough to keep me away from my friends.

As if.

And now Dad and I fought, seemingly all the time. He would threaten to send me to military school; I didn't believe that for a second. Meanwhile, Dad knew—he had zero doubts about this—that the company I was keeping was threatening to derail my life.

The truth is, even though he knew that for a certainty deep inside him, he really had no idea how bad some of these guys could be. There were shootings and stabbings. Some of these guys saw the inside of the county jail, and not just once.

To be honest, as a young teen, there were times when the gang-related lifestyle held real appeal. That whole bad-boy image—girls liked that image, right? Some of my friends seemed to know an awful lot about various street gangs. But I was never a gangbanger, never in a street gang. Not ever.

I surely knew, though, what was there, if that's what I wanted. One of my buddies once called and said he had to talk to me about his cousin in Tacoma. The cousin's car had just gotten shot up by some rival gang members. He said, "You want to roll down there?"

"Roll down there? For what?"

"We have to retaliate, man."

I said, "Uh—I can't."

Then there was the time I was hanging around and some older friends picked me up. They had just stolen a car. That movie *Gone in 60 Seconds,* about a master car thief? That was a laughable amount of time to these guys; they could liberate a vehicle in *ten* seconds.

I asked, "Whose car is this?"

"Don't worry about it," they said.

I said, "I don't want to be rolling in a stolen car."

"Don't be tripping. Relax, dude."

I looked in the backseat of the car, and there were a bunch of television sets. They were in the midst of robbing houses. I was in the eighth grade.

At another point, these same guys had a bag with them. I asked, "What's in the bag?"

"Some weapons."

I was thoroughly scared—as I am now—of guns. This bag held a collection of guns: 9-millimeter handguns, some .22s, some .45s.

That's the moment I asked myself: *What am I doing?*

———————

THE ONLY PART of my life that offered anything like an answer was when I was at the rink. What was I doing? I was getting better and better.

Plus, I had really started to compete.

The U.S. Junior World Championship Trials took place in January 1996. I was still only thirteen, four months away from fourteen. Going in, I remember, I was ridiculously nervous. Now I wonder why. Who expected anything of me? I was the farthest thing from a name, a proven commodity, a favorite. I was just a thirteen-year-old kid.

Overall at those trials, I finished fourth.

And it should have been higher. During the 1000-meter event, racing in third, trying a pass, I bumped one of the top guys. Instantaneously, I felt bad about it, and so, right there as the race was still going on, I punished myself. I dropped to the back and stayed there until the end as a string of questions flashed inside and around my head, frantic thought bubbles registering one after the other in my mind as if ripped from a cartoon: *Who were you kidding, trying to pass like that? Did you think you could win? Who said you were allowed to think that way? Did you think you were even going to make the team?*

Really?

I was only thirteen.

My mental game had a long, long way to go—not that I could articulate any such thing back then.

At the same time, what was obvious, and increasingly so, was that I had talent at speed skating. By that spring, I had won a number of championships, including the U.S. short-track overall title for my age group. Around one of my meets, up in Red Deer, Alberta, Canada, it happened that the U.S. national team and the Japanese team were also scheduled to race. That meant the U.S. coaches and officials were on hand. This meant Dad had access, and he had a topic in mind.

Me.

Dad found Jeroen Otter, who was then the U.S. national team's senior head coach, and said to him, "I don't know what the next step is. I don't want Apolo's short-track career to slow down or even come to a stop because I don't have the information we need to help him."

Otter knew about me. My name was circulating in short-track circles: *Did you hear about the up-and-coming kid, the one from out in Seattle? Did you see that race, or hear about it, maybe it was in Milwaukee, Wisconsin, where the kid was wearing a two-piece skin suit—or what he thought was a skin suit—an old Nike shirt that was too small and a pair of tights? The kid is thirteen, maybe fourteen, years old. And he doesn't have, like, any money—but what he's got is talent.*

So in the heat box, some other kid takes a look at what the Seattle kid is wearing and starts making fun of him for the outfit. And the Seattle kid says to someone else—I think it's that Shani Davis kid from Chicago—"I'm going to beat that guy." The Shani kid says, "Do you know who that is?" The Seattle kid says, "I don't really care." By the way, it's some kid the Seattle kid has no business beating. So the Seattle kid goes out there, and he's all relaxed, and he stays with the kid who had been making fun of him. He keeps the pace, keeps the pace—and at the end, the Seattle kid lays the hammer down and ends up beating the other kid.

And the really amazing thing is that this Seattle kid hasn't had any real training. No real coaching. No weight lifting. Nothing like that. He's doing it right now on raw talent. And he's got an unusual first name: Apolo, with one l. *You hear about him yet?*

Otter knew.

"Apolo has promise," Otter told my dad. "You know where he should go? Lake Placid, New York. That's where the U.S. junior development team trains."

The development program is designed to identify promising young skaters and immerse them in the sport. It would include on- and off-the-ice training. I would live in a dorm. And I would go to school.

There were just two little problems: First, you had to be fifteen to be in the program. I would be fourteen.

But Dad was hardly going to let one little number like that stand in the way. He picked up the phone and called Pat Wentland, the junior development team coach; they discussed my wins, my times, my potential.

Pat was convinced—Apolo should be in Lake Placid. He said to my dad, "Mr. Ohno, we'd love to have your son be part of our training program. We think he has a ton of talent. We think he could be somebody." After that, Pat went to the entrance committee and argued my case. The committee then agreed to make an exception and admit me.

This all happened amazingly fast, in part because the program was due to begin in just weeks.

Now the second problem: No way did I want to go. Absolutely, positively, no way in the world did I want to go.

It was nearing the end of the school year. That meant summer was beckoning. Summer vacation meant the beach, barbecues, camping out, hanging out, water parks, parties—the life. I had things to do, people to see, and none of it involved Lake Placid or New York, and it especially did not involve leaving my friends or undertaking a program that sure sounded like it involved regimentation and conformity. Nor did I have any desire whatsoever to confront the jumble and rush of wild emotion this notion had clearly ignited, even if at the time I couldn't have articulated it so clearly.

Now, though, I can: I would have to leave home and everything and everyone I knew. I would have to live in a dorm among strangers from strange parts of the country who surely had never met anyone who looked like me, an Asian kid from the Pacific Northwest. I would have to commit myself to skating, and thus to finding out how good I was and could be. What if I wasn't good enough? What if I genuinely, truly put myself out there, with all my heart and all my soul, and it wasn't enough? What if I failed? What then?

Dad and I fought. And we fought. And we fought some more.

He insisted this Lake Placid thing was the opportunity of a lifetime. "Chances don't come around every day," he would say. "If you don't grab them, they never come back. Everyone gets one big opportunity, not several. That's the way life is."

"I don't care," I would reply. "I am not going."

Naturally, Dad saw Lake Placid through a far different prism than I did. He saw it as an opportunity, yes, and so much more. Here, unexpectedly but most fantastically, was a karma-laden pathway. This opportunity had abruptly presented itself to me because he had simply followed his instincts and asked for advice. Obviously, this was a sign—indeed, a lifeline. Moving me to upstate New York would remove me from the orbit of all those distasteful, disruptive, and potentially devastating influences in the neighborhood. Dad had no desire whatsoever to be separated from me so early; even so, he was willing to make that sacrifice for the greater good, not just for my skating but for my entire well-being.

Understandably, Dad had no qualms about my ability to go off in a new direction at fourteen. At that age, he was already plotting for himself a new life that wasn't in Japan. And then there was my grandfather, who as a teenager had dared to dream of something other than a farming life.

Finally, Lake Placid was likely to be an adventure, and I might very well be on my way to realizing my destiny. That was a great thing. What more in life could one wish for?

Dad's mind was made up.

I was going to Lake Placid.

No, I was not, and every time he brought it up, it was bad, or worse.

Dad refused to be deterred.

We screamed and yelled at each other.

That solved nothing. Still, we screamed and yelled, a lot. It got to a point where it seemed that if something didn't break, him or me, the house itself might well explode. A couple of times Dad almost took me to the police station. We would drive by, and he would say, "I'm going to drop you off here."

I would say, "Do it—I'm not scared."

I was supposed to fly to New York in early June. By late June, I was still home. It seemed like we shouted at each other all the time. It was as if there could be no other topic in the house unless and until this matter was resolved. Dad pushed and pushed. The more he pushed, the more I resisted.

Dad would say, "Apolo, you are going."

I would reply, "Oh, no, I'm not."

Or he would say, "Apolo, you are so going. I see the kids you're hanging out with. That's not the path I want for my son."

I would reply, "I don't care and you don't know—you don't know me, and you don't know my friends."

Or maybe I would take the offensive. I would say, "Why don't we wait until next year? Maybe I can try next year?"

He would respond, "No, Apolo. You've got to go."

He might ease up for a bit. Then he would come back with a different tack.

"This," he would say, "could be your ticket to the 1998 Winter Olympics. They're in Japan, you know. In Nagano—up north. Your grandparents might even come."

"Oh, please."

"There'll be older kids in Lake Placid. Look, you like hanging out with older kids."

"I'm not going to Lake Placid."

"The coach and the team are there. They're there already. They're waiting for you."

"Don't care."

"Give it three months. If you don't like it, you can come home. Three months—just give it three months."

"I'm not going."

"It will be fun. It's a new place. You're going."

In late June, Dad literally packed my bags, told me to get in the car, and drove me to the airport. His mind was made up, for sure. If I missed this opportunity, he felt certain, it would never come back. It would go to someone else.

Probably it would all work out for me across the country, way over there in Lake Placid. Or maybe it wouldn't. But at least I would have gone. He understood that this way I would have zero regrets.

It was June 29, 1996.

June 29 was a Saturday.

That Thursday and Friday, we had been in Portland, Oregon, at a regional in-line skating event. We had gotten back home so late Friday that it was nearly Saturday. Dad's plan was now to get up before dawn on Saturday, send me on a long run, tire me out, drop me off at the airport, dispatch me to Lake Placid, and get back to make an appointment at the salon at one-thirty in the afternoon.

He had his plan. I had mine.

The flight, Northwest 154, was due to depart the Seattle-Tacoma International Airport at ten thirty in the morning. I was going to connect in Minneapolis to fly somewhere else, I had no idea where, and somehow all the connections and all the flying were going to end in Albany, New York. There I was supposed to get picked up and driven to Lake Placid.

Dad, of course, was up early. He got me up at five. Sunrise wasn't even due for another fifteen minutes. Because Weyerhaeuser, the lumber company, is based in Federal Way, there are wooded trails around, and that's where I went running.

Then we piled into the car.

By now, my dad had given up on the Rabbit. He had replaced it with a reddish-colored Dodge Colt that featured a hatchback and peeling paint. It was very quiet in the Colt on the way to the airport, an uncomfortable silence indeed.

When we arrived, we wrestled the luggage out. We got my boarding pass. There wasn't a lot to say. He tried. He said, "Good luck, Apolo." He gave me a hug.

"All right, Dad, whatever."

I grabbed my stuff, and Dad turned away. He wasn't waiting. He headed for the car.

I killed a few minutes, just long enough to be sure the Colt was gone. I walked directly to a pay phone. I picked it up. I called a friend.

"Yo," I said, "I'm at Sea-Tac. Come get me. My dad brought me here so I could go to someplace in New York. I'm not going."

REACHING

I love this saying: Reach for the unreachable.

When you reach for that branch in the tree and
you can touch it—great. That's your goal.

More: That's your destination.

When it's your destination, that changes
everything about how you approach the way. An
Olympics, for instance—that might be four years
away. There are innumerable ways to get there.
But those four years are going to speed
by amazingly fast. An Olympics lasts seventeen
days. The cauldron goes out and it's over.
I've arrived—or have I?

Afterward, while I surely remember the
Games themselves, I mostly recall the moments
on the way. The strength you gain from that
is remarkable. You've lived the experience—
really lived it, fully.

CHAPTER 3

A few days later, Dad's phone rang. It was Pat Wentland.

"Mr. Ohno?" he said.

"Yes," Dad said. "That's me."

"Mr. Ohno, the invitation to Apolo is still open. We want to be sure you understand that. But we haven't heard from you, and we were wondering if you were still sending your son to come see us."

"What? You lost my son?"

"Excuse me, sir?"

"Mr. Wentland," Dad said, "I'll get back to you."

From the airport, my buddy and I had gone to his house and dropped my bags. Then we were off to a party. For the next several days, I went to more parties, to barbecues, to the fair, to the movies. Perfect. This was precisely how I had seen my summer playing out. I bounced from one friend's house to another. I maybe bunked one night in Federal Way. Then the next in South Seattle. Anywhere and everywhere. I didn't have a schedule. I did whatever I wanted to do. It was summer. There was no school. I had no rules. I was fourteen, and I had committed myself to an extraordinary act of rebellion.

Being fourteen, I figured I could live this way for at least a year, maybe two, perhaps even longer. I mean, I had friends all around the Pacific Northwest. I could stay with a particular friend for a few days—until his parents figured out something was not quite right—and then move on to another.

Easy.

This was fun, I thought. I was just hanging out, doing stuff. Nothing bad. Just dumb stuff.

Being fourteen, there must have been a part of me that secretly, desperately wanted to get caught. For one, I would sneak back home to get clothes while Dad was working; I knew his work schedule, of course, but maybe something would go wrong and we would be forced into a rousing confrontation. Also, I had—um, accidentally—left a list of my friends and their telephone numbers in my bedroom.

In all, I bounced around for about a week.

Not surprisingly, Dad actually figured out through my friends what I was up to. But he decided to let the situation play itself out for just a bit before he drove over to get me at a friend's house.

He felt shock, anger, bewilderment, frustration, guilt, blame—all of it. In essence, his son had run away. *What,* he kept asking himself, *have I done? Have I really made life that miserable for him?*

Dad drove over to where I was camped out. It was, he says, one of the worst moments of his life. He had to ring the doorbell and ask to see me.

The mom there hadn't seen any reason while I was there to have checked in with my dad, even to tell him I was there. She just assumed I was there because it was summer vacation. What did sleepovers matter when there was no school in the morning?

Dad waited at the doorway for me. He was shadowed in the bright sun. I walked into the front hallway and just stood there. My father started crying.

"Apolo," he said, "you have to come home."

Nothing else. He didn't say anything about how I might be forgoing a huge opportunity or about how I was obviously making a huge mistake. Nothing of the sort.

"Apolo, you have to come home."

That's all.

He was so shaken. It was clear that in that moment he felt he was losing me.

I was unmoved. Or at least that's how I played it. I looked at my father, eyes cold and hard, and said, "No, I'm not coming home."

Dad turned and slowly walked away. He says now that he walked back to that Dodge Colt feeling an enormous sense of rejection. *My God*, he thought, *am I really that much of a loser? Lacking so much in love? Have I somehow not provided anything near enough?*

Dad was a hardheaded realist enough to know that the decision to come home ought to be mine, if that was possible.

It was, and it wasn't.

Three days after he appeared in that doorway, Dad found me again.

"Apolo," he told me, "you have to come home with me. You have to come home with me right now."

And I did. It simply was time for me to go home with Dad.

July 8 was a Monday. Northwest Flight 68 left Seattle that morning for Detroit. Instead of dropping me off that morning at Sea-Tac, Dad parked the car in the airport lot. From there, we walked together to the gate. He walked me to my seat. And then he sat down, too.

It wasn't until that instant that I realized what was up. This time, Dad was going with me.

We flew together to Detroit, and then on to Albany, where he rented a car and we drove to Lake Placid, winding past green pine trees and brown hills. The only conversation in the car came when I volunteered just how awful all of this was.

"The air is clean here," he said.

"It's clean in Seattle," I said.

By the time we got to the training center, it was late at night. But it was not so dark that I couldn't see that there wasn't much in Lake Placid to see.

Lake Placid is a village in the Adirondack Mountains. A village, with all that entails. It's not big. Even so, Lake Placid staged the Winter Olympic Games in 1932 and again in 1980. For the 1980 Games, they spent millions to bring in snowmaking systems and other equipment and to build venues, too—even a new Olympic Village, which later became a state prison.

At those 1980 Games, Eric Heiden won five gold medals in long-track speed skating, an absolutely amazing, astounding, probably never-to-be-duplicated feat. He won every single race at every single distance, the sprints and the distance events—500 meters, 1000, 1500, 5000, and 10,000. There were thirty-seven countries competing in Lake Placid; Heiden won more medals by himself than Sweden, Liechtenstein, Holland, Italy, Canada, Great Britain, Hungary, Japan, Bulgaria, France, or Czechoslovakia. He cut quite the figure, too. Everyone who saw Heiden on television remembers him in his golden skin suit. They also remember the story of how Heiden took the night off before his final medal, the 10,000, to watch the event those Games are probably most remembered for, the "Miracle on Ice" hockey game, because a couple of his buddies from the University of Wisconsin were on the U.S. team. The Americans won the hockey game, beating the Soviets. Heiden overslept the next morning; he calmly woke up, ate a few pieces of bread for breakfast, and then went out and broke the world record by more than six seconds.

When I arrived in Lake Placid, I knew none of this. Those 1980 Games were two years before I was born.

Since that "the invitation is still open" phone call on June 29, Dad had been in touch somewhat regularly with Pat Wentland. "We're coming," he would say.

Pat had no idea why it had taken so long for me to get to Lake Placid. That night, at the training center, Dad and I met Pat, who said graciously, "Hello, Mr. Ohno."

Dad shook his hand, looked him in the eye, looked over at me, and said, "Good luck"—as in, *Good luck with this kid because you're going to need it.*

Pat shot us a look that said it all: Oh, boy, what am I getting myself into?

That next morning, I needed a road bicycle for bike training. Some of the athletes there had custom-made bikes, machines worth thousands. Dad went into town and bought one for precisely $623.28. That very day, I rode the bike with the others. I didn't feel a thing. I wasn't tired in the slightest. I rode like an animal.

Pat told Dad I could be one of the best skaters in the world. Dad said he didn't know if I was going to stay in Lake Placid for even three months. "If you can keep him that long," Dad said, "I'll be happy."

Meanwhile, Dad said to me, "If you don't like it, you can come home in three months. At least then, that will be your choice."

Day Two: Two hours on the ice.

Day Three: A timed bike trial. I came in third.

Day Six, Sunday, July 14: Dad went home to Seattle. He was hardly going to stay forever. And he had appointments at the salon on Monday.

As he was leaving, Dad did his very best to be as loving as possible. After all, he had gotten his way—I was in Lake Placid—but this was no time to claim victory. He didn't say much, not even, "Train hard." He said, "I'm glad you're doing this. You won't regret this opportunity. You are going to be very, very good."

He said, "I love you."

And then he went back to the West Coast. I was on my own, in Lake Placid, New York.

———————

PAT WAS MY first real coach. It didn't take even one full year for him to turn me into a champion.

Pat was intense. He could be strict. Pat had his ways. Pat also knew what he was talking about. He was a two-time national champion. He trained with us, on and off the ice. He became a force in my life—a force for positive change. Which I needed, because for that first month in particular, I was predictably homesick; the food at the training center was predictably repetitive; and I was, predictably, tired and sore.

A typical day would include running, skating, school, and weight lifting. Then we'd get up the next day and do that all over again.

I went to public school in Lake Placid; it's right next to the training center. There were only about two dozen kids in the class, and so, in a change from middle school in Federal Way, I had to pay attention. That's not, though, why at the beginning I felt so strongly out of place there.

The kids in the school were, for the most part, white. Where was the diversity? I had grown up surrounded by Asian kids, black kids, Latino kids. Here it could seem as if everyone's family had been in Lake Placid for generations—everyone's except mine, of course.

That first month, I not only acted with defiance, I *felt* defiant, through and through. I didn't want any part of anybody, not in school and not on the team. Everyone just seemed different. They all listened to different music than I did, dressed differently than I did, acted differently, talked differently.

I didn't like it. I didn't like being around all of that and all of them.

Dad called every week. I'd act like I was still put out. He'd tell me it would all be okay. I'd tell him right back that I hated everything.

Not surprisingly, I didn't want to follow any rules. Mostly, I just went through the motions. We would go on these afternoon runs that started about two. The course wound from the training center around what's called Mirror Lake, then back; we would do loops of this course. Along the way, we would pass a pizza place. I was easily one of the slowest runners on the team. Many a time another skater, Chul "Eric" Lee, and I would lag well behind the others, so far back that no one could possibly have noticed when we'd duck into the pizza joint. He'd buy a large pizza. We'd eat the pizza, and then as the team was going by again, we'd fall into line—that is, way back at the end of the line. No one had any idea.

Hence, however, the reprise of my nickname: Chunky.

At some point, the sports medicine people took the body fat percentage of everyone on the junior development team. Mine was the highest on the team. I came in at 12 percent; everybody else was in the 6 percent to 8 percent range. That made me very uncomfortable. I thought, *I can beat some of these guys—and I'm fat?* That somehow just didn't seem right.

This body fat test proved to be the trigger I needed. Clearly, I had skills. I had talent. I might even have a special gift. And Pat saw that. Pat hung back and let me do my thing. He didn't apply any undue pressure.

At some point that summer, I went to Pat to tell him, "I don't know why, but I have, you know, kind of started to really enjoy myself."

I was thoroughly enjoying both the progress I had made physically and the sport itself. I was also thinking, *You know, I really could be pretty good.* But I had no idea how good.

"Pat," I said, "I want you to make me a machine."

He laughed and said, "Oh, yeah?"

I said, "Is it too bad if I get to be too good too young?"

He laughed again. "Don't worry about that type of stuff, Apolo," he said. "You just have to give me your best effort. You have to commit yourself, Apolo. If you can do that, you can be one of the best."

"Okay," I said. "Make me a machine. I want to be the best ever."

That August, I called home. "There's a World Cup race here in October," I told Dad, "and while usually those are for World Cup racers only—the best guys in each country—this one is also going to have a junior team competition between us and Canada. Pat has picked me as one of the skaters."

"Congratulations, Apolo—I'll be there."

Dad flew out to Lake Placid in mid-October. He saw me at practice, and what he saw was me growing into an athlete. Short-track wasn't just about fun anymore—that is, it was fun and work, inextricably tied together. What he saw was me living the life of an athlete.

Two days after Dad got there, as practice was winding to a close, I fell on the ice—hard. The Zamboni that had been used to clean the ice had been brought in from outside; it had apparently dropped some sand, maybe a little bit of dirt, on one of the corners. My blade caught and knocked me down, and I went sprawling into the wall. The hamstring muscle in my left leg was hurt. My right leg, too. Even my hip. I couldn't walk and had to be carried off by trainers.

Dad said, "Apolo, don't worry about the race," which was three days away. "You just need to get better."

I said, "Dad—I'm going to race."

For Dad, this settled it. I had come into a new world. Maybe I truly could grow to become a serious young athlete.

On race day, as the others zipped around the track in warm-ups, I glided slowly, trying to loosen up and warm up. Every time I moved my hip, though, I felt a sharp jolt. Brutal.

Breathe, I told myself. *Try to calm yourself down. Just breathe.*

When I lined up at the start line, I felt no pain. I had blocked it out or something, because after the race, it was back to throbbing. But I went out there and raced, and won, an American beating all the Canadians. In the niche world of junior short-track racing, that got everyone's attention.

It got mine, too.

My injuries healed, and for the next several months, I attacked my training. I showed up at the junior world trials in December 1996, in Milwaukee, Wisconsin, in great shape and in a great frame of mind, convinced I was going to make the U.S. team and thus get to travel the world.

Didn't happen.

Even before I stepped onto the ice, it all fell apart. My blades weren't right; consequently, I didn't have any feel for the ice. That good vibe— gone, almost immediately. In its place, a mental *yech* that animated and intensified my frustration. I made it into the finals for only one race, the 1000 meters. I then won that race but came in third overall. They took only the top two for the team.

Dad drove me back to Lake Placid. He was upbeat. I was down.

"You did a wonderful job, Apolo. Even with something wrong with your blade, you proved you could still perform."

"Yeah, right," I said, sarcastic as could be.

"You didn't quit, did you? You could have fallen and gotten injured, right?"

"I guess so."

"You should be proud. You won the 1000-meter with a bad skate."

Back in Lake Placid, I trained harder still. Pat came back after traveling with the junior team. "Relax," he said. "Relax into it and go tighter around the corners."

There's a fine line in everything between going too hard and just feeling the flow. Suddenly, I felt the flow.

I'd come to Lake Placid with significant advantages of a sort that in 1997 were only just beginning to be understood, because cross-training was not yet fully appreciated. For six years, I had been a swimmer. Beyond that, I had been an in-line racer; in-line training makes for great resistance work because of the friction the wheels produce. Indoors, in-line racing was on a very short track: 100 meters. Practically, that meant there wasn't much glide, recovery, or weight shifting, but there was a lot of pushing—all in all, a different sort of hard work compared with the smooth surface of ice.

Pat had helped me exploit all that. And now, suddenly, I was feeling the flow.

The senior world team trials were scheduled for March, in Walpole, Massachusetts, a town that sits between Boston and Providence, Rhode Island. Two weeks before the event, we were doing practice nine-lap trials. I clocked a 1:28.3; there were only a handful of guys in the United States who went under 1:29, let alone 1:28.5. The truth is, for most of that timed nine-lap trial, I was going easy. When I was on the ice, and I was feeling it, I suddenly wasn't worried about anything. Dad, school, girls, friends, the general angst of being a teenager—it all went away.

It felt . . . pure.

It's why I liked the sport so very, very much. It was a departure from everything else. Even, it seemed sometimes, a departure from reality.

I went hard in that nine-lap trial only with two laps to go, and then because Pat said how many laps were left. I figured, okay, time to push it. We tried to keep that 1:28.3 a secret, but when we showed up in Walpole, people were talking. I remember hearing it all around me, from parents and other coaches: *This kid is the real deal, this kid is the future of short-track.*

In Walpole, I was up against guys like Andy Gabel. He already had competed in the 1988 Games, when short-track was a demonstration sport, and then in 1992 and 1994, when it was a full medal sport, winning a silver in Lillehammer on the 5000 relay.

That March, Gabel was thirty-two. I was still fourteen.

In the warm-ups, I was rocking baggy clothes; my sweatpants sagged low. To complete the look, I had really long hair. Anyone taking a look at me might well have wondered, *This is the future of short-track?*

A nine-lap time trial separated the top sixteen from the rest of the skaters; I won. A four-lap time trial came next; I ripped off the fastest split times all the way through to the last corner, when I slipped and slid on both hands, knees, and chest across the line—good for third. Then I won the 1500. I took fourth in the 500, got shut out in the 1000, and grabbed second in the 3000.

Overall, because of the way the point system worked, I had just won the U.S. title, making me the youngest short-track winner in American history.

My time in Lake Placid was abruptly done. I'd be moving to Colorado Springs to train with Otter and the senior national team, because of course I had made the U.S. team, and not the juniors but the real deal, even better. The top two from these trials were to represent the United States on the World Cup circuit—me and, as it would happen, Gabel.

For Pat, for me, for my dad, here was undeniable proof: I could be somebody.

The 1998 Winter Olympics were about eleven months away.

BY ALL RIGHTS, I should have been the closest thing to a lock for the 1998 Olympic team imaginable. But in sports, as in anything, there is no such thing as a lock. That would become all too plain to me over the next several months.

I left Lake Placid on such a high—number one in the United States. I packed up, said good-bye to Pat and to my friends, and flew to the Olympic Training Center in Colorado Springs.

What happened after that would—if this were business school—make for a classic case study in how to, or more precisely how *not* to, integrate a new guy into the culture of the particular enterprise. There was plenty of blame to go around. Including on the new guy's part.

Every entity—business, nonprofit, a professional sports team, an

Olympic training squad—has its own distinct culture. In this instance, a lot of things from the get-go were working against me. I was not only younger, I was very much an outsider. When the senior trials ended, the then-president of the speed-skating association didn't come over to say hello to me or Dad or even to shake my hand.

In Colorado Springs, obviously, the other skaters were older, and in some cases much older. They all knew one another, and in some cases had been friends—rivals, yes, but still friends—for years. A related piece of that dynamic: nobody had ever gotten to the top of American short-track as quickly as I had. The others had, for the most part, worked their way up, in many cases together, through the junior and senior ranks, and it's fair to say that as a consequence, some skaters had little intention of accepting me as the number one guy on the team.

For his part, Otter had never before trained a fourteen-year-old. I was lumped in with fifteen others; everyone else had worked with him before. I would have gotten the most out of a more personalized workout regime—running, biking, lifting, skating. That didn't happen. Related to that, in turn, was that: None of the grown-ups took direct, personal responsibility for figuring out how to help me succeed. And I was, still, fourteen.

Yes, I had lived away from home for nearly a year. But that was in a much more structured environment. Now I had to learn the most basic of basics; for instance, why snacking on pizza on those Lake Placid training runs might have seemed snarky and funny, but a regular diet of cold pizza and candy late at night in Colorado Springs was the farthest thing from optimal.

And even though I had been to skating meets for years, this was different, and in two ways. This would be the World Cup, not an in-line event in Nebraska. Moreover, I was the number one guy, at least in theory. But I had no idea what being number one meant, except that it seemed clear everyone would be, or already was, gunning for me. Also, I had no idea of the practical realities involved in traveling the world:

how to pack smart and how to take care of my gear, how to deal with international travel and how to manage jet lag, how to stay smart on the road to minimize the risk of getting sick. And more.

My first world championships arrived in that spring of 1997, in Nagano, at the White Ring, the dome-shaped arena where they would hold the short-track competition in the Olympics the next year. It did not go well. Not at all.

For starters, this was all new to me, and I allowed myself to wonder whether I belonged in the same arena with the Koreans, Chinese, Japanese, Italians, Canadians—everyone from all over.

I had so much going on in my head. "Hip in," I wrote on the skin suits we wore as racing gear. Too bad that wasn't the only piece of advice I had to think about, and you can't be running down some checklist when you're racing. Plus, it seemed that every single one of these guys, no matter where he was from, had been programmed to perform without showing any weakness or even any doubt. Did they ever get tired? If they did, would they show it?

Not only that, they skated in packs that were so tight I wasn't sure how or where or when to make my moves. Hesitation leads to doubt, and doubt is a confidence and performance killer.

And then, once again, my blades felt off. Whom was I supposed to turn to for help? A mechanic? Did we even have a mechanic? One of my friends? None of them was there in Japan with me. Otter? It wasn't his job to look after me and only me.

I got thrashed in every race. Overall, I placed nineteenth. Leaving Nagano, I felt extraordinarily discouraged. Which is why I decided, as only a fourteen-year-old can, that I'd had enough.

At least for a while.

———————

I NEEDED A break. I wanted to take the summer off. I missed Seattle and my friends there. I thought it would be best if I went home and took a long, long vacation. Dad was inclined to agree, believing it would be healthy to restore a measure of balance to my life.

What did we know? We did not know that there is no way you take three months off, and especially in an Olympic year.

The idea in short-track is to peak in the winter, for the worlds or the Olympics. But that doesn't mean you slack off in the other months, even in the summer. Summer is when you build your base; that is, you work on your endurance and overall fitness.

In 1997 I did not train from April until almost August. I went back to being the me I had been before I went off to Lake Placid. I went right back to doing the same things I had been doing and to hanging out with the same crew, except they were by now a little bit older, a little bit badder, and doing things they shouldn't have been doing.

I slept late. When I finally got up, midmorning, I'd call one of my buddies, go over to his house, and hang out. Maybe we'd go to the beach. Or the mall. Or someone else's house. At night there were barbecues or movies and, after, maybe a party.

Otter had told me to put in lots of miles on the bike while I was in Seattle. I didn't. I also did not run or lift or stretch or even skate, at least very much. I did eat a lot of junk food. I gained—oh, a conservative guess would be maybe 25 pounds.

By August, the 1998 Olympic Trials were just five months away. The U.S. team assembled for a training camp in Chamonix, in France, up in the Alps. I was the only one there who hadn't biked all summer. Every day was a lesson in how painful—literally and figuratively—it was to be a slacker. I ran at the back of the pack. I biked at the back of the pack, my lungs burning. The weights I managed to lift were puny in comparison with everyone else's amounts.

On top of which, I got the flu.

Otter suggested I go home, get better, then put in two or three hard weeks on the bike. After that, he said, I could come back to Colorado Springs and get ready for the World Cup circuit and the Trials.

I went home, all right. And once I got back home, it was as if I had never left. There were barbecues and movies to go to and people to see. Same as it ever was. From the day I got back until the Trials, however, I was behind, or sick, or both, and it seemed I could never catch up. My room was littered with laundry and half-packed bags. It was a mess, and so was I.

Instead of putting the focus on things I needed to do, I was messing around. I didn't dedicate myself. There was no want in my heart. I had no clue what it really took. I went through that summer and fall giving half the effort I had in me—if that much. I turned defiant; I mouthed off to coaches. I quit races. I quit competitions. I quit on myself and everyone around me.

I simply didn't understand what it meant to become an Olympic athlete, and I didn't understand the rarity of the gift I had, an opportunity before me that you can't buy. I clearly had talent. And I was throwing it away.

I dragged myself to the Trials in January 1998. I showed up not wanting to make the team—at least, that's what I was telling myself. I didn't even really want to skate at the Trials. I already had it fixed in my head that I wasn't going to the Games, so why bother to show up merely to be humiliated?

Looking back, I wonder now how it all might have turned out if I had trained hard before those 1998 Trials. Would I have made the team? If I had, would everything else be different? Or is it the case that everything is supposed to happen just the way it does?

The Trials, back in Lake Placid, stretched over two weekends. The first featured a nine-lap time trial. I hadn't done any nine-lap trials that entire year; 1:28.3 was a long, long time gone. As the race went on, I became exhausted. I got no points and didn't qualify for any of the weekend finals. The second weekend featured a four-lap trial. Again—nothing. I didn't make any of the finals.

Between races, Dad would try to say something encouraging. I didn't want to talk to him, or to anyone.

As the Trials ground on, Dad became increasingly infuriated and exasperated. He liked to think of me as a young lion. Now his young lion was out of the hunt. No—the young lion had been taken out of the hunt, lacking appropriate direction, guidance, and training. The way he saw it, the other skaters, older and more experienced, were just waiting for the young lion to stumble, and then they wasted no time in mauling me.

Dad was devastated. The coaches said to Dad, "Please bring Apolo back after the Olympics. He'll make it back for the World Cup as a full-fledged member of the U.S. team."

Dad was so angry. Didn't they have a responsibility to me, to develop my talent? Where was *their* investment of their time and energy in me? *Why*, he thought to himself, *should I leave my son with you?* In that moment, the primary thought in his mind was, *I must keep my son away from these people. Maybe*, he even thought, *this is it for short-track. Maybe Apolo goes back to swimming.*

For all Dad's anger at the coaches around me, the blame was mine. I was fifteen. I didn't care.

The Trials ended with me dead last, sixteenth of sixteen.

After the last race, I saw Pat and told him that maybe I had skated my last race ever. The year before, I had gone from nobody to first. Now I had gone from first to last. I was disappointed and embarrassed, humiliated and ashamed, and more. Pat said, "Go home and get in shape. Take some time and think about things before you make a decision about anything."

Dad and I finally got a quiet moment. He said, "Apolo, please listen. I don't care that you didn't make the Olympic team. This, though, is what I do care about: I am afraid you are throwing away a talent, an opportunity that doesn't happen to many people in this world. You have that kind of talent, an amazing talent. You have in front of you a path that you can follow, a path that can lead you to places you can't even imagine right now, places likely to be very different from those of your friends back home—and maybe even a path very, very different from anyone else's."

"You," he said, "have found your passion. You have found your craft. You have to allow it to blossom within you."

He was talking about speed skating. And so much more.

He was teaching me right then and there the most fundamental thing: You have to dedicate your heart and soul to something. Then you go forward; you don't look back. And you don't hold back. You go after whatever that thing is without being afraid to fail.

I had told myself before these Trials that I was going to fail and lose, and I did just that. That was one thing.

Another was the underlying fear, which he understood I had tried like hell to avoid by not really trying on the ice: What if I gave it my very best and still didn't make it? Would that mean I wasn't, at some level, good enough? Would that reveal a profound set of personal inadequacies?

It's not as if I was simply playing it safe, which at least might be a course you could try to rationalize.

There was so much to think about, and yet the conclusion, to my father, was obvious. I was not there yet, and he knew the only way for me to get to that ultimate understanding was by myself; a life marked by regret was worse, way worse, than trying your best and maybe coming up short.

Did I have the courage to confront that? And if not now, when? How could he help me get to that place?

It was a long, long series of plane rides back to Seattle. The minute we would land in Seattle, he figured, was the start of a new chapter, maybe even a new life. What was that going to look like?

I needed direction. How to provide it?

FINDING EMOTION

As a man, as an athlete, being stoic and cold often comes with the territory. It's a facet of a persona—the aura of invincibility.

Especially when you're younger, it may feel indisputable that you need at certain times to adopt that persona, to use it as a tool to become stronger and better.

But in the end, you become truly stronger when you acknowledge that you are not invincible.

Obviously, I tried in my own preparation to make sure I had as few cracks as possible in my armor. But to see myself truthfully is to admit that, like anyone, I have weaknesses and insecurities. And once you open up to that, you can be much more comfortable about them.

I am a die-hard competitor. It's that killer instinct that certain athletes have. And when I'm training, I'm a different person. I'm a fighter.

That's why I can laugh about what we wear when we race. We wear tights.

CHAPTER 4

O n the flight to Seattle, my father suddenly understood what to do.

"Apolo, the ocean is calling you."

As metaphysical, even mystical, as that might seem, that made immediate and thorough sense, especially given our shared history at the shore.

This, he decided, was what he had to do for his son. As soon as we landed, he would take me to the ocean—that is, he would take me back to the ocean, to Copalis Beach and Iron Springs Resort, a place of total isolation. He would leave me there essentially alone to think about who I was, who I wanted to be, and what I was willing to do to get there.

I needed a place of safety and security that was also removed from everyone and everything.

He didn't consult me, didn't ask whether I thought it might be a good idea. This is what my father decided. Before we landed, his mind was made up. Shortly before we landed, Dad told me the plan.

As Dad well understood, on one level it was brutal. I had just been defeated. He was running the risk that I might feel he was simply abandoning me in a time of need. Another approach to this situation, after all, would have been to take me home, give me a hug, and put me to bed with a bowl of warm soup.

Then again, as he saw it, I was at a critical juncture in my life, and there was no time like now to do what needed to be done. It was tough love, and he believed I needed a dose of that most. I was so hard-headed, so defiant that he believed it not only was the best option, it truly seemed the only option. As he saw it, I was at the top of a cliff. I had just been kicked off, straight down. Now I would have to climb up—a steep climb, to be sure—and I would have to do it myself. No matter how torn or defeated I was, I would have to steel myself for the climb. And in doing the climb, I would show him I was strong. More important, I would show myself the strength I could already wield at fifteen and unleash the potential for even more within me as I went along.

In that way, my father was giving me a gift.

He had seen me growing up so fast—at least, physically. He realized that if I was ever going to realize my potential, maybe even make the Olympics and win medals or become a world champion or both, I needed to have unbelievable mental strength. If he could, he needed to accelerate my mental maturity dramatically. He probably couldn't articulate all that then, but if he hadn't believed that I was strong enough to handle being left alone, he would not have done it.

And at a level surely well beyond all words, he trusted me enough to let me take control of my own destiny.

Federal Way is not all that far from Sea-Tac. When we landed, Dad said, "Apolo, we are going to the grocery store, to get you food. Then we're going home for about two seconds; we're going to pick up your cat, Tiggie. We're going to grab some other things. And then we are going out to Copalis."

It was roughly three hours in the Dodge Colt out to Copalis. When we arrived at Iron Springs, it was pouring rain.

"Here is the situation," Dad said after we unloaded the car.

"You have a choice. I don't care what path you go on in life. I don't care if it's sports or academics or business. Whatever it is, it's all fine by me. But whatever that is, you truly have to do it one hundred percent. Dedicating yourself to your craft—that's what is important to me. You're going to contribute one hundred percent to this sport, and you're going to give one hundred percent; you're going to sacrifice because you want to give that one hundred percent, because you want to be the best. Or you're not going to do it at all. You need to come to a decision, Apolo. Do you want to skate—or not? Do you want to swim? Do you want to go to school? What do you want to pursue?

"Apolo," he said, "you are going to stay here, and you are going to figure out what that is—what you want to do with your life.

"I will accept whatever you choose. If you want speed skating, I accept that. If you want to quit speed skating, I accept that. Just know that if you want to quit speed skating, what then will you do? You have to decide something.

"There is only one answer that is not suitable: 'I don't know and I want to come home.'

"Call me," he said, "when you have made your decision."

At that instant, all I knew was that I did not want to be in Copalis Beach, Washington. As my dad turned to go to the car and the long drive back to Federal Way, I said, "Whatever."

IT'S NO SECRET it rains a lot in Washington State. In the winter, in particular, it rains and then it rains some more. When I woke up in the morning, the rain was pouring down in sheets, the wind howling in off the ocean. The color of the sky and the sea reflected my mood: somewhere between gray and black.

Here, as I looked around and took stock, was the situation:

Except for Tiggie, I was completely isolated. Dad had not even told the management at Iron Springs that he was leaving me there by myself. The cottage had no phone. There was a pay phone down the road; that was it for communication with the outside world. We had brought from home a small TV, a VCR, and some skating tapes. We had also brought a stationary bike so that I could, if I wanted, exercise without having to deal with pelting rain. We had stocked the refrigerator and freezer with frozen dinners and other food.

I got on the bike and, for the first two days, pedaled away.

Who was I kidding? It was a stationary bike. I wasn't going anywhere or getting anywhere.

On the third day, I began to write in a journal.

Day 3
1-21-98, after the Olympic Trials

9:15 a.m. *Got up. It was very cold, so I cranked up all of the heaters. Tiggie was sleeping in my bed, nice and comfortable. I made juice consisting of yogurt, one banana, carrots, orange juice, and broccoli. I had two bowls of cereal, one bowl was with blueberries. Built fire and ate right next to it. Made Tiggie some toys to play with while I ate.*

10:30 a.m. *Started to write in daily journal and thought, I want to go and jog today between the worst rain. While watching Tiggie play, I noticed that she always makes me smile.*

10:40 a.m. *If I come back and try to skate at the World Team Trials, my goal is to be able to skate at 150 pounds, and to be very lean, with no muscle loss. I need to work on my endurance,* *jogging and cycling. I want to be more agile on my skates. I need to watch videos of other skaters and I need to work on my dry-land technique.*

If I do skate at World Team Trials, I am skating to WIN, not second, not third, but FIRST and only that. If my dad helps me and I keep faith in God, myself, and my dad, I think I can do it. If for some reason I can't do it, then I know at least one very important special thing. I gave something 110 percent. If I could do that, I believe I'd be one of the top skaters in the world.

__12:20 p.m.__ I'm going for a walk outside, even though it's raining . . .

Outside, it was cold and damp and miserable. I briefly thought, *Maybe I'll call Dad*—but then I followed up that thought with the realization that I had nothing yet to tell him. I ran—jogged, really—for maybe ten minutes. Back inside I went. I turned on the TV and VCR, and turned my attention to skate videos. I couldn't stand being inside any longer. Back out I went. This time I ran—ran—for about an hour.

__5:00 p.m.__ My run was intense. I am very bored and pretty lonely right now and wish I had someone to talk to or that Dad would come up and visit me. I very truly believe that I can make my goals, but I need to SKATE and be coached on my technique. Without skating, it is idiotic to even try this goal. I want to give my goal 110 percent every day because I know I'm capable of that and it would help tremendously when I train.

__5:10 p.m.__ Watch more tapes and take a shower.

I had brought only some crummy sneakers with me out to Iron Springs, a pair of beat-up old Mizunos that I never liked. I don't know why those were the shoes I had with me; they were hardly the sort you'd use for long runs. But I had no other option. And all of a sudden, I powerfully felt the urge to go on long, long runs.

Day 4
1-22-98

8:30 a.m. *Got up and made eggs with cheese, toast, and blended juice.*

9:20 a.m. *Just finished breakfast, and I want to go run at 10:30 until 12:30 p.m., a two-hour run. Pray time ... "Dear Heavenly Father ... Thank you for giving me the opportunity to be here. It is very lonely and I would like to go back home. I have started training hard again. Will you help me keep on training so I can give my goal 110 percent? Pray by Jesus's name. Amen."*

9:50 a.m. *Watch tapes, then run.*

The rain never seemed to stop and drenched me to the skin as I ran along the steep, curving roads. The wind roared in from the shore and buffeted me further. I didn't just get blisters on my feet; I got huge blisters. My shins hurt from the repetitive pounding on the asphalt. My lungs hurt because I was in god-awful shape.

I was hurting.

Still, I didn't let up.

Actually, I poured it on. I began to work out three times each day.

After long runs in the mornings, I'd ride the stationary bike through the afternoons. Then I'd watch skate videos, on the lookout for detail. In the evenings, I would run again. My sweatshirts started to smell. My sweatpants were getting nasty.

The days started to blur together. I was out for another long run, ninety minutes, maybe two hours. I was pounding along a two-lane road. The rain was still pouring down, the sky and sea still so foreboding. I stopped.

What, I thought, *am I doing? Why am I here? Why am I running? From something? Toward something?*

Emotions of all sorts welled up inside me. How much more alone could I be?

But was I really?

I looked around. Of course, there wasn't anyone else on the road. There hadn't been anybody on that road since I had been running it that entire week. A boulder, huge and flat, perched over the sea. As the rain beat down, I sat on the rock.

There isn't really any money in short-track speed skating, I thought. *It's not likely that I'm going to get rich or famous doing short-track. So why bother? Why? The Winter Olympics in Japan haven't even started, and then it's going to be a long, long four years until the next Olympics, in Salt Lake City. Am I in this for the long haul?*

I stood up, off the rock. Then I turned back toward it and kneeled. "Give me guidance," I began to pray. "Give me the strength to make a decision. Give me—give me something. Give me the courage to be strong. Give me the strength to keep going through the physical pain and through the moments of doubt. What am I doing? Why am I here? Why am I doing this?"

I love skating, that's why.

It was at once that complicated and that simple. *I love it. It's what rings true to me.*

When I got up off my knees, I knew with certainty that I faced first a fundamental choice. I could resume this run, heading out as I was away from the cabin on a full loop out and around. Or I could turn back toward the cabin, walking, and this particular part of my journey would be complete.

My choice.

I looked down at my thrashed Mizuno sneakers, headed out away from the cabin, and began to run. After I finished the run itself, I jogged down to the pay phone. I called my father. "Dad," I said, "I've made a decision—will you please come get me?"

———————

NINE DAYS AFTER dropping me off, Dad came to pick me up.

In that call from the pay phone, I hadn't said anything to him about what decision I had made. On the car ride back home, I told him. "I want to try this," I said.

"Are you willing," he asked, "to really put forth a true effort? From the bone?"

I told my father: "I want to skate."

With clarity of purpose, everything suddenly seemed different. I didn't just want to skate—I loved it. I realized, too, that while I had to want to buy into the training, the discipline, the self-sacrifice, I needed direction and guidance, too. You truly can't get there by yourself. I needed not only to truly and profoundly depend on Dad for help but also to welcome those—coaches, trainers, others—who could help me along the way.

"I'm in," Dad said.

The U.S. team was in Colorado Springs getting ready for Nagano. After the Olympics would come the U.S. championships, which doubled as the qualification meet that would decide who would represent the United States at the forthcoming world championships; thus, in speed-skating lingo, this event was also called the world team trials. "I think," Dad said, "you're going to have to go to Lake Placid to get ready for the world team trials." The very next day, I headed out there, on a red-eye from Seattle.

As soon as I got to the center, I started working out like a fiend. I would go for extra runs. Two workouts per day? Three.

A few days later, a coach called my dad. "Apolo is working out so hard," the coach said, "we're worried he's going to burn out."

From Lake Placid, I watched the 1998 Winter Olympics on television.

The next month, at the world team trials in Marquette, Michigan, I proved competitive in every race. As the meet played out, I had to beat two other guys in the last race, a 3000-meter event, to make the team—which I did. That earned me the fifth and final spot on the world championship team.

Upside: I was on the team.

Downside: as an alternate.

The two best skaters get to compete in the individual events. Four guys skate the relay. The fifth guy is typically there as insurance.

The worlds that year took place in Vienna, Austria. I actually did get to skate, in the relay heats, but mostly I observed. I watched other guys skate, and I vowed I would never forget what it felt like to watch those other guys skate in races I thought I deserved to be in. The whole time I was there, I was also making promises to myself and writing them in my journal:

> *I'm not going to mess it up this time. When I go home, I really am going to be the different person I decided in Iron Springs I would be.*
>
> *I know what I want to do. I want to be the best I can be. I want to be the best in the world.*

I didn't know quite yet how I would get there. But I was clear, and I had no doubt—that's what I was after.

SEEKING LIFE'S TESTS

The first Special Olympics were held in Chicago in 1968. Eunice Kennedy Shriver opened the event with these words: "In ancient Rome, the gladiators went into the arena with these words on their lips: 'Let me win. But if I cannot, let me be brave in the attempt.'"

Everyone, in his or her life, faces tests.
These tests make for markers in your life,
gauges of how you're doing.

The Olympic Games, for instance, are magnificent. But they're nonetheless a kind of a marker.

The Games afford a setting for a test, with the advantage that the result comes straightaway; it comes with no ifs, ands, or buts.

The Games would compel me to meet my insecurities, those inner voices, to confront the thoroughly human emotions of fear, of freezing up, of not performing to my ability.

It is at the Games as it is in every arena in life: I have a choice. I can give in. Or I can fight—I can test myself. Perhaps I prevail; maybe not. If I am supposed to lose today, then let me be brave while I'm trying, because I am going to try, no matter what.

Isn't that what life is? Isn't that the true meaning of accomplishment?

CHAPTER 5

Every one of us has choices, and the way we frame them and make them sets us on our paths. After the worlds in Austria, I could choose where to spend the summer: Colorado Springs or Seattle?

This was the summer to prove I could keep those promises I'd made to myself. The distractions that had so bedeviled me before would again be all around me.

Now, though, I would not be tempted.

Seattle.

It all started that summer with that very first choice. After I went home, I made another. I did not call even one of my friends. Dad and I set up a gym of sorts in the garage. We bought a better stationary bike. I put a little TV we had in the house, a seven-inch Sony Trinitron, next to the bike, along with a VCR and a small fan. For two hours a day, dripping sweat, I rode that bike and watched skating tapes.

The bike was just the start of my summer workout regime, a program I wrote myself and that had no logical progression, not even really any rhyme or reason. In essence, my plan was to go hard and then go harder. At night, when no one was on the track, I ran three times a week at the local high school, Decatur High. When Dad came home from work, we would do what's called dry-land training: exercises that focused on strength, flexibility, and balance. Or we'd drive to a nearby park trail so I could in-line for mile after mile while Dad kept me company on his bike. I read books about nutrition. I cut out what seemed like every single trace of fat from my diet. I also started taking online classes, working toward my high school diploma. The months rocketed by, and as the summer drew to a close, I went back to Colorado to report back to the team and get back on the ice. What, I kept getting asked, happened to you? You look lean.

I smiled.

We went out for a training ride. I led. Pat—who was the newly appointed head coach—told me to slow down on the hills. I just kept dropping people. I couldn't help it.

Not only was I the fittest guy there, I was obliterating every other guy in the program, hands down. I was doing double the work of everyone else, and it was easy.

I was attacking the sport with a completely different mentality.

It's not too grandiose to say that was when I started changing the sport.

At the same time, an important and irrevocable change had come over me. I had just turned sixteen. But once back in Colorado, I knew with certainty that I had left home for good. I might go back for a summer or for the holidays, and I would always call Seattle my hometown, but Colorado Springs was now where I was supposed to be. I was on the way to becoming who I was to be, and as I achieved a measure of independence, as I made my way toward becoming my own person, some of the realities of growing up were truly upon me, and I embraced them.

I thought then about how it was when I had first arrived in Colorado Springs. The entire team went out one night. I not only couldn't order a beer, but it would be five more years until I could order one legally. Five years! Crazy.

So maybe I couldn't party with everyone. But I didn't want to be looked upon as the baby of the team; I wanted to lead the team. And if I couldn't lead as the captain or as a veteran of many years on the international scene, I could nonetheless do it with my performance.

That summer, something else changed, too. I met Dave Creswell.

At the time, Dave, who was from Lincoln, Nebraska, was a student at Colorado College. Some professors there had turned him on to sports psychology. The U.S. Olympic Training Center nearby was a great lab. Moreover, Pat was a great believer in the potential and power of sports psychology. Pat also thought that having an extra set of eyes and ears couldn't hurt, and so he invited Dave to become the short-track team's resident advisor.

Dave was more or less our age—in his early twenties. *If they won't listen to me*, Pat thought, *maybe they'll listen to Dave.*

Dave moved into the dorms with us that August. In the beginning, I did not like Dave. He seemed like a complete geek. He was still in college and didn't yet have a degree to formalize his expertise. What could he possibly know?

Dave watched practices and workouts. Gently, with no pressure at all, he suggested that each of us start keeping a logbook—to write down goals especially, but also thoughts, experiences, anything that came to mind.

No way, I thought.

I had kept a journal those few days in Iron Springs, and also on oc-casions such as the worlds in Vienna. But in general, I didn't see the point in setting goals or in committing to writing a continuous record of my development.

"Dude," I said to Dave, "do you play sports? I mean, who are you?"

A pretty fair badminton player, that's who Dave was, as fate would have it.

The U.S. Olympic badminton team is based in Colorado Springs, at the Training Center. I had become friends with some of the guys on the team, who had taught me to play. Anyone who says that badminton is a foo-foo sport hasn't seen it played at a world-class level; the sport is all about speed and athleticism. See it once live, and you see how cool badminton can be. Dave was a very good tennis player, and thus a natural at badminton. He and I started playing together; I would put in six or more hours each day doing short-track work and then connect with Dave for two more hours of badminton.

Dave would kick my butt in badminton.

How, I would think, *could I possibly be losing in badminton, of all things, to Dave Creswell, of all people? Wasn't I back to being in ridiculous physical shape?* Even so, I kept losing, making the same mistakes time and again. It was not only irritating, it was exasperating. When my frustration would show through, Dave would quietly ask, "Do you know why you just did that?" Or, "How do you feel about that last shot?" Or, "Tell me what you feel before you serve."

"Dave, shut the hell up," I would retort. "Let's just play."

Dave was undeterred. If he would win several points in a row, he would ask, "Are you losing your focus—and why? How could you handle this situation differently?"

For the first time, I was being prompted to think consciously about the mental aspect of being a world-class competitor. Maybe, I decided, Dave was a pretty cool guy after all. He and I started running together in an area in the northern reaches of Colorado Springs called Garden of the Gods. As we ran through canyons of red rock, Dave would talk about things I had never heard about before: visualization, meditation, breathing exercises.

Breathing exercises? "Yes," Dave said. "If you pay attention to your breathing, not just how often you breathe but whether, for instance, those breaths are shallow or deep, you can not only bring real focus to bear on what you're doing right then and there, you can also teach yourself to be calm no matter what's going on all around you.

"You can start meditating simply by paying attention to your breathing," he would say. "Feel your breath passively going in and out. If you feel your attention drifting away, bring it back by focusing on your breathing. In, out. In, out. Center your focus on just that: in, out.

"You'll see."

At first, I did not see. Schedules, workouts, laundry—I had all this mental clutter. Plus, this was a new skill. New skills sometimes take time. But practice makes, if not perfect, at least better. And what became blindingly obvious was that this could be huge.

In any sport, but particularly in short-track, you have to confront the pain of lactic acid buildup and the malaise of fatigue. Either can produce the voice inside your head that announces, *That hurts,* or *I can't.* Together, they're absolute performance killers. The way to dull that voice, make it go away, even, is to concentrate and to relax. Dave showed me how to transfer the exercises I'd been doing to practice, then to travel, then to the heat box, and, ultimately, to the start line.

Because I was the fifth guy on the travel team, I didn't skate much at all early in the 1998–99 competition season. Pat gave me a chance that October at a World Cup exhibition event in Saratoga Springs, New York; I did so well I earned a slot at a World Cup event in November in Székesfehérvár, Hungary, near Budapest.

A long name for a little town, and for me a breakthrough moment on the world stage.

All the big boys were there, the fastest short-trackers in the world, among them Kim Dong-Sung of South Korea, who just a few months before at the Nagano Games had won gold in the 1000 and silver in the 5000; Marc Gagnon of Canada, winner of bronze in Lillehammer in the 1000, gold in Nagano in the 5000 relay, and a world champion multiple times over; and Fabio Carta of Italy, who had just missed out on a medal in the relay in Nagano, the Italians finishing fourth.

Dong-Sung was so on fire at this event that he set a world record in the 3000. He won the 1500, too. But wait: I finished third in the 1500, a flash of a skate behind Fabio. This was the first time an American had medaled at that distance in a very, very long time.

In the 1000—in the final—it was me, Dong-Sung, Fabio, and another Korean, Lee Seung-Jae. To say I was the underdog would be a gross understatement. But because of my work with Dave, my mind was ready. Even without fully understanding it, I was in the zone. With a couple of laps to go, I made a phenomenal pass to go from fourth to second, ahead of Dong-Sung, just behind Fabio. Dong-Sung not only saw it, he felt it, felt what was happening; he felt me, and I could feel his uneasiness. It was as if I could read his mind: *Who is this kid? How did he sneak into that space?*

Those tapes I had been watching while pounding the bike in the summer—I had been studying Dong-Sung and Fabio in particular. And now I understood the tempo and rhythm of their skating beat. I knew what they did, their mannerisms, their tics. I knew what would happen if they would win or lose. I knew these guys on the ice per-haps even better than they knew themselves. I had studied them to exhaustion.

So I knew that when Fabio would go hard, he would take two hard crossovers to get into the corner. In skating lingo, it's called taking two ins. He did it twice, and I did it right behind him. I knew, too, that this little display was his max speed; I knew to a certainty that I would take him.

With a lap and a half to go, I tried to pass Fabio. He came over on me; I didn't have enough room. At that instant, I said to myself, *I'm going to go bust or go home; I'm going to win this thing or get nothing.* I was willing to take the risk. Not just willing—eager and ready.

On the final corner, amid a rush by all four of us for the line, I passed on the inside, an ugly pass that was technically not very pretty but nonetheless beautiful indeed: an ugly pass of all heart. A beat later, my skate was first across the line—my first World Cup win and one of the first for the United States.

I screamed in joy. Pat screamed, too, while the other coaches from other nations looked dumbfounded. You could see it especially in the eyes of the Chinese coaches: *Who is this kid?* They didn't even have anyone in the race, but nonetheless they knew the sport had just changed.

What's more, it felt easy. The action all around me slowed down; I was relaxed, concentrated, confident. I was in control and in the zone. Just like Dave had suggested it all would be, could be, and should be.

I went back to Colorado with proof positive of two things: One, I could not only compete with, I could beat the best skaters in the world. Two, Dave was obviously a genius. I was clearly wrong to have harbored even the slightest doubt about him at the outset. And I wanted more of what he had to give. We practiced more meditation techniques. We discussed positive affirmations. I practiced the art—and it is an art—of talking to myself in a constructive fashion. I began to visualize, to play out in extraordinary detail not just what I wanted to happen in training and races but also how I wanted such events to play out.

"Imagine," Dave would say, "the distractions that might come up while you're racing. You know full well, Apolo, that there are multiple races a day in short-track, and the course of even one day in a meet that stretches over several days can be jangling to anyone's nerves. What if, for instance, you accidentally fall in one heat and then you have to go again in another not even an hour or two later? It's easy to say, 'Oh, I have to put that fall behind me.' So let's talk about how. What is your plan? What is your calming routine? How do you visualize that next race?"

In his gentle way, Dave was reaching a place of depth inside me. But now I was genuinely starting to see, and to understand, the potential and the power in the mental edge.

That next race, the next significant occasion to put our work together to the test, came in Montreal, at the junior world championships in January 1999.

The night before my first race, Dave and I went together into the
arena, the Maurice Richard Arena. We walked high up into the stands.
"Go sit down," Dave said. "Pick a seat—anywhere, any row, doesn't
matter. I'm going to leave you in that seat; I'll come back in an hour. I
want you to visualize how you want the day to go tomorrow. What do
you want to have happen tomorrow? Imagine potential problems. Produce solutions. Not just what you might do or what you could do—but
what you will do."

He walked away, and I sat there alone in the empty arena. First I set
about settling down physically, getting myself comfortable, feeling a
quiet calm settle on and around me. Then I developed race strategies:
detailed strategies, the moves I not only wanted to pull off but might
have to execute if circumstances dictated. Then I produced a vibrant,
full-color, all-senses picture in my mind of what was going to happen
in each race.

With every breath, I took in strength.

With every breath, I let go of anxiety and felt a relaxed sense of calm
purpose.

Now I could feel myself as Dad had liked to imagine me: as a young
lion, the undisputed king of all it surveyed, a very big cat that was also
very soft, very light on its feet, exceedingly patient, waiting until the
very last moment to strike in a ruthless attack that would be both
hugely explosive and ferociously fast, a turn that would unleash fear,
confusion, and chaos in my rivals.

Throughout these junior world championships, I'd see Dave between races and say, "How'd I look out there?" He'd come right back:
"How did you feel?" Now I understood. It was on me to find that place
of quietude before, during, and after races.

The shortest distance between two points is, of course, a straight line. It's why in short-track an inside pass is easier; it takes more technique but less power. To execute an outside pass takes more of everything. More speed, strength, stamina, endurance, explosiveness, power, technique, lean, centrifugal force, kinetic energy—and, consequently, more mental toughness. At these championships, I had to execute outside passes repeatedly because of an intriguing bit of Korean strategy. On the sidelines, the Korean coaches would yell instructions; at the same time, someone—it's not clear who—would blow a whistle whenever it appeared a Korean skater was in position to be passed. The whistle would blow, and whatever Korean skaters might be on the ice would immediately change tracks to block a pass—before it could take place, that is. Each time I set up for a pass, I'd hear a whistle, and what do you know, the passing lane that was just there would mysteriously be gone.

A coach can say or yell anything he or she wants on the sidelines. But team skating—when skaters from one nation get together to help a particular racer from that country win—is very much against the rules, and what was going on here would naturally raise suspicion. If this was in part a mind game, I was prepared. I stayed calm. If outside passes it had to be, they were part of what I had envisioned, and I was ready; I would execute those passes with quiet resolution. The championships came down to the 1500 "superfinal," as the race was called; if I won, I would win the overall title. I got to the line and, in what would become a common theme, I became keenly aware of the energy levels the other skaters were projecting. I could literally feel it. The guy next to me, for instance, was already fatigued and just didn't want to show it. It was like a secret whisper on a communications frequency to which only I could be attuned.

My energy out there was blunt and direct: *I want it bad. I'm here to win. I'm young, hungry, naïve, neither thinking about nor afraid of any consequences.*

With about three laps to go, it became obvious what I was going to have to do and where I had to go: outside. I heard the whistles. I kept going wider and wider. I passed everybody, on the outside, and pulled away to win.

Afterward, I was asked by reporters about what had happened. I could articulate it with precision because I had seen it all play out beforehand in my mind: "I felt strong, mentally and physically, and I was just going for number one."

No American had ever before won a junior worlds. Dave couldn't have been happier; Pat, too.

Me, too. This race made me a firm believer, not merely in my physical skills but in the power of the mind.

Winning can carry with it an altogether different set of expectations and pressures. But you can't be afraid to win. This was what I discovered in Montreal in 1999. I could allow myself to win, allow myself to want it, allow all the hard work I had put in to come to fruition.

To execute a plan without regard for consequence, to jump in with no fear—this, I discovered, meant I could allow myself ready and real access to the belief that anything was possible.

It is sometimes said that great athletes are great because they hate to lose, that while others may want to win, the truly great ones hate that much more to lose.

That's only part of it, though. It's not simply that you want to win. That's far too simplistic. You have to believe wholeheartedly that you can win and will win, and you must prepare to win.

It is still the case today, remarkably so, that the mental aspect of what it takes to win is relatively ignored by far too many. If more athletes were to give training the mind even a quarter of 1 percent as much focus as they do the physical aspects of gearing up, records would fall by the bushel. I am a walking example of the truth that the most challenging opponent in any endeavor is you. It was Lao Tzu, the ancient Chinese philosopher, who said, "He who conquers others is strong. He who conquers himself is mighty." Or, in a far more contemporary context, I am a fan of Dan Millman and the book he published just a couple of years before I was born, *Way of the Peaceful Warrior.* He once sent me a shirt. On the back it said, "Peaceful Warrior." On the front, "Here and Now, Breathe and Relax."

———————

ALL ATHLETES ARE taught to push through pain.

The trick is to know what is enough and what is too much.

Actually, the trick is more than simply knowing; it's learning when you're genuinely hurt. When that's the case, you need help. It's okay not only to ask for help but also to lean on others, sometimes literally. Sometimes, too, those lessons come the hard way.

The world team championships were held in St. Louis that year after the junior worlds. The world team championships bring together the top eight skating nations. The skaters are grouped into brackets; you skate once at each distance, and whoever does best in his bracket during the heats, quarters, and semifinals moves on to the finals.

I won the 1000 and went into the 500 finals full of confidence. I was chasing down François-Louis Tremblay of Canada, an excellent sprinter, and had just caught up to him when my skate kicked one of the blocks. Off balance, I went down and skidded out of control toward the wall. I hit it hard and fast. The impact knocked the wind out of me; I could barely breathe as Pat and others urged me to finish so we could get points from the race. I got up and I finished; afterward, the medical staff looked me over and said I had bruised some bones in my back.

It wasn't for many more months that I would understand the truth: I now had a chronic back problem, and it needed real attention.

Instead, I pushed through. At the 1999 world championships in Sofia, Bulgaria, I won silver in the 500, behind Li Jiajun of China. But my back ached. Overall, I got fourth.

That summer, now seventeen, I went back for a few weeks to Seattle.

If being a world-class athlete meant ignoring pain and pushing your-self to new limits, I was in—and I mean in a big way: three workouts a day, running, biking, dry-land.

Of course, very few knew about my back, and when it was go time, there was no way I was about to let show even a hint that something might be amiss.

That December, at a World Cup event in Changchun, China, in front of the kind of huge, screaming crowd that at the time was virtually unknown in the United States for short-track, I proved again that I was a force with which to be reckoned. I took first overall—my first World Cup overall title. In China, I became famous instantly, an icon for defeating Li Jiajun. The Chinese reporters couldn't get enough of me. I would walk out of the arena and would be recognized on the street.

It was hardly like that back home.

In February, the U.S. championships went off near Boston. I had skipped some smaller meets after getting back from China, but, no question, I was bound and determined to skate in Boston. This was the national championships as well as the selection meet for the upcoming Goodwill Games, worlds, team worlds and the following season's World Cup team.

As before, the nine- and four-lap time trials were worth considerable points; I won the four and took second in the nine. Then I won the 1500. And then came the 1000.

In that 1000, I fell and hit the wall so brutally hard that I dislocated not just one but both kneecaps. Even now, it hurts just thinking about what it was like having both kneecaps out of place. Stabbing agony. It is perhaps a credit to my willfulness that I put one of the kneecaps back into its proper position while I was still on the ice; that way, I could stand up. The only consolation for a very long day spent with Dad at the emergency room was that my points total was good enough for second. I would still get to compete just a few days later, in the Goodwill Games, back in Lake Placid.

It is, again, a credit to my willfulness that I wanted to compete. I wouldn't seriously entertain any other notion.

As before, Dad said, "Don't worry—you don't have to go to Lake Placid."

"I'm going," I said.

Your kneecaps do not like it when they are pushed violently out of place. Even when they go back in, they're unbelievably sore, and everything around them is sore. On top of which, I had just gotten a new pair of boots; boots need to be broken in. I was determined I would break them in while skating in Lake Placid.

In the 1000, I fell—again.

All this was prelude to the worlds in March in Sheffield, England. I ran a high fever; I couldn't stop coughing and couldn't sleep. My red blood cell count was way low, my white count high. Dad cruised the Sheffield health food stores in search of homeopathic remedies. I appreciated his effort but didn't want to take anything for fear it would be contaminated with a substance on the banned list. I did the only sensible thing—took antibiotics—even though I don't like taking them because they make me feel sluggish and slow. My best finish in Sheffield was hardly a surprise: seventh place.

FROM DAVE I knew the import of critical self-analysis.

What are my strengths?

Perhaps even more important, what are my weaknesses? And how do you go about turning those weaknesses into strengths?

Clearly, after Sheffield, I had work to do.

I was a young lion, right?

I was now eighteen. This coming season would be the critical pre-Olympic year, the time for a young lion to roar in full voice. That summer I stayed in Colorado Springs, determined after reflection—and after the sick bug went away—to turn things around.

My way.

Sue Ellis had taken over as head coach before the 1999–2000 season, the one that had just ended. Her training focus was long on drills, leg strength, body mass, and lactic capacity. My focus had always been elsewhere—on biking and running, for instance. Her methods had me doing lots of weight training, and that training got me leg pressing roughly 1,500 pounds.

Strong. But, well, heavy. I weighed 180—up 15 pounds, at least, from where I ought to have been. The consequence was that while I had the strength to get to the front of the pack, I often felt wiped out after a race; I didn't have the ability to recover like I should have.

I told Sue I was going to do my own training. Probably a good idea, she said.

Pat was in Colorado Springs—not coaching—and he and I, along with his wife, would go on long runs several times a week. That was just the start; I rode my bike up and into the mountains for hours; I worked on the StairMaster. Two months later, my weight was back to 158, my body fat down 8 percent.

I also worked that summer with a new assistant coach, Steve Gough. Steve had been on the 1994 Canadian Olympic team; he had a great technical eye, and he made my blades feel good.

On the ice, Rusty Smith and I pushed each other. Rusty was the 1997 junior worlds overall silver medalist and a 1998 Olympian, an extremely fast sprinter, a first-rate training partner, and a good friend.

I was going faster. It was obvious. I could feel it.

Three months in, meanwhile, my blood work had come back to normal. It was a mystery why it had been so off in the first instance, maybe something as simple as having overtrained.

"You're going to surprise a lot of people this year," I was told.

I knew I was going to do well, though, and it was no surprise. That summer, I was working just as hard, maybe even harder, at the mental edge.

We had a new sports psychologist, Doug Jowdy. My interest in Eastern philosophies and particularly in mind control—that is, using my mind to control my body—was intensifying; I wanted to take myself not only to a level I had never before experienced but to a place few had ever gone.

"Doug," I said, "I want to handle a level of pain and fatigue that would seem impossible to other athletes."

The number one thing in short-track that inhibits you from going faster is your pain tolerance—in scientific terms, your lactate threshold. When you feel it and respond to that pain, your technique changes. You get choppy; you start coming up out of the skating position, meaning you're sitting higher and therefore are less aerodynamic; your strokes are shorter; your pushes are shorter. You start wasting energy while at the same time you throw in all kinds of excess body movement.

It's a downward spiral.

To use another metaphor, it's not just letting off the gas pedal. It's letting off the gas pedal while opening the window and the sunroof and turning the car into a convertible, and then, just to top it off, unfurling a parachute behind the car.

What if my pain threshold could be ramped way, way up?

Pain is temporary. Lactic acid is simply a chemical, a by-product of what happens when your muscles are working. It was obvious that a mere fifteen or twenty minutes after a workout, all that pain was gone. Other guys might say, "I can't deal with that pain," or, more likely, "I don't want to deal with it." Or "I'm just not good at it."

I saw it as entirely within my control.

Doug came back with exactly what I wanted to hear: "Let's do it."

Doug had been hired the year before; Dave had left Colorado Springs to pursue a PhD at UCLA. Doug's hiring was actually a small part of a big program undertaken by the U.S. Olympic Committee in advance of Salt Lake and the 2002 Games, an initiative that was dubbed Podium and called for the investment of millions of dollars—in specially targeted areas—to each of the winter-sports programs. The speed-skating federation wanted to hire a sports psychologist; it turned out to be Doug.

Doug played hockey in college and then worked as an assistant hockey coach at Penn State. He arrived in Colorado Springs, it would turn out, with unbelievably hilarious stories of these two seniors on his team when he was a mere freshman—a personalized Jowdy version, times two, of the Socrates character from Dan Millman's *Peaceful Warrior.*

The first guy, the team's starting center, stood six-three and weighed maybe 180. He played, though, like he was much bigger. He played with no fear. This guy's pregame meal consisted of all of maybe ten French fries with a few drops of ketchup. Doug would say to this guy, "Don't you need to eat more?" The guy looked up from the fries and said, "You got to go in there freaking hungry—freaking hungry, I tell you." Before every game, this was the ritual, his recipe for being mentally tough. He ate a bowl of fries. And he played as if he were freaking hungry.

The other guy was one of the starting defensemen and loved, as hockey players do, to hit people. Jowdy was playing defense, too, and this guy—when you looked at him, he inspired comparison to Charles Manson, only bigger—was, frankly, intimidating, especially to a lowly freshman. The other guy, as some hockey players do, had a penchant for beer. Sometimes even between periods of a game. Jowdy would look over, and this guy might pull out a can and take a swig, and Jowdy would say, "Okay, I'm in for some of that, too." Here was a way, albeit unorthodox, into the zone. From a psychological perspective, who had the time or inclination for any sort of worry? Everything was cool.

Jowdy's stories came with time, as he and I built a relationship of loyalty and trust, and as I made the switch after having worked with Dave. Doug is soft-spoken; his gentle manner belies the raging force and incredible drive within him.

When he was interviewing for the job with the Olympic Committee, the human-relations specialist asked him, "You've been working at a hospital with heroin addicts for the past three years. How would that apply to Olympic athletes?" Doug had a long history by then of working with athletes, too; he'd been at that hospital because full-time sports-related jobs were hard to come by. He said, "Isn't Olympic sport about addiction? It's all about addiction! You work really hard; you develop a tolerance; you develop an aerobic and anaerobic threshold, and then you want more; then you want even more; then even that much more isn't good enough. An exercise physiologist tells you to rest—you go ride your bike for fifty miles or play two hours of basketball. Performance is performance.

"Okay," he conceded, "it's a different kind of performance. A person with a drug addiction is trying to stay sober one day at a time; an athlete is trying to set a personal best or win a gold medal. But there are certain psychological challenges that are very similar. In sports, the results are more tangible, more quantitative, and you get a different kind of approval. Either way, it's what's going on mentally.

"In your HR department," he went on, "I bet you have people who don't have the ability to communicate, who aren't organized, who have a hard time concentrating at certain times of the day, who aren't motivated, who don't believe in themselves. It's the same thing with Olympic athletes."

"You're hired," he was told. "Oh, and maybe you could come over to the HR department and talk to us sometime?"

When we first met Doug, at a team meeting, he shared his philosophy about training for the psychological side of sports and made it plain that his style was to let us, the athletes, make the first move when it came to working with him individually. The pattern in these situations is fairly consistent. Some of the guys would talk with Doug while he was skating on the ice during practice but never come to the office. Some would get him in the locker room but not in his office. Some might grab him on road trips but never in the office. Some might venture a thought or two while standing around in a group but never even think about venturing into his office.

I went to his office. Not immediately but soon enough.

Doug's office was small. It had a desk, a chair, and a La-Z-Boy—this huge, comfortable chair. When I came in that first time, I took the chair from behind the desk and sat in that. "You take the La-Z-Boy," I told him. "This is your office; you deserve to be comfortable."

Doug has said many times since that he knew from the get-go that working with me was going to be different.

At the outset, in an effort to get to know all the skaters better, he had handed out an eighteen-page questionnaire.

"I would like to become a machine, no mistakes," I wrote—this was in October 1999, when I was still just seventeen. "Be able to focus to my potential every time I skate."

The second-to-last question on the questionnaire read, "What questions would you like answered that would help improve your training, performance, and quality of your life?"

I wrote, "Am I going to heaven? And am I leading a good life?"

The last question asked, "Is there any other information you think would be important for me to know in order to help you reach your goals this season?"

I wrote, "I want seven world championships, six gold medals, and to be a legend in speed skating."

Another questionnaire Dave gave us was entitled a "Survey of Athletic Experiences." It asked various questions and asked us to rate our response this way: 0 meant almost never; 1, sometimes; 2, often; 3, almost always.

"The more pressure there is during a game, the more I enjoy it," the survey said. I rated that a 3.

"To me, pressure situations are challenges that I welcome." 3.

"When I fail to reach my goals, it makes me try even harder." 3.

"I improve my skills by listening carefully to advice and instruction from coaches." 3.

"I make fewer mistakes when the pressure is on because I concentrate better." 3.

After our first session in his office, Doug worked up a mental training program for me. "This is going to take an enormous amount of effort," he told me. "To become skilled at this will take persistence and dedication—you're going to have to keep a journal, set goals, and reevaluate them, watch videotape, practice various forms of meditation and visualization."

"Okay," I said. "I want whatever you've got."

I had seen other guys get in the zone by listening to music. But intuitively I understood that in terms of building the kind of mental strength I was seeking, that had to be but a grain of sand compared with what was out there.

If, as a premise, all world-class athletes had physical talent, what could separate one guy from the rest? Since everything else had to be equal, it figured that the guy who could make the best use of the mental edge would consistently be in a better position. A central theme of Doug's work was that sports psychology too often focused on competition and overlooked the import of training. "Let's really focus on training," he said. "That's where everything begins."

Because he would be on the ice during workouts—the hockey player and coach in him—Doug and I could talk then and there. If others would split after whatever coach might be running an on-ice session left the arena—warming up and cooling down may well be for many athletes the least favorite part of working out—I made a point to stay, to run for just a bit, and then stretch for a good twenty or thirty minutes. Doug and I would check in with each other there, too. If others couldn't stand the cooldown and stretch, there was a distinct reason I embraced it. It was a perfect opportunity to concentrate my mind on each stretch, on each movement—and on the breathing that went with it. Weight training was another perfect time, Doug said, to work on strengthening your mind, to use strength training as a form of meditation, and to focus your mind to achieve discrete goals.

"These are just some of the techniques," he said, "that we're going to use to train your mind to transcend pain and fatigue."

Before heading to the weight room, then, I would lock in.

First I would focus on my breathing, to calm my mind and my heart rate, to center myself. In, out. No counting. Just focusing on the breaths themselves, allowing whatever distractions there might be to dissipate.

With my body awareness up, I would visualize how I wanted the workout to proceed. What were the goals I wanted to achieve during this session? How was I going to do it? How, specifically, was I going to attack that workout?

During the workout itself, I would bring intensity and passion. *Tired? Not an excuse. Bring it.*

I would tell myself: *No regrets.*

I would even say it out loud, the words echoing around the weight room: "No regrets."

"This weight," I would say if I were doing squats, "is not going to defeat me. I can and will move it. I am going to put this weight on my back and explode out of this hole like I am breathing fire and move this weight."

And I would.

That summer, Doug gave us another questionnaire. It asked, among other questions, "What can you do to improve your psychological skills? In other words, what can you do on a regular basis to improve your ability to concentrate, deal with pressure, stay motivated, be more confident, cope with pain and fatigue . . . work well with coaches, etc.?"

My answer was lengthy and underscored both the progress I was making and my emerging interests:

For me personally, I need to be much more consistent when doing my meditation, really work on how I meditate, feel my chi more focused but relaxed at the same time. I really want to start learning chi gong and [begin] using it every day to improve my imagery, healing, circulatory skills. I want to be at a competition, and when I am not jogging, I need to be meditating. I believe that when I prepare mentally for a workout beforehand, I am much more efficient during the workout and I feel much more confident. On a visual basis, I am pretty good with self-talk. I think that I need to mentally start using the meditation skills for recovery. I have to learn how to push myself but at the same time be very smart about my recovery. This all leads to the Olympics. For me to become an Olympic champion I need to be doing mental work all day every day. While eating . . . while working or [doing] school work I really need to be focusing on the moment. Most important— consistency.

I signed it "Apolo Ohno aka Chunk Dog."

From the Training Center in Colorado Springs, what locals call the Incline beckons from seemingly right outside your dorm room.

To call the Incline a hiking trail is to do it grave injustice. It is one of the great cross-training tools in all of the United States, and a place where I could, indeed, push myself.

The Incline, a scar on the face of the mountain several miles west of the Training Center, essentially goes straight up—to be precise, just over 2,000 feet of vertical gain in almost exactly one mile by way of thousands of railroad ties and crushed granite. The average grade on the Incline is 40 percent; the steepest is 68 percent.

Essentially, the Incline is a StairMaster cut into the face of a mountain. You top out at an elevation of 8,585 feet, after about 3,000 steps. Just for a comparison, it's a gain of 1,224 feet and roughly 1,860 steps to get to the observatory on the 102nd floor of the Empire State Building.

Climbing the Incline, it's unavoidable: the air is thin. It can hurt just to breathe. The thousands of lunges up those stairs produce a burning sensation in your quads and your butt, in your back and your calves. Even your ankles feel it. All of this triggers the brain, which says, *Slow down—catch your breath.* This was the biological process. But I didn't have to be a slave any longer to that process.

True, the harder I went, the more my body would produce that lactic acid, and the more that acid would tell my pain receptors, *Ouch, this hurts, slow down.* I acknowledged all of this in my head. It's the natural human reaction to pain. And then I let it go. Pain and I—we could be acquaintances, but we need not be more. The fact that I felt pain did not mean I would immediately, inexorably, and irreparably *be* hurt. That I felt pain did not mean I needed to fear it.

And so I went harder up the hill.

The guy I often went to the Incline with became a very, very good friend, Mark Fretta, a triathlete who was also based at the Training Center.

Fretta was an endurance athlete. I was always looking for ways to maximize my endurance; I thought, *Triathletes are freaks at endurance. That's what they do.* Fretta, I noticed, was amazingly good at biking and running, and I wanted to be stronger in both. "Look, man," I told him, "I want to start doing the Incline with you—I hear you're a monster."

At that point, I had done the Incline in 25 or 26 minutes.

No one beats the Incline. No one, not ever. You never conquer it. You simply learn how to go up it faster.

Fretta holds the Incline speed record: 16 minutes, 42 seconds. I learned how to do it in about 17:15.

The Incline became our thing. "Fretta," I would say to him on the phone, "I'm doing the Incline in half an hour. You in?" Or, "Fretta," I would say, "today we're going to go up this and we're not breaking any records, we're just going to talk." Or, "Fretta—today I really want to work this."

Fretta was always, always in.

One of the ways back down the Incline is along a trail that runs four miles, through switchbacks that loop through the pines. Sometimes we did that. Other times, I would stand at the top of the Incline for sixty seconds, enjoy the view, and then head right back down the stairs.

At the Training Center, I also found myself increasingly drawn to the group of wrestlers living or working out there. They had about them an undeniable warrior mentality that I was eager to tap into. You could look around, for instance, and see Rulon Gardner, who would go on at the Sydney Summer Games to do the unthinkable: defeat Alexander Karelin, the man mountain from Siberia. You can't measure the potential and power of human will, and that's what I reveled in around the wrestlers. When a wrestler walks out onto the mat, when a boxer climbs into a ring, I would sometimes remind myself, he has to have supreme confidence. It can come off as arrogance, but without supreme confidence, he is nothing. Think about what Rulon is up to. When he goes to Sydney, there's Karelin, who hasn't lost a match of any kind since 1987, winner of three straight Olympic gold medals, a guy who at the 1993 world championships won gold even though he had broken a rib in a preliminary round but carried on because a broken rib was, as he put it, "a trifle."

I loved that die-hard mentality. I would imagine myself in a boxer's place. He's going into battle with another man who's trying to make his face look like meat loaf. Any hesitation or doubt in your ability—it's lights out. *Be supremely confident, like that boxer,* I would say. Didn't Muhammad Ali say it best? "I am the greatest!"

Ali had insecurities—sure, he did. He admitted afterward that a lot of times before he fought, he was scared. But did he ever show it? Never. He transcended his fears. He convinced himself he was the greatest of all time and the other guy in the ring was simply—and about to be demonstrably—inferior in all ways, foolish even to dare to get into the ring with him.

At the Training Center, the wrestlers also had their own sauna. It was nasty. It smelled awful.

I loved it in there.

In my years at the center, I believe I was the only nonwrestler allowed by the wrestlers into their sauna, which is right off their practice floor.

Dad had suggested that I start practicing some of my meditation techniques in a sauna. Frankly, the idea had not occurred to me, but for Dad it was a natural. The bath is central to Japanese culture, with its emphasis on the *onsen*, the hot springs. You clean yourself at an *onsen*, but not just physically; the emphasis is on the spiritual, a cleansing of the body and of the soul.

The wrestlers would say to me, "Hey, man, why are you in here? Do you have to cut weight in your sport, too?"

"No. It's not that way in short-track."

"So why are you putting yourself through this torture?"

For them, indeed, it was akin to torture. It sometimes seemed borderline psychotic, what these wrestlers were doing—deliberately losing 20 or 30 pounds to make weight, all to go fight another man in hand-to-hand combat? There were guys in there weighing 200 pounds, ripped, with a physique that ought to have been featured in some six-pack abs special, and they'd drop down to 180 or 170. Yet through the power of the human spirit, they somehow would be able to bring it, and bring it hard, when it came time on the mat.

If these guys can do that, I would tell myself, *I can tap into that. I can take my mind and body to that place, too.*

So when I was in the sauna, I would remind myself, *You can hang with these guys. It's just pain.* I would be in there for a half hour. Or more. Maybe once a week some of the wrestlers would do what they called the Russian sauna: a sequence that started with forty-five minutes in the heat, followed by twelve minutes out; then thirty minutes in, eight out; then twelve final minutes back in. After that, you'd wrap yourself in hot towels and drink hot tea.

They were all in; I was all in.

As time went on, meanwhile, the sauna became for me a far different place. My body acclimated. The heat no longer felt threatening or suffocating. Instead, it felt welcoming, the sauna now a quiet place of recovery and stillness.

"Read this," Doug said to me one day, handing me *The Inner Game of Tennis*, the 1974 classic by Tim Gallwey, mindful that I had a lot of time in the sauna, or back in my dorm room, to think. "Here's what you're looking for in this book," Doug said. "Gallwey talks about 'Self 1,' the thinker, who is constantly telling 'Self 2,' a silent doer, what to do: bend the knees, watch the ball, follow through. Gallwey says that when you master the inner game—you confront fear, doubt, lapses of concentration, dealing with negative thought and low confidence—the scoreboard, the outer game, will take care of itself. To do that, you have to learn to control Self 1.

"Think about this, too, while you're reading," he said. "Short-track lends itself to personality types who are of course highly achievement oriented but simultaneously both compulsive and perfectionistic. Any of this resonate, Apolo? Haven't you seen it around you that someone has a bad workout and then can't feel good unless and until he has the good workout that he thinks makes up for the bad one? But he puts so much pressure on himself that he sabotages that next workout—or, worse, and as the case may be, that next heat? He starts obsessing on what seems like the smallest thing and can't get off it?

"Self 1 is the voice that keeps running in your head. Self 2 knows what to do if Self 1 will only let him," Doug said.

Fascinating.

"Let's do this, too," Doug said at another point, introducing me to the neurofeedback machine. "This device measures brain waves. We can use it to help you achieve a state of deep, relaxed concentration.

"The more you relax and focus, the slower and slower the lines on the machine's display will get. You want the line to drop and then to go *tick-tick-tick*. Like this. Watch."

He hooked himself up, took a breath, exhaled, and—*tick-tick-tick*.

I got hooked up. I took a breath. The display looked like one of those old-fashioned Pong video games, with peaks and valleys all over the screen. I couldn't stay focused on anything for more than two seconds, it seemed. I tried counting. *Eee-boop, eee-boop*, the machine would grunt, a soundtrack of sorts to the Pong-style up-and-down on the video.

"Calm," Doug said. "Work at being calm. This machine will give you immediate feedback. When you learn how to control this, it's probably one of the most powerful ways you can go to control your thinking. And when you can do that, you're putting your mind in the state most conducive to peak performance. *When* you learn—not *if* you can learn."

Maybe three of us on the team made use of the machine. The others tried it five or six times, Doug would say later. I did maybe two dozen. Over time, I could make the machine do what I wanted. It started making the most satisfying, soothing sound: *tick-tick-tick* . . .

———————

IT DAWNED ON me that summer: I wasn't racing against other guys or other countries. Not really. I was racing against myself. If I allowed myself to be who I could be, the possibilities were endless.

As soon as the first group of skaters arrived in Colorado Springs to prepare for the upcoming winter season, it was clear that things were different. Some of the others were huffing and puffing; as I sailed along, I felt only that I was on the right track. Also, I had gotten a pair of new boots from a company in Australia called RBC; with these boots I had great feel.

The first World Cup that fall of 2000 would be in Calgary. The week before, we held a pre-Cup competition there called CODA, an international get-ready meet.

It was obvious I was so much stronger than anyone else. But in practice, I fell; the fall tweaked my blades. Negativity, that old demon, started creeping in. *Your feel is gone,* it said. *Oh, you tried so hard, but so what? All that hard work you did this summer—all for nothing.*

No.

The blades got fixed.

I vowed things really would be different.

I acknowledged the negativity.

Then I let it go.

One of the last races in the pre-Cup CODA event was a long skate—3000 meters, twenty-seven laps. Instead of hanging in the back, my usual style, this would be the event that would show everybody just how strong I really was. I told Sue to direct me during the race to attack, to sprint as hard as I could until she said stop; the attacks ought to come not in sequence, so that I could prepare to go all out and then get ready for the next one; instead, I would attack whenever she said, however many times that would be.

It's very difficult to run those sorts of sprints for the same reason that it's difficult to run fast in a marathon or other track and field distance event without a rabbit setting the pace. Mentally, it's a huge challenge to chase your own rabbit, if you will. In those twenty-seven laps, Sue ordered seven sprints. She wanted to see, and I wanted to know, how many such attacks I could sustain during a race. Seven, for sure, we learned, because the lap times I threw down were not those of an endurance race; they called out the numbers you'd see in a sprint such as the 500. When I finished, everyone murmured, "Apolo is on it."

Truth be told, it hurt. That race hurt. But I didn't show that to anyone. The pain was momentary. It went away, and I was left with the satisfaction of knowing I was so strong.

The next week, at the World Cup stop, the rest of the world would find out how strong I was.

Now Kim Dong-Sung was in Calgary, too. Marc Gagnon. Li Jiajun.

I won the 500, 1000, and 1500, and I set American records in the 500 and 1500. I crossed the line first in the 3000, too, but was disqualified after the referee ruled I had interfered with Kim. I won the meet overall title, my second career World Cup overall, and around the rink you could see the other coaches assessing this new dynamic: *We could be in big trouble. The Ohno kid is ridiculously strong this year. He can do things nobody else can do. He is strong. He is patient.*

Dong-Sung came up to me after one of the races and said, in English, "You're number one. You are the best."

Marc also made sure to get me by myself to say, "Good luck, man— you're the only guy who can beat the Koreans."

I thought that, too, but to hear that as an affirmation from Gagnon, one of the greats of the sport, cemented it for me.

At the next World Cup, in Provo, Utah, I fell in a 1000 heat but repeated in the 500 and this time won the 3000. Afterward, speaking about me to a reporter for one of the Salt Lake City newspapers, Sue said, "He probably has the best skate control of any skater I know. The guy should have been a world-class figure skater."

The next two World Cup stops were in Asia in December, first in Nobeyama, Japan, then back to Changchun, China. In Japan, I won the 1500 and 3000. In China, I won the overall.

When the Asian swing was over, reporters asked the Korean and

Chinese coaches, "Who is the best short-track skater in the world?" The answer came not only quickly but with unanimity: "Apolo Ohno."

That Christmas, Dad came to Colorado Springs. The other skaters had all gone home. We had the run of the place, pretty much all to ourselves. We hung the pads on the walls; I would skate. Dad, as ever, would time and videotape my laps.

Over to Colorado College we would go, so I could run the bleachers. Dad wrapped himself against the cold and watched me run, up and down. It made for a truly great holiday—just me and Dad, together.

The World Cup season wrapped up about a month later in Europe, in Austria. I won the 500, 1500, and 3000 and again won the overall title for the meet.

So for the season: three overalls in five World Cups; second-place finishes in two other World Cup events; I won at least one race at every distance; and I was awarded the overall World Cup title for each distance and for the entire year.

I was without question number one in the entire world.

In this one season, it's not too much to say that I changed the sport. I changed the way people raced, the way they trained, the way they viewed the sport, the sport's technique—and set in motion a search for talent all over the world that would ultimately ignite a wave of new Korean, Chinese, and Canadian skaters recruited with but one goal in mind: beat Apolo Ohno.

Salt Lake City and the 2002 Games were a year away. It was readily apparent that no American male had yet to win even one individual Olympic medal in short-track; Cathy Turner had won two, both golds, in 1992 and 1994, and so all around me the story line was slowly but surely starting to take shape: maybe Apolo could win not just one but four.

Just one thing. There is never any predicting the future.

MENTAL EDGE

Mental edge is everything. It's everything in life, of course, and all the more so in sports, and particularly at the Olympic level, where everyone has talent. The mental edge not only can be a difference—it is *the* difference.

Breathing techniques, visualization methods, meditation pathways—these are just some of the ways to train your mind the way you train your body.

There is great wisdom, too, in one of my favorite books: Gary M. Walton's *Beyond Winning: The Timeless Wisdom of Great Philosopher Coaches*, the stories of men who were successful in sports and in life.

There are all kinds of ways to tap into the mental edge. It doesn't need to be complex, and it doesn't need to be expensive. When I go to the gym, for instance, I like to wear a T-shirt that says, "No Weakness." I have another I like, too. It says, "B >yesterday," which means "Better Than Yesterday" or maybe "Bigger Than Yesterday." When I put on those shirts, I'm ready to go.

CHAPTER 6

No one ever expects to get injured. When you're younger, you think you're bulletproof.

The world team championships were scheduled for March 24, 2001, in Japan. The very next weekend, the world championships were to be held in South Korea. Three days before the world team championships, already in Japan, I went to do a little light weight lifting. No big deal. In fact, a totally typical thing to do before and even between competitions. As I was lifting, I felt an awful pain in my back. Not a tear, not a pop, but a deep, savage pain that literally took my breath away.

Three days until I was supposed to race. The trainers suggested ice and massage.

Race? I had trouble even standing up straight.

That weekend, I got on the ice and raced. The team needed me. Somehow I won the 3000.

The back spasms got worse. There wasn't time to figure out what was wrong and how serious it might be. My back had been hurt the year before, but then I'd done so well. Had I aggravated the prior year's injury or was this something entirely new?

What I knew for sure was that these worlds in Korea were the first championships I was going into with a real chance not only to win but to dominate, if I could push through the pain. In the 1500, I hesitated and got fourth. In the 1000, I hesitated again and got second. I went nowhere in the 500. That left the 3000. With three laps to go, I was in the lead. Inexplicably, I hesitated again. Gagnon jumped right up behind me. Around, around, around we went. Marc, who was in position to win the overall title if he could win the race, was looking for an opening. Me? I was looking for at least the one individual win and second overall.

I had enough in me to hold him off and win the 3000. Later that same day, in the 5000 relay, we Americans won: me, Rusty Smith, Daniel Weinstein, and Ron Biondo, our first-ever relay world title.

In the moment, it was easy to forget about the pain in my back—two world championship golds and one silver, a great finale to an amazing season.

As soon as I returned to the States, I should have gone into rehab. I didn't, though—the young lion and all, and the feelings of invincibility that went that spring with turning nineteen. Indeed, when I got back, I didn't just take part in practices with the men's team, I worked out with the women's team, too. I would do back-to-back practices. That was no good for my back. What was I thinking?

I wasn't, obviously.

I used to use a weight vest regularly—that is, I'd skate with a weighted vest the same way that a baseball player slips a weighted doughnut over the bat in the on-deck circle so the bat seems lighter when he's up at the plate swinging for real. I used to do sixty laps minimum with the vest; I would push myself to do eighty.

Now, though, I couldn't even do twenty.

What was wrong with me? The Olympics were coming up in mere months. It wasn't possible that I was going to be a wreck in 2002 after bombing out in 1998. Was it?

Finally, reluctantly, I went to a chiropractor in Colorado Springs, Scott Rosenquist. He ordered up X-rays and an MRI scan. "Hmm," he said. "Here's what's going on. Your legs are really strong, but your lower back is really not. Here's why. To make a long story short, you have tears in two muscles, the psoas and the quadratis lumborum. The QL connects your pelvis to your spine and helps you extend your back; the psoas is part of a muscle group called the hip flexors, and when you do a sit-up, it's those muscles that flex the spine upon the pelvis.

"Got that?" he asked.

"That's the start. The other muscles in the area are so tight they're going into spasm every time you're bending over to skate. And because they're so tight, they're causing a disc in your lower back—it's called the L5-S1—to bulge, and that's pressing on your nerves, and that's what's causing you all that pain.

"Got that?

"Good news, bad news," he said. "Good news: You'll almost certainly be fine. Bad: You're going to take at least two months off. In those two months, you're not even going to think about getting on the ice. In about three months, you'll probably be about eighty percent."

This was May.

Three months—that would take me through June, July, and into August. The Olympics were in February, six months after that.

Rehab is no fun, and it was particularly no fun because I knew full well that within the niche world that is short-track, the word would get out, if it hadn't already: *Ohno isn't ready.*

Did you hear? That awesome season he just had—maybe that's it. Maybe he won't even be able to go to Salt Lake City. I hear he's hurt pretty bad.

My job was to block out all of that, to stay focused, to let the noise go by for what it was—noise. My job was to look within myself, will myself to get better, be calm, stay calm. My job, too, was to project that calm. That would convey strength, too. Anyone looking at me, looking for any sign of weakness or vulnerability, would see only calm and strength.

The first two World Cups that fall came early—in late September, in Asia. We did not go.

The horror that was 9/11 intervened. The terrorist attacks on New York, Washington, DC, and Pennsylvania stunned us, shocked us, left each of us on the Training Center campus hurting, especially for those who lost family or friends. The horror of watching the two planes crash into the World Trade Center towers in New York—it remains unspeakable.

At such moments, sport can seem awfully trivial. Yet there is something about sport, and about the Olympic Games in particular, that speaks to the best in each of us, to our hopes and dreams, to our vision for a better world. We honor the sacrifice and carry forward the struggle, each of us in our own way.

My way was to skate and to represent the United States of America, and to assume both of those responsibilities with renewed dedication.

We stepped back onto the World Cup stage in Calgary, in the third week of October. My blades weren't right. I wasn't 100 percent, and I knew it.

Wait: be calm, be focused.

I won the 1000, passing Kim Dong-Sung. I took second in the 3000.

"He is, after all, Apolo Ohno—everyone else, frankly, is not," the U.S. team leader, Jack Mortell, told a reporter from one of the Salt Lake City papers.

It was huge to medal. Only a very few knew the entire backstory, the newspaper reporting that I had a "stubborn sore muscle" in my lower back and Sue saying, "It has kept him from staying over his hips and going into the turns as hard as he'd like."

I met the press wearing a "Salt Lake Fire Department" T-shirt and said, "You've got to show the rest of the world your face. Short-track is about the psychological edge as much as anything." So at least I was back on my skates, back into it—and then, suddenly, I was not. During a heat in the 5000 relay, I came around a corner, lost my edge, and flew headfirst into the wall. The impact was so intense that my helmet flew off my head. I tried to stand up; I couldn't. I tried to get up; I couldn't. Finally, I got up and off the ice. I was not only done for the day, I had sustained a concussion.

Another obstacle to confront.

Be calm, be strong.

Be smart.

I flew back to Washington State. A close family friend had recommended I see Dr. Lawrence Lavine, a specialist in osteopathic medicine whose office was in Tacoma. I figured I still had time before the Games to get myself back to 100 percent; my recovery, though, seemed to have hit a plateau. I needed to get back that last 20 percent; maybe he could help.

Oh—he could help, all right.

Osteopathic medicine, surprisingly not all that widely known, has been around since the 1870s. It is based on a philosophy that focuses on the unity of all body parts, with the muscles and bones a key element in positive health; the emphasis is on a holistic approach and on certain manipulative treatments designed to spark the body to heal itself.

Dr. Lavine's list of credentials was long and incredibly impressive. He was board certified in, among other specialties, emergency medicine and neurology. He had earned a master's degree in public health from Columbia University in New York.

"You've got the expected chronic strains," he said after the initial workup. "But you should also know that multiple energetic axes have been shifted off their normal positions. We can relieve some structure and tissue restrictions. That will allow your body to begin healing itself more rapidly."

I had never heard anything quite like it or met anyone quite like him.

"Imagine a piston with the sleeve bent," he said. "How does that piston work? Not well, obviously. But if you straighten the sleeve, now the piston can work correctly again. That's what we're going to do.

"We'll get you better," he said.

After our first treatment together, he warned, "The next day, you're going to feel like you got hit by a truck. But after that, you're going to notice just how much better you feel.

"You'll get better," he said.

And I did.

Whatever Dr. Lavine did, his methods seemed a little bit voodoo. But they worked extraordinarily well. I worked back to training six days a week, sometimes seven. There was a lot to do in what was now looking like not a lot of time.

Beyond the training time, I now had other obligations: meetings with potential sponsors, interviews with newspapers and magazines and with NBC, which would be broadcasting the Games.

———————

A LITTLE MORE than two weeks before the Olympic Trials, Shani Davis—who had become a good friend—and I were driving home from practice. I was behind the wheel. The road seemed slushy, nothing more. Abruptly, my Toyota 4Runner started pulling to the left, across traffic. We had been in the far right lane on a divided six-lane road; I had been going thirty-five miles per hour, ten miles under the speed limit. Maybe somebody bumped me from behind and I just didn't feel it? I looked in the rearview mirror—no one there.

The car kept sliding, across all three lanes.

At that instant, as we slid into the median, we had no idea what was going on. Only that we were not in control of the situation.

We had hit a patch of black ice—which we would only discover later.

The car slid off the pavement. I said to Shani, "You okay?"

He didn't even have time to respond before the car flipped and rolled—three, maybe four times. It came to rest, wheels up, on the other side of the road, all the way over in the far lane. We were terrified, scared beyond words. Both of us were sure we were going to die. If some eighteen-wheeler came along the road, we were sitting ducks.

In one of those moments when you have to believe that fate is whispering—*You have things you still have to do, Apolo, and you, too, Shani*—there was no oncoming traffic.

The 4Runner was totaled.

But we were still very much alive.

Still inside the Toyota, we surveyed the wreckage, ourselves, each other. I looked down at my legs. I counted my fingers. Everything was still working. Shani looked himself over; amazingly, he was in one piece, too. Each of us had been wearing a seat belt. If not for that, surely one or both of us would have been catapulted out onto the road in a hail of glass.

Time kept ticking. Still no cars coming. We needed to get out of the 4Runner.

The doors were stuck.

There was only one way out. The windshield was already cracked and crumbled. We would have to kick it out and then wriggle out over the hood.

Good thing we had strong legs.

———————

"YOU'LL BE FINE," Dr. Lavine said.

Until almost the very moment I left for Salt Lake City, and the Olympic Trials, I was at it in the gym, in the weight room, on the ice. Morning till night, I was intensely focused, the goal now in sight: to make the 2002 Olympic team and, more, to be one of the top two skaters at every distance so I would have the chance to compete in all four Olympic events.

I knew full well whom I'd be racing against here.

Rusty Smith, Dan Weinstein, and Tommy O'Hare had been on the 1998 Olympic team. Ron Biondo—and Rusty—had been on that world championship 2001 relay team with me. Shani had been the overall winner at the 2001 U.S. junior short-track championships. J. P. Kepka, who was seventeen, had won the 1999 junior elite trials. Adam Riedy had finished second—behind me—at the 1999 U.S. junior nationals and had raced on the World Cup circuit.

We were teammates, and we might be good friends, but this was no time to be friends. It made no difference that we had lived in the dorms together, or trained together, or traveled together. In Salt Lake, I even took the extra step of staying at a different hotel from the others.

There would be time after the Trials to go back to being friends. This was business.

For me, as everyone knew, it was unfinished business.

The Trials ran over two weekends. The first day of that first weekend, I won the nine- and four-lap time trials. The next day, I not only won the 1500 but also did so in unofficial world-record time. Over the next several days, I kept my practices short, my training light.

The first day of the second weekend, I not only won the 500 but also set an American record.

As we neared the end of the Trials, it was all good. In seventeen races, including heats and other qualifiers, I hadn't been beaten; I led the Trials by such an overwhelming margin of points that I was already in line to skate the three individual distances at the Games. There's no 3000 at an Olympics; instead, the program consists of the 500, 1000, 1500, and the 5000 relay.

The final race of the Trials would be the 1000. Now I had a strategic decision to make. Winning eighteen races merely to win eighteen races was not any kind of goal; it wasn't and would never have been. I knew—and only those closest to me knew—the injury ups and downs I had been through over the past several months. So I could go out there, mix it up, and try to win, mindful of the possibility of some freak injury. There's always the risk of contact in short-track, and the risk in this kind of race was sure to be elevated because a place at the Games was at stake for others who were going to be in the race.

Or I could play it safe.

Emotions were high all around, and then everything got ratcheted up even further because Adam—who might well have made the team—had been diagnosed with multiple sclerosis, his left foot too numb for him to race to expectations.

The Trials were almost over. One more race. The situation with Adam. Everybody all keyed up and run down simultaneously. I could just play it safe, particularly with so much else at stake. Shani, for instance, had to win to make the Olympic team. If he won, it would be a historic moment. Shani would become the first African American to make any U.S. Olympic speed skating team; he would also be the first to tell you he does not concentrate on making black history.

Shani was ranked eighth in the overall standings; a win would boost him to sixth, the final spot on the Olympic team. Before the 1000, Shani hadn't placed in the top three at the Trials in any event. Then again, he was the American record holder in the 1000; he had set that record just two months before at a race in Calgary.

To add to the dynamic, in the semifinals, Shani had defeated Tommy. That result sent Tommy to what's called the B final—a consolation race, if you will—and meant that Tommy no longer controlled his 2002 Olympic destiny. If Shani won the A final, Shani would be on the team; if Shani took any place other than first, Tommy would be on the team.

There would be four skaters in the race—me, Rusty, Shani, and Ron—and one more layer of complexity. I had earned one of the two spots in the individual races at the Games; as things stood, Rusty had the other. Ron was chasing Rusty.

Shani broke to the lead early; Rusty sat behind him in second, drafting, sniffing for a chance to pass. About halfway through the race, I lost my footing. I almost went down. *Easy*, I told myself. *Relax. Play it safe and smart.* Around and around we went, the final few laps—Shani, Rusty, me, Ron.

And that's how it ended—Shani, Rusty, me, Ron.

Shani was, of course, thrilled. And I was happy for him; he was, after all, a good friend. I caught up to him about a half lap after we crossed the finish line and gave him sort of a hug.

"It's like a dream," he said afterward. "I'm overwhelmed with joy right now."

I had raced a safe race; I had let the others battle.

Did I give 100 percent? No.

Did I have to give 100 percent? No.

Was I obligated to give 100 percent? I'll answer that question with two questions: What, to win an eighteenth race that held no bearing on what I'd be doing at the Olympics? Given all the circumstances, weren't the Games the time and place to go all out?

Was it smart of me to be especially concerned about injury? Yes.

Given my recent history? Of course.

Given that on the very same day, in the semifinals of the women's 1000, Brigid Farrell and Allison Baver went down, one of Allison's blades cut into Brigid's side, and Brigid finished the race with her uniform soaked in blood? All the more reason.

The week after the U.S. Trials, at Japan's Olympic qualifiers, Takafumi Nishitani, the gold medalist in the 500 in Nagano, broke his ankle. The sport can be truly dangerous.

Would I have won if I had given 100 percent? I don't know. No one knows. Shani was, after all, the American record holder.

Because I didn't give it my very best effort, did that cost Tommy the 2002 Olympics? No. Wasn't losing to Shani in the semifinal his real undoing—not anything having to do with me? Did I cut Shani a break so that he could make the Olympic team? No way.

I don't play those kinds of games. I definitely don't do that—not only didn't do it in this instance, but never would.

Tommy left the arena without talking to anyone.

Immediately after the Trials ended, Dad and I went to Los Angeles for a Nike photo shoot. Then we went up to Tacoma to see Dr. Lavine. After that, I flew back to Colorado Springs, where all hell seemed to be breaking loose.

———

SHORTLY AFTER THAT final 1000 at the Trials, Tommy filed a formal grievance alleging that Rusty and I had conspired to fix the race, thus depriving Tommy of a spot on the Olympic team.

The allegations were untrue; I had done nothing wrong. Nonetheless, the press had itself a controversy, with me cast in a leading role.

The irony in all of this: at the Trials, Dad had tried to encourage Tommy. Of course, Dad had known Tommy for years. "You're going to make it," Dad told him at one point when Tommy seemed down. "You're a great racer, and you'll make up those points."

Now Dad reminded me: "Shut your ears. Don't listen to the television or the reporters. Focus on the journey and your future."

The controversy reached its peak in late January amid three days of hearings in Colorado Springs, at the end of which Tommy withdrew his demand for arbitration.

Meanwhile, the arbitrator in the matter, James Holbrook, took the extra step of issuing findings. They were emphatic. The race had been run fairly, he declared, the results valid. I hadn't violated any rules or any codes of conduct, and neither had Shani or Rusty. The chief referee had the authority to restart the race if there had been irregularities, the arbitrator noted. But he didn't do any such thing. Further, the referee certified the race.

That should have been that. Instead, the matter was hardly over.

A columnist for the *New York Times* wrote, "In some ways, Ohno is still on trial, with the Olympic oval as his next makeshift courtroom."

Sports Illustrated featured me on the cover of its Olympic preview edition, the left sleeve of my skin suit purposely ripped to make me appear edgy, the cover screaming, "Ohno? Oh, Yes!"

Inside, a long article about me declared near the top of the story, "Here comes 19-year-old Apolo Ohno, the name summing up divine talent and ungodly trouble," adding a few sentences later, "Now comes Ohno, a diamond stud in his ear, a whiff of scandal in his wake."

On NBC, Bob Costas said I could be a "shooting star of these Games." He described me as a "young, hip, marketable" athlete who "comes here having survived the most serious charge that can be leveled against any athlete: an accusation of fixing." Eric Flaim, the winner of an Olympic silver in long-track in 1988 and another silver in short-track in 1994, who was working at Salt Lake as an NBC analyst, said, "It's a real testament to the strength of Apolo as a skater that people think that he needs to win every race. He says he didn't want to risk injury and skate safe. But personally for me, when I went out and raced, I went out to win."

"You're somewhat suspicious?" Costas asked Eric.

"Well," Eric replied, "I understand Apolo's point—he was on the team at that point, so he really didn't need to win the race."

Ron, meanwhile, had gone off to practice for a while with the Australians, who were already in the States—actually, in Colorado Springs—gearing up for the Games. Then he came back; we were, after all, the defending world champs in the relay, and if he wasn't going to be skating in any individual events, the relay was what he had. Two days before the opening ceremony, all of us on the short-track team sat for a news conference. Jack Mortell, as ever the team leader, interrupted reporters talking to Ron to say, "Help us pull the team together instead of pulling the team apart."

To add to the mix, most Americans didn't know much if anything yet about short-track; the Salt Lake City Games were planned to be the sport's breakout event. Could it still be? Could I handle the intense glare of the spotlight?

Eric Heiden—who was now, in his early forties, an accomplished orthopedic surgeon and was on hand in Salt Lake as a volunteer team doc for the speed skating team—said about me in that *New York Times* column, "I do worry about him. The pressure can be overwhelming as it is. Now he has things other than skating to worry about, but I don't think he should avoid the issues. If he's honest, people will respect that. If he's straightforward, he can put this behind him.

"It's so important to be able to focus on training. I can remember going to the grocery store, standing in line, and thinking about skating. I'd go to bed thinking about it and wake up thinking about it. Something like this is not healthy."

Pat Wentland, meanwhile, who was genuinely trying to be supportive, wondered out loud how I would handle being the favorite when skating before a largely American crowd. He told the Associated Press, "Being the guy that everyone is after is hard. Sometimes he struggles with that. He skates well as the underdog, but that's not going to be the case this year."

On top of everything else, security was extra tight because of 9/11 just five months before. In all, there were about ten thousand soldiers and police officers on duty in and around the Olympic venues, many with automatic weapons at the ready.

Focus on the journey and the future.

I told Costas, "I really don't feel like I have anything to apologize for. I went into Trials with goals. I wanted to be the top two in every distance. I wanted to skate well, skate strong. I wanted to come out injury free. That was my number one goal. To be able to skate, to have the spot secured, just skate safe, was the number one thing, and be able to get off the ice knowing I did my job—I was very, very happy with that."

In a perverse way, it would turn out that all the publicity, though decidedly unwelcome, made for an unexpectedly positive turn. Suddenly, a lot more people knew my name.

And Dad and I were definitely closer than ever. I was really proud of that. When I was younger, I'm not sure I ever thought it would, or could, be like this: me on the ice, him a constant presence in the stands, videotaping my performances and scribbling thoughts and notes. In that *Sports Illustrated* article, I said, "Skating as well as I am—that's special," then added, in a reference to the Trials and all the controversy and distraction, "To be able to come out of that mess as I did is special. To be able to improve my relations with my dad is special. I'm happy with the way my life's going, the way I'm growing up as a person. Skating has changed me. I've had a lot of chances, and this is my time to shine."

I had no idea, of course, just how true that would prove to be.

But I totally, wholeheartedly believed it. The 2002 Olympics would be my time.

As soon as I stopped throwing up.

Getting some extra training off the ice in Salt Lake City.

Hanging out on the red carpet in Mt. Hood, Oregon, with my first fan, my dad.

My dad and I plot some strategy right before the World Cup in 2009.

At the end of the day, it's all about taking care of my body and taking care of my skates.

John Schaeffer, trainer extraordinaire, pushed me to the limit before the games. Two months before Vancouver, you can see how lean I'm getting.

Here's the famous "weekend luxury meal." A normal meal wouldn't have had that pasta on the side!

My dad looks a little worried about this crazy workout regime, but he was pretty proud of me later when it all paid off.

The place where I do some of my best thinking—and where I conceived of a lot of this book: the sauna.

An unusual training exercise, the low walk, made more intense by doing it on a sandy beach in Michigan.

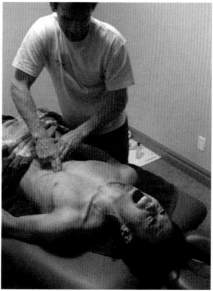

(Above) John Potsma is actually a horse massage therapist. He says there are seven layers of muscle. I think he found an eighth one when he worked on me this particular day!

After a long day of training, I decided a little extra workout on the stairs would help. Here, Jae Su Chun, one of the "masters of short-track," gives me some technical advice.

My favorite sweatshirt, and some words to live by.

No weakness doesn't mean
there aren't any surprises.

Sometimes it's good to be in front, sometimes it's good to bide your time.

Despite having a mild case of H1N1, I managed to win the 1000-meter World Cup in Marquette, Michigan. Here is a cool picture that really captures what it is like to be going forty miles per hour on two pieces of metal . . . on ice!

In the final relay, the last race of the Vancouver Olympic Games, I got to share a medal with my teammates. We captured bronze; Korea, silver; and Canada, gold.

(Right) I congratulated Lee Ho-Suk, not just on this race, but on the entire 2010 Olympic Games.

Here I am with Australian skater Steve Bradbury, one of the sport's quirkiest competitors.

Gold medal figure skater Evan Lysacek.

With Travis Jayner on the day we arrived in Vancouver.

One Saturday afternoon in Marquette, Michigan, Shani Davis and I met fans and signed autographs. Believe it or not, there was a time when I was taller than Shani!

I told Bob Costas that I'd be taking over his job one day. "I don't think so!" he said without hesitation, making me and the rest of the room laugh really hard.

At the start of our early morning ice training, the cameras caught me telling a joke to Shani and the rest of our team. Yes, we did get used to having the camera crews and press following us around.

I'm always ready to goof off
when there's a camera nearby.

Me and my friend Oscar.

Meredith Vieira
wasn't my usual
dancing partner, but
she had some pretty
great moves.

(Above) The first time I returned to the stadium in Salt Lake City where I had won Olympic gold was to film an amazing commercial for AT&T. It was surreal to be back there in such different circumstances but still dressed to skate.

We had quite a party in Las Vegas to celebrate my twenty-eighth birthday.

No matter what happens, I'll always need my quiet time to be sure my head is in the right place.

ON WINNING

Vince Lombardi, the Hall of Fame football coach who became a legend as boss of the Green Bay Packers, once said, "I firmly believe that any man's finest hour, the greatest fulfillment of all that he holds dear, is that moment when he has worked his heart out in a good cause and lies exhausted on the field of battle—victorious."

I don't think he's talking about actually winning. Some people will naturally disagree. To me, though, being victorious is not necessarily about standing on top of the podium.

After all, what does winning mean? What does becoming a champion really mean? What does that truly mean? Crossing the line first? That's part of it, absolutely. That's why we crown a champion.

But for me, and especially with respect to the Olympic Games, and thus by extension to the goals and dreams each of us has in all areas of life itself, "winning" connotes something very different. It means the display of winning qualities and a championship mind-set. It means effort, emotion, and sportsmanship. It's that never-give-up, never-say-die mentality.

CHAPTER 7

Ultimately, the only thing that would shift the focus off the Trials and onto the Olympics was, predictably enough, the start of the Games.

The opening ceremony proved spectacular, marked by an outpouring of patriotic American feeling. President George W. Bush was greeted by a huge roar as he arrived in the stadium. During the parade of nations, the American team was led in by Amy Peterson, a short-track speed skater; we waved small American flags. The French team, meanwhile, waved double-sided flags, the French tricolor on one side, the Stars and Stripes on the other. Midway through the procession, the French began doing the wave. It quickly spread across the stands. Even the Mormon Tabernacle Choir joined in.

The stadium hushed when a tattered flag recovered from the wreckage of the World Trade Center was carried in by an honor guard of U.S. athletes and New York City police officers and firefighters.

The 1980 U.S. men's hockey team lit the cauldron, and President Bush formally opened the Games from a spot in the stands, surrounded by the American team. He had been sitting next to figure skater Sasha Cohen. She had used her cellular phone to call her mom and then put the president on the line.

Now the president said, "On behalf of a proud, determined, and grateful nation, I declare open the Games of Salt Lake City, celebrating the Winter Olympic Games."

Mitt Romney, the president of the Salt Lake organizing committee, said, "Following September 11, there were some people who wondered if these Games could be pulled off. Now they seem more important than ever. They can be a source of healing, not only for our nation but for the world."

It was incredible. It was awesome. I was so glad I was there.

Even so, one of the quiet secrets about the Olympics is the intriguing dilemma the opening ceremony presents. As an athlete, do you go, or no?

The decision would seem obvious. It's not. It's a complex decision that comes loaded with variables.

On the one hand, you're privileged enough to have a place of honor at a great show that's designed to pay tribute both to the Olympic ideals and to you—that is, to all the athletes of the world. Moreover, everyone knows going in that most of the competitors aren't going to win a medal—there are roughly 2,500 athletes at a Winter Games—and so for most of them the ceremony serves as the emotional high point of the entire experience. For seemingly everybody, at least for this one night, no matter who we are or where we're from, whether in the stadium or watching on television in the farthest reaches of the globe, we all allow ourselves to share in the hope that our world can be a more peaceful, gentler place.

Who wouldn't want to be touched by the light of such idealism and goodwill? How could you even give thought to missing such a thing?

The challenge lies in balancing the ephemeral and inspirational with the very real logistical. When, for instance, was the last time you sat outside in the night air, the temperature well below freezing, for roughly three hours? It began to snow, almost as if on cue, just as the ceremony got under way that Friday night in Salt Lake City; at show-time, the thermometer read 19 degrees.

If you had to compete the very next day, would you go, even if the ceremony was very likely to be a once-in-a-lifetime experience? Even if, like me, you weren't due to compete for a few days, would you go if you were that much more likely to come down with the flu and get so sick you didn't know if you'd ever get out of bed, much less race at the Olympics?

That night, it was snowy and wet. We did a lot of walking. None of us really knew what to expect. Everyone was riding a superhigh, and that kind of energy demands attention.

Here was a lesson: bring snacks.

That night, I did not have enough snacks with me. By the end of the night, I was not only tired, I was run-down.

I had the flu.

It came on quickly: a sore throat, chills, vomiting, fever, sniffling, watery eyes, feeling dizzy, the whole package.

Four days before my first competition at the Olympics, the prelims of the 1000, I was put in quarantine, moved at Jack Mortell's direction from the athletes' village to a room at the Marriott Residence Inn in downtown Salt Lake City.

Why was this happening? When I could summon the strength to think, that's what I thought. Why now? After all my training? After all I had overcome?

I mean, I was at the Olympics. My back was finally feeling better. I was so geared up to go. And now I was flat on my back, and all I wanted to do was sleep. The medical staff said, "Antibiotics. We know you react strongly to them. We know you don't like the idea. But at this point, roll over and let us stick this big needle in your backside. We even know that you'll feel like you won't want to get out of bed for a day after we do this, and you'll be wondering why in the world you let us. You have more time than that. Roll over now, okay?"

Dad was right there with me at the hotel. "It's going to be fine," he kept saying. "Drink some water. You need to stay hydrated—it's the best thing you can do for yourself."

I did not get better overnight. But by the time the prelims rolled around, I did feel much, much better. Not my best. But there was no question I would race. And I had a history of gaining strength through adversity. To become a true champion, you have to overcome obstacles. You come out stronger; you come out a better person.

For me, this was as good as it gets. I was going to lace up my skates and race at the Olympics.

———————

I HAVE ALWAYS had two race-time quirks:

One, I put my skates on at the last minute.

Two, I put the left one on first. If I'm not paying attention and put the right one on first, and then the left, and I realize it before it's go-time, I must sit down and take them both off and start all over, left one first. There have been times when I've been in the heat box and put on my right skate first and tied both and almost missed a race because I've had to untie both skates and start over from scratch.

No double knot, either. Just a bow, and it has to be just right.

For this first race, I put on a black bandana. There's no rhyme or reason to the color of the bandana I wear—red, blue, whatever. It's whatever color comes up when I reach into my bag and grab. For these Games, I had special black Nike bandanas to choose from as well.

There's no great mystery why I started wearing a bandana in the first place, in my early teens. It was not meant to be fashion forward. It was all function. My hair was long, and I needed something to keep it out of my eyes. Besides, the bandana would keep the sweat off my face.

Similarly, there's hardly much of a backstory to the soul patch.

When my beard first came in, that's where you could actually see hair: there, nowhere else. Maybe at first I was trying to look older, and then I thought the patch just suited me.

Our skin suits in Salt Lake were red on top, silver under the arms, blue from the waist down. The red was a dark red, the blue dark, too. At these Games, my helmet cover—black numbers on a stretchy yellow background—said I was racer number 369.

Number 369 stepped onto the ice, and the place erupted. There were tens of thousands of people in the arena, and because NBC had already featured me on TV in the pre-Games buildup, they knew what I looked like, and they chanted my name, time and again—"Apolo! Apolo!"— mixed in with the home-crowd fervor: "U-S-A! U-S-A!"

It was so loud out there on that ice—outrageously loud. A crowd of 15,900 people had turned out; this was the largest crowd to watch short-track in Olympic history.

The place quieted as we were called to the start line. Kim Dong-Sung—the Korean suits featured a shockingly bright yellow and blue pattern trimmed in red—and two others were in the heat. Two of the four of us would go through to the next round.

The other two, Arian Nachbar of Germany and Battulga Oktyabri of Mongolia, were inexperienced. They were not my concern. Dong-Sung was.

And I knew that I was his.

The Koreans were undefeated in the 1000 in the Olympics. Three times the event had been run at the Games; Koreans had won all three, Dong-Sung in 1998 in Nagano. Dong-Sung had been a force on the international scene for years. In 1997 he had made history as the first guy to be the best at both the world championships and the world junior championships. Even so, both Dong-Sung and I knew which of us had won so convincingly in Calgary roughly sixteen months before—a race so dominating that he had been moved to show me great respect.

The gun sounded.

The 1000 goes for nine laps. At the outset, I was content to hang back, behind Dong-Sung, just measuring his tempo and rhythm, feeling his energy. With five laps to go, the pace picked up, and with two and a half left, Dong-Sung went hard. I went with him.

With about a lap and a half to go, I made a move to pass, accelerating first on the outside. But I didn't pass. I just moved right up next to Dong-Sung. My point in moving up was simply to show Dong-Sung that I was there, that I had strength. I could have passed but chose not to do so. I knew it; I wanted him to know it, too. I moved up alongside Dong-Sung, really, just to look in his eyes.

With exactly one lap to go, as we flashed across the ice, I cut to the inside and looked to my right, at Dong-Sung. It wouldn't be all that unusual for him to be skating with a decided arrogance. I wanted him instead to feel doubt. He had gone hard, and yet I was right there with him, and he would know that now and he would know it even further when he got off the ice and looked at the video: *Dong-Sung, is that all you've got? I'm here, and I can pass you anytime I want.*

That same night brought the semifinals of the 5000 relay. All that controversy, and Shani wasn't one of the four guys on the ice. For that matter, he wasn't even the alternate. The decision had been made the day before race day. Sue said that Shani's comparatively slower times in practice were the reason. At any rate, Shani had gone to the coaches and, with an eye toward the junior worlds in long-track in Italy the next month, offered to withdraw. That made the decision easy. No matter what, the history books say he was on the 2002 Olympic team.

"I'm happy with everything, actually," he told reporters. "I got my experience at the Olympics. I'll just take it one step at a time.

"Maybe in the next four years I won't be in the position of having to rely on coaches to put me on a relay."

The relay is forty-five laps. Rusty put us in front. Dong-Sung and

I skated the next two laps together, me in front. I made sure I didn't even put an arm down in the corners—again, for show. Dong-Sung would notice. So would the Korean coaches. So would everyone else.

Dong-Sung especially would know how fast we were going. He would feel it. And he would see that I was so strong, so calm, so relaxed.

With twenty to go, about half the race left to go, we Americans were in front. The race was setting up for a great stretch run. Then Min Ryoung of Korea went down.

He went down and skidded across the ice. He slammed into the pads, and he didn't get up. Min took an Italian skater, Nicola Rodigari, with him.

The officials stopped the race. Min was taken off the ice on a stretcher. The Koreans were disqualified—they wouldn't make it to the medal round—and the semifinal restarted from the beginning. Min would end up banged up but not seriously hurt; he was treated at a local hospital and released.

On the ice, what had happened at the U.S. Trials had to be forgotten, and it was. Dan, Ron, Rusty, and I—we now had to skate, in essence, a relay and a half.

No problem. This was the advantage of training at altitude, in Colorado Springs. With eight laps to go, the crowd screaming "U-S-A!" I turned on the jets. *Boom.* Fabio Carta told me afterward that it was scary to watch—scary good. I simply had that extra gear. We won easily; the Italians qualified second; the Australians lagged behind in third.

Long after the race was over, the stands were still full, the arena buzzing. People didn't want to leave. It's like they were saying, *This is the coolest sport we have ever seen.* Later, I heard that tickets in the far reaches of the upper arena were going for as much as $1,000. Everybody wanted in.

When I come off the ice, I always—always—look for my dad first. On this particular night, I couldn't find him. I had to call him later. "Dad," I said, "it was the most electric environment I have ever skated in."

———————

AND THAT WAS just the warm-up act.

The semifinals and the finals of the 1000 took place three days after the prelims, on a Saturday night. The final went down about a half hour after the semis.

The noise and the buzz in the arena that Saturday thoroughly dwarfed the prelims. It was hard to imagine the crowd could have been any louder. But it decidedly was; it felt as if the place might explode.

This was a night to make history.

Dong-Sung skated in the first semi. Unbelievably, and disappointingly for me, he finished last, after a fall—and it wasn't until they showed the video of him afterward that you could see why. I'd had the flu; now he had the grunge. His eyes were so swollen it looked as if he could barely see.

Gagnon, meanwhile, had been eliminated in a quarterfinal, disqualified.

Two of the top guys—gone.

I skated in the second semi. Another black bandana.

The new factor was another Korean, Ahn Hyun-Soo. He was sixteen. He weighed all of 117 pounds. He wore wire-rimmed spectacles and looked like Harry Potter on skates. You'd be tempted not to take him seriously except that in practice he had turned laps in 8.3 seconds; 8.3 is quick. Hyun-Soo was serious.

Hyun-Soo went to the front and tried to stay there.

With two laps to go, on an inside pass, I seized the lead and stayed there. I was so in charge that I made the pass with both arms still on my back. Fabio and Hyun-Soo jockeyed now for second, first Fabio and then, ultimately, Hyun-Soo.

I felt in command, set up for the race of my life. In the finals, it would be me, Mathieu Turcotte of Canada, Hyun-Soo, Li Jiajun of China, and Steve Bradbury of Australia. Mathieu and Jiajun were veterans, both skating well. I knew now about Hyun-Soo. And then there was Bradbury—one of the great characters in short-track, immensely likable, with a personal history that almost defied belief. So did the skating strategy he'd been using at the Games.

Steve had been on the international scene for a long, long time. At the 1994 world championships, he had been involved in a crash that cut his leg so badly he needed 111 stitches and four pints of blood. In 2000 he fell during practice and broke two vertebrae in his neck; he had to wear a neck brace, bolted to his skull, for six weeks.

In Salt Lake, he knew how to stand out from the crowd—streaked blond hair, a goatee, and, to top it off, a pierced left eyebrow.

Steve was only seventeen when, in 1991, he was one of the four guys on the team that won the 5000 relay at the world championships; that gold made for Australia's first-ever world championship in a winter sport. In 1994, in Lillehammer, the Aussies took bronze in the relay—Australia's first Winter Games medal. Steve was thus already something of a hero in Australia. But by Salt Lake, nobody figured him for a gold medalist. In his many previous individual Olympic races, he had never finished higher than nineteenth.

His strategy here in Salt Lake had been—in a word—unique. He would deliberately lag behind, way behind, the main pack. If you were being generous, you might call it a safe distance. You might also call it 20 to 30 meters. Then he would wait for everyone else to fall down. It seemed almost laughable.

In the quarterfinals, two guys ahead of him fell. Steve advanced.

In the semifinals, two guys ahead of him fell and another was disqualified. Steve advanced.

The night before the semi and the final, Steve, under little illusion about his chances, had emailed me. He had a favor in mind. If I won, he asked, maybe I could remember to mention the name of the boots I was wearing?

Those RBC boots, the Australian ones that were by now fully broken in—the company was the brainchild of a guy named Clint Jensen, once one of Australia's top skaters, too.

Training for the 1998 Games with Steve, he had become frustrated at the six- to twelve-month lag time it took to make a pair of custom boots. They thought, *We can do better, especially if we do it together.*

Those boots—I loved those boots. They were called the RBC AR1. They were silver. They didn't look like anything special; in fact, they didn't look like anyone should feel the slightest bit good in them. They were clunky, with a lot of padding, the farthest thing from stream-lined. And yet in these skates it didn't feel like I was skating. It felt like I was walking. It felt incredibly natural. There was something about the way the boots locked my ankles in, the way they fixed the angles in those ankles and in my hips. It just felt so good.

I always wear two pairs of socks when I race. Not liners; two pairs of socks. The socks aren't special. They're just socks. I can feel the ice so well that I don't like to feel all the ridges and bumps; it's too intense. The two pairs of socks act as something of a cushion. In these RBC boots, with my two pairs of socks on each foot, I had such incredible feel for the ice. Truly—they were incredible and it was incredible.

We stepped to the line for the 1000 final, Steve in his RBC AR1s, me in mine, the crowd alive with sound and noise.

My plan was to let Hyun-Soo lead. I knew he was out to do the same thing he had tried to do in the semi. He couldn't pass yet on his own—he didn't have the experience—so he would try to win from the front. Have at it. I was going to use him to control the pace; he would make it faster and faster.

I also wanted to make my move earlier than normal, with two laps to go, maybe even a little more, and when I made that move, I was going to make it big. Until then, I would just more or less hang out.

I had the race planned out. I had it visualized, every twist and turn. I was calm and prepared; I was ready for anything. Anything—even, as it would turn out, the wildest, most unpredictable, craziest ending in Olympic short-track history.

No matter what happens, I reminded myself, *keep your cool, maintain your focus, be in the moment.*

Dad was down on the side of the boards, taking it all in, in a gray fleece sweatshirt and black gloves. He had shown up at the arena four full hours before the finals would go off. The NBC cameras kept turning to him. He only had eyes for the ice.

The announcer called my name. I took two deep breaths.

I had drawn the middle start position, number three.

The gun went off, the crowd exploded, Turcotte went hard for the lead at the first turn. By the end of the first lap, though, just as I had seen it happening in my mind, Hyun-Soo was in front. With seven laps to go, Turcotte went back out front. I sat fourth.

Six to go, five to go—Hyun-Soo was in front.

With four laps remaining, I went hard on the backstretch, to the inside, passing Jiajun and Mathieu. Now I was second, right behind Hyun-Soo. Perfect.

Three to go. Hyun-Soo first, me right behind.

With two and a half to go, I drove hard to the outside, by Hyun-Soo, and into the lead. Just as I had envisioned it. As I moved to extend my lead, Jiajun dropped Hyun-Soo into third. Mathieu was fourth, Steve a distant fifth.

The bell sounded. One lap to go. I was nearly a quarter of a lap ahead of Steve.

Half a lap now. Jiajun was a full stride behind me. I felt it: this was the best race of my life. I knew exactly where everyone was; I knew exactly what was going on.

As we rounded the final corner, Jiajun tried to pass on the outside. He was trying to go over the top. He grabbed at my shoulder.

At that exact instant, Hyun-Soo tried to move up on the inside. He was small—but not that small.

There simply wasn't any room there.

Around the curve, after grabbing at me, Jiajun lost his balance and went spinning out, into the pads.

Even as Jiajun was flying out of the race, Hyun-Soo lost his balance. Because there was no room, he had nowhere to go but down, and down he went, out of control, taking out both Mathieu and me.

The force threw me onto my back and sent me into a full 360-degree spin. It slammed me into the boards. My head bounced off the padding. I could feel the wind at my fingers, and the next thing I knew, I was in the boards.

Everybody in the race but Steve was down.

Be ready for anything. Never, ever take a race for granted until you're over the line. Finish. It doesn't matter if you're in a daze. It doesn't matter how quick everything is happening all around you, no matter how crazed. What happens to you is up to you. Finish.

I got up, onto my right skate. I turned toward the line as Steve, his arms at his sides, sauntered by. He coasted across the line, the winner. Your gold medalist.

I couldn't hold my balance. I fell again, face-first, but at least aimed toward the finish. As I was sliding, I twisted myself around and stuck my left foot out over the line. Silver.

Mathieu was right behind. He slid across the line like a baseball player executing a hook slide, left foot first. Bronze.

Jiajun would ultimately be disqualified. Hyun-Soo took fourth.

Steve raised both his arms and smiled. You could see later on the video that it was a smile of absolute disbelief. He would later say, "Maybe I'm not the most deserving guy, but I got the gold, and I'm stoked about it. I thought maybe two would go down and I'd get the bronze. Then I saw them all go down and, 'Oh, my God.' "

Later, the Australian government would feature Steve, holding his gold medal, on a 45-cent postage stamp. He wrote a book—he called it *Last Man Standing*—and the phrase to "do a Bradbury" has become part of the Aussie vocabulary. It means to achieve something against all reasonable odds.

Good for Steve. Circumstances played out so that he was supposed to win that race.

I headed off the ice. *I need to see some video to figure out just what happened,* I thought. Something had happened, and it was mayhem.

Wait—what's with my left leg? Why so insistently itchy all of a sudden?

Uh-oh.

I looked down to see that my left thigh was gashed wide open, on the inside, just above my knee. I had apparently slashed it on my skates when I went down. On the ice, in all the frenzied excitement, I hadn't even noticed. It wasn't until I got to the locker room and peeled off my skin suit that I could see how bad it was.

It was bad. I could look into the leg down to the bone. The wound was not bleeding. It was a clean, open cut. But it was huge, and it was nasty.

Mathieu, it turned out, was also cut—a big slice on his backside.

"The phone, the phone, I need a phone, get me a phone!" I said, talking out loud to anyone who might hear. "I need Brent Hamula, my trainer."

"Brent," I said when we connected, "could you please come to the locker room?" He showed up a few moments later with a big smile. "Man," he said, "that was a crazy race." Brent and I had worked together for four years. He was rock solid. I looked down at my leg. I said, "I cut myself."

Brent couldn't have been cooler. "Okay," he said. "Let's get you stitched up."

We made our way to a nearby office as he made a call or two. Who walked in but Heiden, who is also an orthopedic surgeon. Superfast, superefficient—as always—he put six stitches in me. I threw a bag of ice onto my leg and dropped into a wheelchair. After all, I had to get to a ceremony. I had a silver medal to collect, and I was thrilled about that.

It was, after all, the best race of my life.

I didn't lose gold.

I won silver.

Some were already crying for the race to be rerun. That's not the way it works, and that's not the way it should work. Life isn't certain; short-track isn't certain. Even when something seems certain, you're coming around the last turn, in position to win—it's still uncertain. My goal was to get off the ice and to be satisfied with the effort I'd given, to have no regrets, and on this particular day, in this particular race, I had indeed given all I had. How, in any way, could I not be delighted with silver?

They brought me out to the medals ceremony in that wheelchair. I hobbled onto the podium, and they put the silver medal around my neck. I hopped up and down on one leg, flowers in my right hand, medal on me, waving to anyone and everyone—thankful and grateful for everything.

Back in Tacoma, Dr. Lavine had seen the race unfold live on Canadian television. "If anything drastic happens," he had told Dad before the Games, "get these into Apolo," a couple of packets of homeopathic remedies; they included arnica, which has been used for centuries to reduce redness, swelling, and bruising around cuts. Watching the TV, Dr. Lavine decided immediately that whatever had just happened qualified as drastic. He called Dad's cell and said, "Yuki, remember those packets? Get those packets into Apolo as soon as you can."

The next morning, it was Dad's turn to call Dr. Lavine. "How fast," Dad said, "can you get here?"

The next night, Sunday night, I sat for a few minutes—medal around my neck still—for a televised interview with Costas, who introduced me with a smile as "a man who had won a silver medal . . . on his back," then said, rolling the tape of the 1000 final, "This was wild near the finish line."

I said, "I pretty much just went into that race just to be able to skate my heart out. I definitely walked off the ice with that impression."

Video of me on the podium played behind us. I clapped for Steve and shook his hand. I reached for Mathieu and shook his hand, too. "You were extremely gracious afterward," Costas said. "A lot of people felt real good about you, the way you handled yourself.

". . . A lot of people said, 'Well, he's got a chance to win three, maybe four, golds.' Now you have silver. Some people would term that a disappointment. But by your demeanor, you don't appear disappointed."

It was easy to tell the truth: "Oh—not at all. My goal, my journey, my quest, everything I've been working for for four years wasn't toward the four gold medals. It was—the number one thing was to be able to just step on that line, come as prepared as possible, and get off the ice satisfied, skate the best race of my life at the Olympics. That was definitely my time to shine. I was definitely shining as bright as I could out there on the ice."

"Any doubt in your mind that, no collision, you win the gold last night?"

"No doubt, no doubt. I could feel it. I was tasting it in that last corner, going into that last corner, that I was going to have the win under my belt. But—this is short-track and, you know, maybe it just wasn't my day to win."

Later, Dad would receive a forwarded email from James Holbrook, the arbitrator from the Trials controversy. It read, "Apolo Ohno's humble and gracious remarks last night reflect great credit on himself, his sport, his team, and our country. I know you are justifiably proud of this remarkable young man."

Dad told me later how proud he was. He said a father can only hope that everything he has tried to instill in his son—about winning, about losing, about facing challenges—gets through. "When you stepped onto the podium to get your silver medal," he said, "I was so proud of who you had become."

———————

WHEN I MET reporters after the 1000, I made a small joke about the gash on my leg. I said, "Maybe next time I'll be a little bit farther in front."

Everyone laughed.

What everyone really wanted to know was when that next time would be. The 1000 final took place on Saturday night. The 1500 heats were Wednesday. That gave me four days. "I'll be okay," I said, adding, "I'm just lucky the injury is not more severe."

What I didn't say was that I had to keep racing. Had to. For me and for the sport. "After Saturday night," I told people, "I don't know what people will think of short-track, but I do know that every person out here was turned on by the sport."

I didn't get on my skates that Sunday, the day after the 1000, hoping that keeping still would help the leg heal faster. For fear of being groggy again like I was with the flu, I didn't want to take another dose of antibiotics. Enter Dr. Lavine, who assuredly didn't want me to take antibiotics. After presenting his bona fides to the Olympic medical staff, convincing them he wasn't out to do voodoo for real, he got to work.

There were essentially two challenges. One was making sure I would be strong enough to compete. The other was keeping the wound itself closed enough so I could compete.

Dr. Lavine focused on the first of the two. "You'll be fine," he said. "I got here within twenty-four hours. On average, it takes twenty-four hours for an injury to set itself up in the system. If you get to what's wrong in those first twenty-four hours, it's amazing what we can do to make it seem like it had never happened.

"We have to get you breathing right," he said.

"You banged your head hard on the pads," he said. "Let's work on that."

"We're going to reset some energies all over," he said.

I got back on the ice on Monday. The cut ripped open.

We took Steri-Strips and glued them to my leg.

The cut ripped open.

We even tried Super Glue to keep the sides of the cut together.

The cut ripped open.

The challenge was simple; solving it, not so much. My thighs were huge to begin with; when I skate, they fill with blood and lactate and get bigger still. The cut kept ripping open. To this day, when I press on the scar, it still feels like it's cut.

Who knew how dicey it was? Very few people. When I'd had the flu earlier in the Games, I hadn't broadcast that; I wasn't about to start saying now that I still had a big hole in my leg. I wasn't even going to acknowledge that I might not possibly be 100 percent. And I certainly wasn't about to start talking at length about how I was truly scared.

It was indeed a nasty cut. For his part, Dr. Lavine had done fantastic work; there was no sign of infection or swelling.

That Wednesday we glued it, stripped it down, wrapped it, and an enormous roar went up from the stands as I took to the ice. It felt like "Welcome back, and thanks." Ted Robinson, who was calling short-track for NBC at the Games, was truly gracious. He said on air amid the roar that the way I had handled myself had given "all of us, even those of us much older than him, a tremendous lesson in maturity, in grace, and in Olympic sportsmanship."

In the stands, they were waving American flags and sporting—wait, were those fake soul patches on so many chins, even on the girls?

The 1500—assuming my leg didn't explode—was my best shot for gold, considering in particular the unofficial world-record time at the Trials just weeks before and the four of five World Cup wins the year before at this distance. This was the first 1500 in Olympic history; the event was new for Salt Lake. We would run the heats, the semifinals, and the final on this one night.

My heat was the second of six. There were five of us in this heat. Three in each heat would move on to the semifinals; there were three semifinals; the top two in each semi would go on to a crowded six-man final.

The main thing, of course, was to get through the heat, and to get through using as little energy as possible while making it look like I was just as strong as ever. In warm-ups, though, the cut bothered me; it felt like someone was stretching at either side of the cut, pulling at it the way you might open a bag of potato chips.

When the gun went off—the pain was gone. I went out strong early and stayed at or near the lead the whole way, finishing second behind Fabio. It was more of the same in the semi, about ninety minutes later. Out to the front of the pack early, took the lead with two laps to go, finished in second behind Fabio.

Dong-Sung was apparently over the grunge. In his semi, he had set an Olympic record. No, there hadn't been many Olympic 1500s run yet; yes, he was apparently feeling fine.

The finals: Dong-Sung, Li Jiajun, Gagnon, Fabio, Bruno Loscos of France, and me. The field was stacked, even Bruno. He had never before made the final of an international event, but in Salt Lake he had found something.

I knew for a certainty that Dong-Sung's strategy would be to go to the front early and hard. He knew I was cut, and he was going to try to burn me out. If I did try to pass, moreover, Dong-Sung would do every-thing in his power not to let me pass. From his standpoint, it had to be better to lose that way than to let me pass cleanly, because a clean pass would prove unequivocally who was stronger, and they would write about that thing in the Olympic history books, tell that story for years and years to come.

To know Asian culture is to know how important it is not to lose face.

Meanwhile, Dong-Sung also knew something else, and I did, too: if I were leading, he wouldn't be able to pass me. In October, in this very arena, in this very same race, the 1500, I had beaten Dong-Sung.

In the heat box immediately before we were called to the ice, I yawned—the TV cameras caught it. I wasn't bored. This was just a piece of the calming techniques that by now had become a part of me.

"This is a sport that was known by very few in the United States until a week ago. Now, suddenly, it is spawning hysteria—all because of a young, hip teenager from Seattle," Robinson said on air as the NBC cameras panned over fans holding signs and waving American flags.

". . . What many others saw as unjust on Saturday night," he also said, "Apolo Ohno saw as occupational hazard."

Dad was perched by the side of the ice, just on the other side of the pads. He was wearing a silver fleece jacket that was accented by silver-framed sunglasses holding yellow lenses. Looking sharp.

Just as predicted, the race slowly got under way. After a lap and a half, I was fourth. With three and a half gone, ten to go, I was last. Eight laps to go, fifth place. Seven, and Dong-Sung made his move, surging into the lead with a pass on the backstretch. Six to go, I was still in fifth.

This was starting to look dangerous. Every single one of the guys in front of me was legit.

Stay calm. There will be space. You'll find it.

With one and a half to go, I found it, just enough space on the inside. On the backstretch, I accelerated and passed the other three. Now I tucked in immediately behind Dong-Sung. The bell sounded for the final lap. We swung around the far turn. I moved up even closer, immediately behind Dong-Sung.

I could hear the South Korean coach, Jun Myung-Kyu, whom everyone in the sport calls Big Jon, yelling to Dong-Sung that I was right there.

In a flash, there it was, again on the backstretch: just enough room on the inside.

I took two strides.

Dong-Sung moved over to his left to block. I was sure we were going to crash and slam into the pads. I had no choice but to slow. I also pulled back and drew up my hands, palms out, instinctively making a signal that everyone everywhere knows—*whatever's happening, it's not my fault.*

Immediately and without any question, I knew Dong-Sung's move to the inside was a foul. In short-track lingo, it's called cross-tracking—a skater who is skating a wide track suddenly changes track. Would it be called?

Some would say later that in raising my hands, I had tried to sell the foul the way a basketball player flops to try to convince the ref to call a charge on the guy with the ball driving the lane. No. What I did was pure instinct.

Without the block, I surely would have passed Dong-Sung. But given the laws of physics and the deceleration the block had precipitated, there was no way now, with only a half lap left, I could pass.

Dong-Sung crossed the line first and raised his arms in apparent triumph.

Um, not so fast.

As I crossed, I pumped my fist.

In the American coaches' sideline area, there was a lot going on. One of our coaches, Tony Goskowicz, was motioning to me that Dong-Sung was going to be disqualified. Another, Pat Maxwell, said to Big Jon, "Jon, that's a blatant cross-track."

"Blocking," Dad said, watching the replay monitor. The overhead shot made the foul abundantly clear.

Big Jon speaks six languages, including English. He didn't reply to Pat. Instead, he thrust his arms toward the sky, making a big victory show. He was hardly about to acknowledge even the possibility of a disqualification.

Dong-Sung set about on a victory lap, holding the South Korean flag high.

I circled around slowly as well. I knew what was coming—assuming, in the face of the Korean victory celebration, the referee, James Hewish of Australia, had the courage to do the right thing.

He did.

I was the gold medalist. Dong-Sung was disqualified. Jiajun was moved up to second, Marc to third.

Dong-Sung threw the Korean flag to the ice in a show of disgust.

I went over to the coaches' box and hugged the American coaches, Sue, Tony, Pat. It was like a dream come true. When you're a little kid, you dream of winning a gold medal, and then you do, and then you have to figure out, exactly what do you do? A big smile on my face, I turned and skated to the center of the rink, leaned down, and gave the ice a big kiss.

The roar from the crowd was deafening.

Dong-Sung, meanwhile, was kicking one of the rubber blocks on the ice. More show.

"You thought you saw everything in short-track on Saturday?" Robinson said on TV. "It just got topped."

———

THAT WAS JUST the start of it.

"No words. No words. Oh, my God. It's an unbelievable feeling. Oh, man—it's great," I said, breathless, speaking for the TV cameras, as I came off the ice.

Later, I found a few. "They can go throw me in the desert and bury me," I told reporters. "I got a gold medal. I'm good now."

I also said, "I just gave my best and I shined, like a star or something. I saw my chance and took it."

Dad and I got in a quick hug. I had to change clothes for the medal ceremony.

This time, I didn't hop onto the podium. I was all smiles as I stepped up to the top, dressed for the occasion in my leather USOC team jacket emblazoned in red, white, and blue.

This wasn't just my moment. It was Dad's, too.

It was a moment as well for everyone who had played a part in my journey. The thousands of cheering fans then transformed the moment into something so very much more. This was, after all, only five months after 9/11; our country was coming together; it felt like everyone there was cheering not only for me but maybe for all of America. So many people wanted me to win. And I was able to deliver, the first male to win a short-track gold for America and Americans. It felt simply amazing. Really—no words.

I kissed the medal.

"Ladies and gentlemen," the public address announcer said, "please rise for the national anthem of the United States." The request proved happily redundant. Everyone, it seemed, was already up, screaming and yelling.

Thirty or so years after my father had left Japan, they played "The Star-Spangled Banner" at the Olympic Games in my honor. My father watched the American flag go up with indescribable pride. Afterward, Dad clapped and laughed and accepted congratulations. That night, he stayed with me—I was still at the Residence Inn downtown—and slept on the floor.

There was the gold medal. It was right there with us. Dad held the medal. But he wouldn't put it around his neck.

I didn't sleep at all that night. I felt the weight of memories. I felt the lightness of so many joyful emotions. I couldn't believe it.

Neither, in his own way, could Fabio Carta. Fabio, who had been moved to fourth in the final standings, had told reporters, "It's absurd that the Korean was disqualified. I don't know what happened."

Watching a replay, Fabio also said, "We should use a rifle on Ohno." *What?!*

Fabio and I were close friends. When we finally got the chance to talk, he explained that what he had said was something of an Italian saying that was then lost in translation. Fabio said he had been asked, "So what do you think of Ohno?" "In Italian," he said, "the saying goes that someone is so strong that the only way to stop him is like the way they treat a bull—to shoot him."

Fabio was near tears. What he had said had raced around the world. There were those who, after 9/11, suggested that his choice of words had been insensitive.

"It's okay, man," I told him. "Don't worry about it."

The worry, as it would turn out, was with the Koreans.

"I saw no foul," insisted Lee Chi Sang, an official with the South Korean delegation.

What was plain to see was that the Koreans were already out of the relay and had come up empty in both the 1000 and the 1500. Used to dominating short-track, they had been expecting—athletes, Big Jon, the other coaches, the South Korean government and corporate establishments, fans, everyone there—to rack up medals. Now they had none, with only the 500 left.

"American journalists only print lies," Big Jon was quoted as saying in the *New York Times*.

Appeals aren't allowed in short-track. It's the rule. Nonetheless, the Koreans appealed the race results to a sports tribunal, the Court of Arbitration for Sport. The sports court said that I had won fair and square. The International Olympic Committee said the same thing. That hardly stopped the deluge of emails, so many—more than sixteen thousand within twelve hours—and some so angry that the U.S. Olympic Committee shut down its Internet server and a Utah state trooper was detailed to protect me.

I wasn't so worried about angry emails. I had two more races to go. That I had so far gone two for two, silver and gold, meant nothing for the 500 and the relay.

———————

OF THE THREE individual races at the Olympics, the 500 is the most unpredictable. Because it's so short, four and a half laps, one little glitch and you're out.

The 500 also demands an explosive start. I didn't feel my leg during the rush that was the 1500. But I couldn't help but be reminded when the excitement dimmed that I still had a big gash in my leg, and you bet I could feel it still.

I was beaten to the first corner in both my heat and my quarterfinal but nonetheless made it through each pretty easily, even sending Fabio out of the race in the quarterfinals.

Li Jiajun, meanwhile, didn't even make the semis; he fell in his quarterfinal race. Nishitani, just seven weeks after breaking his ankle, didn't make it through, either. Rusty, though, was skating great. He won the first semifinal, Gagnon coming in second, eliminating Dong-Sung.

In my semi, I started from the ideal position—on the inside, the number one hole. *If I can just get out of this heat*, I thought, *I might yet be in pretty good shape in the final.* Even so, I got off to a slow start and drifted to the back. With two laps to go, I was third, behind Jonathan Guilmette of Canada and Satoru Terao of Japan. As the bell sounded, I had moved up to second. As we rounded the far turn, Satoru tried to pass me on the outside; we barely touched each other, and he went sailing off into the pads. All my speed and momentum dissipated;

down the backstretch, I was suddenly third, behind Guilmette and Kai Feng of China.

And out.

And formally disqualified, too, the referee ruled later.

I had tried to set Satoru up on the inside. I tried to hold the track. I ran out of room.

Satoru was put through to the final. He came in fifth of five. Rusty got the bronze, Guilmette the silver, and Gagnon the gold; it was Gagnon's first Olympic individual gold. I was happy for all of them and figured, *okay, we still have the relay.*

It started so promisingly, too. Li Jiajun and Gagnon tangled skates; the Chinese dropped way back. Then an Italian skater fell. So it was the Canadians and the Americans pulling away, and a medal seemed right there. We were the world champions, after all; maybe we could win gold in the Olympics, too.

With twenty-six laps to go, though, Rusty fell. He hit a block and skittered away into the pads. We ended up fourth.

If we hadn't gone down, there is no doubt in my mind that, at the end, we would have had the chance to win. But it was not to be. Canada won gold, Italy silver, China bronze. The gold gave Gagnon three medals in Salt Lake, two gold, and five medals overall in his incredible short-track career. Afterward, reporters kept asking, was I disappointed?

No. How could I be disappointed? I had two Olympic medals.

NUTRITION

As an athlete, in pursuit of the Olympics, there
are two different compartments for nutrition.
One is the recognition, even if obvious, that it's
important to have balance, to be happy,
to eat things that make you smile.
The other is the skewed, no-balance approach:
the 100 percent, hard-core, nitty-gritty, not-one-
almond-more-and-not-one-almond-less plan.

When I was in training, that second approach was
typically what I felt I needed to do. I didn't care
about making my belly feel comfortable for an
hour or two after a meal, because I knew, later
that night or the next day, I would regret it.
For me, that made for excess stress.
No one says you should eat like I ate for an
extended period. For sure, I say—don't.

But because I ate the way I did, I am passionate
about nutrition. I see the way it can help improve
people's lives, not just their health but how they
can function each day, the way they feel about
themselves. Eating smart, eating right,
eating not only what but when you should eat—
that's a change everyone can make.

CHAPTER 8

Around me were signs.

Literally and figuratively, signs appeared as the Salt Lake Games were drawing to a close that signaled how my life after the 2002 Winter Olympics could be very, very different from the life I had known beforehand.

"Apolo, God of the Ice," read just one of the many signs in the stands on short-track's final night, the evening of the 500 and the relay. All around the arena, fans had pasted fake soul patches on their chins. One woman showed up, for some reason, with a golden retriever; she and the dog were both soul-patched.

Michelle Kwan, the celebrated figure skater, and Rudy Giuliani, the former mayor of New York, were both in the stands that night, too, and while neither elected to paste on the soul patch, Michelle did hold up a sign that said, "Oh yes, Ohno," next to a drawing of a big pair of lips. Everybody I talked to suddenly loved short-track speed skating, and in Salt Lake City I suddenly was getting to mingle with statesmen, A-list athletes, dignitaries, celebrities, you name it—President Bush, Lance Armstrong, Cal Ripken Jr., Katarina Witt.

I was a nineteen-year-old from Seattle, and these sorts of people wanted to talk to me? And they genuinely wanted to hear what I had to say? Six years before, I had been hanging out with kids who might be juvenile hall regulars. Now the Utah Department of Public Safety was awarding me an official sheriff's jacket and star?

Life certainly moves sometimes in mysterious ways.

On the way to the NBC studios, for an interview at the close of the Olympics, Dad and I sat still and quiet in the back of a car as soldiers and other law enforcement personnel checked it thoroughly for anything that might be amiss. This was standard operating procedure for all vehicles coming into the restricted security spaces around the Games sites—we weren't being singled out—but it nonetheless consistently made for a tense, quiet moment or two. The soldiers would check under the hood of the car. They slid huge mirrors underneath it, checking for bombs. In this instance, as the mirrors were being put away, two police officers checked our identification as we got back into the car. Everything was quiet and official—until the passenger-side door was pulled open, one of the soldiers peering in. He recognized me instantly. He declared, loudly, "Apolo, we're so proud of you! We've been watching everything you've done, and we are one hundred percent behind you!"

It was shortly before the 500 that I'd gotten my first real taste of what my new life might be like. Across the street from the Residence Inn where I'd been staying was an Italian deli and grocery store, Tony Caputo's. During the Games, the sidewalks in central Salt Lake tended to be very crowded; even so, I just happened to be outside, walking. As I was going along, minding my own business, someone recognized me. "Oh, my God! It's Apolo!"

The scene quickly turned to pandemonium—friendly enough but borderline out of control. I ran into the first store I could, Tony Caputo's. The crowd that had gathered stayed outside; no one dared to come in. Tony, the owner, came over and said, "Hey, Apolo, congratulations.

What can I help you with? Some prosciutto? Some mozzarella? What else might you like?"

He ended up giving me a whole bag of goodies, probably three hundred dollars' worth of great stuff. This sort of thing had never happened to me before. "Thanks so very much," I said and turned to go back out and wade through the crowd. The paparazzi had somehow been alerted—*click, click, click*—all these photos.

I made it back to the hotel safely in one piece and started laughing. *What,* I thought to myself, *is going on?*

This, apparently: "Apolo Anton Ohno came here with the prediction trailing him on the part of many that he could win three, maybe four, gold medals," Bob Costas said on one of NBC's closing broadcasts. "He winds up with a gold and a silver. In any case, he accepted his successes and his setbacks with good cheer, and I think a lot of people will leave Salt Lake City feeling very good about that young man."

That sentiment played out in ways I almost couldn't have imagined.

As I was packing up my stuff, just one day after the closing ceremony, Salt Lake City suddenly felt like a ghost town. Thousands of people were leaving or already gone, and all the energy that had powered the Games seemed to have vanished into the wind. There were just a few people still around, mostly tech types hunched over their computers at the Olympic sites, and as I walked by them on my way up to a rooftop interview with a local television station, I thought, *Wow, this is over.*

For me, though, something new was really just starting.

I knew things were going to get crazy when Jay Leno sent a private jet to pick me up. I got a call from Nike: "Hey, Apolo, we want you to dress in Nike gear on Jay's show and, oh, the private jet will be waiting for you whenever you're ready to go." I thought, *What?*

In Los Angeles and New York, I made the rounds of other television shows: *Today, Dateline, Conan O'Brien,* CNN, QVC, MTV. I walked the red carpet at ESPN's ESPY awards. I went on a photo shoot in the Dominican Republic with model Cheryl Tiegs and a number of baseball players.

I got to take part in a made-for-TV "Superstars" competition in Jamaica.

Some of the bonuses I had earned from sponsors and in other endorsement deals meant that I could buy Dad a new house, in Edmonds, another Seattle suburb. Everything about the house has an Olympic connection—even the view, of the Olympic Mountains.

People magazine named me to its "most beautiful" list.

In Washington State, at the state capitol in Olympia, the governor—wearing an electrical-tape soul patch—declared March 14 Apolo Ohno Day. Up in the gallery, a bunch of the teenage pages working at the statehouse had made their own soul patches out of fake fur and double-sided tape. "It's an honor to be here to accept this resolution," I said from the floor, looking up at the kids and smiling.

Back in Los Angeles, I was invited to Elton John's Oscar party. The short-track world championships were being run at the same time, but I'd hurt my ankle in training and couldn't compete. So, there I was: "Hello, Elton, I'm Apolo." "Hello, Denzel, I'm Apolo." "Oh, hi, Halle, I'm Apolo, nice to meet you." "We all know who you are," they said, "and thank you for your hard work and for winning those medals for the United States of America."

This was heavy stuff.

I had brought Dave Creswell with me to the Oscar party. He was in Los Angeles, working toward his degree. "This is just the tip of the iceberg," I told Dave amid the celebrity sightings. "I can do so much more."

More, because while the glitz was fun, then what? There had to be a purpose to all this attention—and that purpose, to me, was obvious. The best part of post–Salt Lake experience was having kids come up to me to say I had changed their lives. Moreover, I knew firsthand the perils of the journey through middle school. If circumstance had made me famous, and being famous thereupon cast me as a role model, then I could do the right thing by reaching out to young people at whatever middle school might have me. I well knew the pressures, profound and in some cases insidious, that start to work on young people at that age. My own path proved some elemental truths: Don't be afraid to reach. It's okay to be unique. It's okay to be smart. What you're here to do is figure out what you really, really care about and then go after whatever that is with everything you've got.

It's okay if you aren't born into something. You're probably not. I wasn't. I wasn't born into speed skating. It doesn't matter where you start from. Look at me. You come from a so-called broken home? What about me? You face gang violence? Look at me. Of course, we are all products of our own environments. But we can get out. Where are diamonds found? Where is gold mined?

It's not where you start, it's where you finish. And it's okay along the way to fail. I failed. It took that failure for me to realize what my potential was and to dedicate myself to something I truly believed in, to understand that it was going to take a whole lot more than going through the motions, no matter how talented I might be.

It's okay if your passion is something different from what everyone else seems to be doing. It's cool to be different. Short-track speed skating is cool. But it's not the NFL or the NBA. It is, for sure, different.

Obviously, I was not a parent; clearly, I was still only nineteen years old. Even so, parents were now asking me for advice. "Be supportive," I would say. "You want to be part of your kids' lives. Look at my dad and me."

Dad always asked me, moreover, "When somebody has a microphone in your face, what do you have to say? Are you going to sit there with a blank look on your face and say nothing? Or are you going to offer something that's going to resonate with people?"

"You know," Stone Phillips said to me on *Dateline,* "of all the athletes out there, you—you were the one who sort of achieved rock-star status."

"I don't know about that," I said. "But after the first day of competition, you know, I was just, like, swarmed."

"I mean," he said, "even the snowboarders and the freestyle skiers were kind of saying, 'That guy's pretty cool.' "

"Well, that's definitely a compliment. I don't know what to say."

"Have you always kind of done your own thing, set your own style?"

"I'm just pretty much normal. You know, I go out there, give my best, and get off the ice and just try to feel satisfied every time."

Dave also went with me on the photo shoot to the Dominican Republic. Toward the end of our time there, he helped me frame my thinking: "You have a new status, Apolo. What does that mean to you and how are you going to handle that? What do you want to do? Where do you want to be in the next few years, and what's your plan to get there? What's your plan to ensure you keep some balance in your life? What do you need to do to minimize distractions? What do you need to do to continue training? Do you want to keep training? Do you want to keep skating? You have a great talent, Apolo. You have a gift. But if you're going to keep skating, it's because you decide to do so. And if that's your decision, why? You have Olympic medals."

"Are we going to see you in four years?" NBC's Jimmy Roberts asked me on live television from the stadium floor during the closing ceremony in Salt Lake.

"I hope so," I said. "I hope so."

That might have been an okay answer at that moment. But hoping wasn't going to get it done. Hoping, by itself, is just not enough.

Life will give what you ask of it. My job was to ask big, loudly, and consistently.

Those months after Salt Lake gave me a tremendous opportunity to see the big lights of Hollywood, to reinforce the considerable respect I felt for actors and for the industry, and to learn that while I was definitely interested, I had unfinished business elsewhere.

I loved the excitement of it. And yet what I noticed was that wherever I was, I would be sure to jump on the treadmill or the bike or venture into the weight room. I would put on my headphones and let go of whatever distractions there might be. To me this felt like purity. Like an expression of my core values. Like where I was supposed to be, still.

Here, then, was the answer. I asked big and loudly; in return, I got unequivocal direction.

In Colorado Springs, I obviously had the opportunity after the 2002 Olympics to move out of the Training Center and get my own place. Frankly, that's what most athletes do after their first Olympics if they're gearing up for another run.

Not me.

I was adamant. For now, I was moving back into the Training Center. It was a bubble, but I wanted that bubble. My room was more or less a sleeping chamber, nothing more. I liked the environment, the energy, and being around other athletes, and the staff like Sherry Von Riesen, dorm mom to us all, and Dokmai Nowicki, who knew the kind of eggs we liked each morning. We called her "Mama Flower." They were like family.

Being at the Training Center would keep me grounded and focused. Being there would remind me that I was in this to embrace the training, the day-to-day of it, the journey.

Around me every day would be athletes who had given up everything else to chase their passion in their sports. I would again be reminded every day of the emotions, see all the sweat, see how bad they want it and the amount of pain they would go through to try to achieve their dreams. And I would think, *Awesome.*

This is why I loved Olympic sports—because of the struggle.

The entire Olympic experience, the Olympic dream, the fact of being an Olympian—all of that was now in my blood, in my eyes, in everything about me. I felt the power of the Olympic spirit. And I wanted to train as if I had nothing, as if I'd had no success. It's why I put my medals in my sock drawer instead of on display. I wanted to act as if I had done nothing, won nothing, yet.

For me, it was now four years to the next Winter Games, in Torino, Italy, in 2006. Four years to train for—as an example—40 seconds in the 500.

If it were just about a medal, that was bad math. It was very good math, though, if the equation were framed differently. For those 40 seconds, I might have the chance to be all I could be.

———————

WHY THOUSANDS OF emails crashed the U.S. Olympic Committee's Internet server after I won gold and Dong-Sung was disqualified in the 1500 in Salt Lake City was, on the one hand, easy to explain: years and years of controversies at the Olympics involving the United States and South Korea. On the other, it was a complex matter that went well beyond sports to matters of geopolitics and perceptions elsewhere— and particularly in South Korea—of America and Americans.

Little, if any, of it had to do with me—that is, me as an individual. I simply got caught in the middle.

And so, for me, a good chunk of the four years between Salt Lake and Torino was wrapped up in an ongoing drama, a drama that didn't need to be a drama and that was intensified by the controversy in that 1500.

The first of the Olympic controversies involving the two countries dates all the way back to a boxing tournament at the 1984 Summer Games in Los Angeles. Jerry Page, an American, won gold in the light-welterweight division. Along the way, he defeated a South Korean, Kim Dong-Kil, in a quarterfinal-round bout that most who were ringside thought Kim had won. Kim was a medal favorite, and the Korean delegation was so angry it threatened to withdraw its team if the decision was not overturned. It wasn't. The delegation and the athletes stayed, but they were not happy.

Retribution came four years later, at the 1988 Games in Seoul, again in the boxing tournament. In the gold-medal fight in the light-middle-weight division, an American, Roy Jones Jr., pummeled a Korean, Park Si-Hun. Park was nonetheless declared the gold medalist. Park was so embarrassed that he told Jones—who went on to one of the great pro careers in boxing history—that he, Jones, deserved to win.

Park's gold hardly put an end to hugely emotional reactions in Korea that many times revolved around the country's sports teams. A few months after the 2002 Olympics, for instance, soccer's World Cup was staged in South Korea and in Japan. The Americans and the Koreans faced against each other in a match that was played in Daegu, South Korea. The game would end in a 1–1 tie; the Korean goal was scored by Ahn Jung-Hwan (he's not related to Ahn Hyun-Soo), who celebrated immediately after the ball hit the net by pretending he was a short-track speed skater. Everyone got the reference. It was immediately dubbed the "Ohno Celebration."

The World Cup stop in November 2003 was in Jeonju, South Korea. It was eighteen months after Salt Lake. This would have been my first trip to Korea since the 2002 Olympics, but the controversy would not go away. I was still the guy who, amid the victory in Salt Lake, was called "the most hated athlete in South Korea" by one Korean newspaper.

An op-ed piece in the *Korea Times* observed, referring to the 1500 in Salt Lake, "Plenty of Koreans . . . find it embarrassing that an incident which in many countries would spark intense but short-lived anger had become almost a national obsession," the writer going on to attribute it "to *pihae uishik*, roughly translated as 'persecution complex.' "

That fall, several threatening messages that originated in Korea and that mentioned me were sent to Internet websites. "You're safe there, but if you come here, watch out," one of the messages read, and others were said to be much more explicit.

There were, it must be said, some rational voices on the Korean side. Kim Ki-Hoon, the Korean short-track team leader and legend, told reporters he didn't think I was the reason for what one story called "such anti-Americanism."

"South Korea had many social problems related with the U.S. even before the 2002 Winter Games," he said. "I think Korean people just found an outlet for anti-Americanism [by bashing me]. People should understand that sport is just sport."

Even so, I really had no choice. No way could I go to Korea. "It is with great sadness and regret that I am announcing my withdrawal from the World Cup stop in Korea," I said in a statement released a week before the event. "Although the Korean Skating Federation has proposed a security plan in great detail, it has become obvious to myself and those that I trust that my security cannot be guaranteed. It is unfortunate that a few people feel the need to make death threats against me. I am an athlete, not a politician. Cyber-terrorism is every bit as dangerous and wrong as any other type of terrorism. Without the arrest of the criminals making these threats against me, I see no other choice but to not compete at this World Cup event."

A majority of the skaters on the U.S. team also voted not to go because of security concerns; our team leaders said that because they buy tickets in blocks, the entire team would go or stay home. Everyone stayed.

That next summer, 2004, the U.S.–South Korea sports rivalry took a new twist, one that further ramped things up. At the Athens Summer Olympics, Paul Hamm won the men's all-around gold medal in gymnastics, ahead of Yang Tae-Young of South Korea, who won bronze, in part because of a judging controversy. The Koreans launched a series of protests. Paul got to keep the gold.

That next skating season, 2004–05, no World Cup events were held in South Korea. But the South Korean team skipped the World Cup stops in Madison, Wisconsin, and then in Canada. The Koreans didn't give any official reason.

By autumn of 2004, two and a half years had passed since Salt Lake. As an indicator of just how tense things still were, though, at an LPGA-sanctioned women's golf tournament in Korea, a Korean-American golfer, Christina Kim, was asked to name an athlete she thought was handsome. She said me. That bought her ten minutes of inquisition by the local press.

"I honestly had no idea I could cause such offense by saying Apolo Ohno was cute," she said in a story reported by Yonhap, a Korean news agency. "I mean, it was such a long time ago. I always think it's better for people to try to put past grudges behind them."

That Yonhap story also said of Christina, who was born in San Jose, California, to Korean immigrants, that she was "questioned, or rather lectured, on how Korean she is, and asked how, as the holder of a U.S. passport, she could presume to take up the Korean LPGA's invitation to play in the annual South Korea–Japan international match in December."

She told the agency, "There are times I go into press conferences in Korea, and I actually feel scared."

It wasn't until October 2005 that I finally competed in South Korea for the first time since the Salt Lake Olympics.

I wasn't scared. We traveled with a special security detail, which included U.S. Secret Service agents. But what a scene ensued at Incheon International Airport near Seoul: upon arrival, we were met by some one hundred police officers in riot gear.

The only other people on hand to meet me at the airport were reporters.

After everything, the week in South Korea went smoothly, more or less. I had wanted to hold a news conference to explain my side of what had happened in Salt Lake City. But the local organizers said no. So

I had to do things like talk with an Associated Press reporter on the telephone while I was on the way to practice.

"A lot of Koreans are not familiar with me," I said. "They only know what they see on the news or what somebody else says. I want to let them know a little bit about me and take it from there. I want them to know I'm excited to be here."

Which I was. I also described South Korea as "the best nation in the world for short-track speed skating." And I said that, for my part, there were no hard feelings. "The Korean public has so many fans of short-track," I said. "This is the place to skate. If you're part of the national team here, you're definitely one of the best in the world."

Predictably, at the rink there were no incidents with fans. As for the racing itself: I was sick with a stomach bug. I also had a sore ankle, which I had sprained severely at the World Cup stop the week before, in China. Even so, I managed to win two races, the 1000 and the 3000.

The stomach flu was so bad that I skipped the traditional after-race banquet. I always make those banquets. Not this time. I felt horrible. I ended up losing 14 pounds in three days.

I went home happy, though, with the crowd reaction while I'd been in Seoul. They understood the sport; I was just one more athlete, competing like every other athlete in the world.

I had grown up with a lot of Korean friends; I had a lot of friends who lived in Korea; I used to be able to do karaoke in Korean. And all this vitriol and bile were directed at me? It was bewildering and saddening. I was the bad guy? For what? Dong-Sung did something illegal and was called for it. What was I supposed to do? That's our sport.

Clearly, then, this was not really about me but about a variety of different matters, in particular an opportunity for certain people to stoke anti-American sentiment.

Then again, there was a part of it that probably *was* about me. Dong-Sung was at the Seoul World Cup as a commentator for a Korean television outlet. He and I didn't speak.

IN THE 2002–03 season, I won the overall World Cup title.

Ahn Hyun-Soo won it in 2003–04.

In 2004–05, I won it.

That made for the backdrop against which we would arrive in Torino. We were the top two skaters in the world. He knew it. I knew it. Dong-Sung had moved on, and Hyun-Soo was now their number one guy.

The Koreans thought they knew everything about me. They were always watching me, always taping me, from 1997 on. They thought they knew my tempo, my rhythm, my heartbeat.

Even if they did, I would show them not a thing, not even on days when I was hurting. They saw so little that you could almost hear the Koreans saying to themselves, *This guy Ohno is so good, he's like a machine.* And in many ways, I was.

I geared up for Torino figuring to be a far, far stronger competitor than in Salt Lake City. I would be older—twenty-three, not nineteen—and with more experience, more wins, and, yes, more losses. The four years from Salt Lake to Torino saw enormous changes in short-track. I saw how the sport was changing. Again, I made myself a change agent. Change, for many, can be paralyzing. I embrace it. Change can be empowering. Change can put you ahead of the curve.

Part of getting that little bit older was getting a lot smarter about what I was eating. If only the pizza on my teenage runs had been my sole dietary sin. When I was younger, I would take a huge stack of Oreo cookies, put them in a bowl, pour milk over them, and eat them as if they were cereal. Now I veered toward the other extreme. I went from not really caring about what I ate to making sure the machine that was me was going to be the best-fueled guy on the line. If the Koreans were going to believe I was a machine, they might as well have good reason.

I love Nestlé Crunch bars. I love M&M's. I love candy. It's human instinct to love it, and I love candy and snacks so much that before this switch, I'm sure I could have eaten a five-pound bag of Crunch bars and not have given it a thought. Now I took all the candy I had and I put it in a bowl, right out where I could see it and get at it anytime I wanted. And I would deliberately ignore it. It never got to the point where I didn't notice the candy, the way you do with some things when they become a familiar part of your surroundings. Oh, no. Each and every time, it would be, "Oh, hello, candy, there you are still in that bowl, calling out to me, sweet and delicious, and here I am, ignoring you."

Two years out from Torino, I made another vow: I was not going to have any pizza until after the Olympics. For me, of course, given my history, this was big. For any athlete, having a slice of pizza every once in a while wasn't all that significant. It wasn't about that. It was the self-discipline and mental fortitude I was proving to myself that I could exert in yet another aspect of my life.

Who else, when we stepped to the line in Torino, was going to be so mentally tough? Who else would have proven to himself that he could do anything he set out to do? In a sport that was always one tick away from being entirely out of control, who else would have done everything he could to take charge of the things he could—and should—control to put himself in position to excel?

It's why my approach toward food and nutrition underwent such a thorough transition, and why I not only had to think about it entirely differently, I had to think about it in the first place. That is, I had to give serious thought to what and why I was eating, as well as to how and when.

"Apolo," Dave used to say, "here's a watermelon. Everyone always says, 'Oh, I wish watermelon didn't have seeds'; that's why they invented seedless melons, right? Eat this watermelon and focus on truly enjoying it even with the seeds. Don't let the seeds distract you." I understood now what he was after; this was another exercise in honing and refining the power of my mind. It didn't come easily. But I finally got to a point where I could forget about the seeds. Instead, the experience of eating the melon became a sensory adventure into the sweetness of the fruit, the juice, the texture, the temperature.

In much the same way, I began now to visualize the benefits of eating right—feeding not just muscles but also ligaments, tendons, fibers, hair follicles, eyeballs, mind. When I ate, I would pay attention to the feeling of those nutrients being absorbed, feel my body becoming stronger, enhancing every aspect of my performance. I could feel the chicken, the fish, the brown rice, the kale going through me, my body absorbing all their goodness.

The real enjoyment I got from eating wasn't so much in the tasting, though. It wasn't any longer the instant gratification of that first bite of whatever it was. To reach the level I needed to be at, the enjoyment I got from eating well came later—the way I felt when I got off the treadmill or off the ice.

I began to pay rigorous attention to the art of nutrient timing, not just what I was eating but at what times of the day, and how such a seemingly simple step could keep both my weight and my energy levels consistent.

At the same time, my interest in appropriate supplements broadened and deepened—the key being "appropriate," because the use of illicit performance-enhancing drugs was never an option.

To repeat: never.

Of course, certain steroids and other performance-enhancing substances are banned. That's the legality of the matter. For me, I never even had to consider the legalities; first and foremost, morally and ethically, the use of such substances is wrong. I could never do it, have never done it, and never—not even for a second—entertained doping as an option. Bluntly, what gives any athlete the right to take what should rightfully belong to someone else?

It would be far too naïve, incidentally, to believe that no one in short-track speed skating has given in to whatever pressures there might be and undertaken a regimen of performance-enhancing doping. That said, doping has always seemed to me to have played the most minimal role, if any, in the sport. Consider this as evidence: who dopes and weighs 130 or so pounds, maybe less?

Before Torino, the U.S. Olympic Committee and the U.S. Anti-Doping Agency asked me to take part—along with Michelle Kwan and U.S. women's ice hockey players such as Angela Ruggiero—in a public-service campaign promoting clean sport. Of course, I said yes. Mine ultimately showed video of me in action while I said, "I respect my sport. I play by the rules. I honor my opponents. I strive to win. I give my all. Real athletes play fair."

The words may have been scripted. The emotions were genuine.

From Dr. Lavine, meanwhile, I had seen the power of Eastern herbs and traditional therapies, substances that have been part of the human experience for thousands of years, proven by research to help not only the best athletes but also anyone in everyday life to cope with stress—what you need and when you need it.

Which led, inexorably, back to the power and potential of the mind.

They say we tap into 3 percent, maybe 5 percent of the true power within the brain. By 2005, we had a new national team coach, Li Yan. She had been one of China's first great female short-track stars: winner of three medals at the Calgary Games in 1988 when it was a so-called demonstration sport and winner of a silver in the 500 at the Albertville Olympics in 1992. Her husband and biathlete, Tang Guoliang, used to practice tai chi and chi gong. All great athletes, whether they realize it consciously or not, are practicing some form of mental training or imagery. Because I love Eastern culture and philosophies, chi gong simply spoke to me on so many different levels, and Tang and I studied and practiced together. At its essence, chi gong involves techniques for dealing with human energy flow. We read about chi gong masters who could control and direct their energies, masters who in the depths of winter in Tibet, when the thermometer would read minus 60 degrees Fahrenheit, the wind chill all the way down to minus 100, would venture outside wrapped in only a white sheet that had been soaked in water. And these masters would be so in control of themselves that steam would be seen coming off the sheets.

Now, that was proof of the power of the mind. These masters were defying laws the rest of us could barely begin to comprehend.

Reading about that, I thought, *That is a path for me to maximize.* In no way, shape, or form am I now, or am I ever going to be, a tai chi or chi gong master. But I could harness my mind to handle an extreme amount of pain and suffering in training.

Doping? Who needs doping? The mind can do so much more. When you get under 2,000 pounds in a leg press, the rational mind might tell your body, *You can't move this.* The logical self might also say, *This is going to crush you.* No. You can do remarkable things if you only allow yourself. Who hasn't read or heard about a mom who picks up a car to save her baby?

How does that happen? Willpower.

I had proven before that I had willpower. Now I not only wanted but needed so much more.

In short-track, the cycle of change can be remarkably fast. In 2000, for instance, the sport was all about brute power, force, and strength. In 2002 it was superhigh speed and a very, very tight track. Now the sport was about sustained efficiency.

I weighed 165 in Salt Lake; Gagnon weighed 165; Carta, 163; Li Jiajun, 168. Dong-Sung was a comparative lightweight at 148.

Four years later, I was 157. Now I was racing guys like Hyun-Soo, who weighed 117. Another up-and-coming Korean, Lee Ho-Suk, weighed 130.

At 117, obviously, brute force meant nothing.

The standard in short-track, a way of testing yourself before a big race, used to be something called a flying lap—you'd do a first lap to build up speed and then get timed over the next two. You'd do this the day or two before the race, to test the ice and yourself. At one time, those two laps served as the standard. Now it was no longer two but seven. What could you sustain over seven laps? At the elite international level, pretty much everyone can do four or five laps hard. The last two are the test.

Imagine getting on a bike and sprinting as hard as you can for twenty seconds, at max watts and max pressure. Now get off the bike and jump to a squat rack that's loaded. Do squats until you feel like you're going to throw up.

That's one rep.

Now get back on the bike and do that same sprint. Then back to the squat rack.

Back to the bike, once more. Then to the squat rack, one more time.

Done? Now you get to race those final two laps. That's what those two laps can feel like.

It was just one of the reasons I loved short-track. Long-track racing, for instance, is about throwing on a pair of skates and hammering against the clock; short-track is like doing the same thing but with a hundred-pound weight on your back, with your body aligned so that the g-forces tear in the corners at your quads and your hips. You have to be so strong—in your core, your back, your legs, your mind.

Before Salt Lake, I would say to my friends when we would watch the Koreans, "If they would ever figure out to just go to the front and hammer, they would have such a better chance of dropping everybody else." Come race time, though, they rarely used that kind of strategy; instead, they would let a race pan out as it might.

In 2005 they finally wised up. *To the front and catch us if you can;* that became their strategy. That kind of racing would demand strength, speed, and efficiency. So my training had to change. It's why I started working extensively with John Schaeffer.

———————

I HAD FIRST heard about John from other Olympians. The boxers referred to him as the "crazy white guy." From the boxers, this was high praise.

John's gym, Winning Factor, is based in Reading, Pennsylvania.

John, it turned out, is the farthest thing from crazy. The only crazy thing about him is how crazy smart he is.

John is a world champion in both kick boxing and power lifting who had turned his expertise toward training, working with swimmers, boxers, mixed martial arts fighters, weight lifters, and NFL players, along with hundreds of high school and college athletes.

I had never encountered anyone quite like him.

Then again, he had never met anyone quite like me, either.

I had heard about John in 2002 but didn't reach out until 2003. I called him; we talked on the phone for four hours. I told him my goals and said that I wanted to hear about why he could help me do the things I wanted to do.

In that call, I did not once say, "John, I want to win gold medals." I said, "John, I want to lose weight and become both stronger and faster." This was about me exploring every avenue to become the best I could be.

This was not about Li Yan, or a rejection of her. She was incredibly strong-minded and strong-willed, and had distinct ideas about what worked. For instance, she never wanted us to ride the bike; she wanted us to jog. She thought the bicycle was lazy because you were just sitting there, even pedaling. Jogging, she thought, was harder. So on our active recovery days, we'd jog. She would always be telling us, "You need to run—no bike." I would joke, "Li Yan, I want some Peking duck—really, I want Peking duck." She would smile and say, "No, Peking duck is too fat. You need to run, boy." One day, we were working out around a lake in Colorado Springs, and I said, "Li Yan, what about those ducks? Those ducks look good. What about those American ducks? Are they the same as Chinese ducks?" She smiled a really big smile and said, "No. Those ducks are fat. They bike—no run."

You could laugh with Li Yan, you could agree or disagree with her, but say this: she knew the sport. In short-track, it's very difficult to bring in someone new. It takes experience to understand the way things work, and that can take years. Moreover, anyone can get stronger, but that doesn't necessarily mean much if you're getting heavier. To be technically efficient, to attain the shape of a short-tracker, is a very sport-specific thing.

In 2003 John didn't know anything about that. But four hours on the telephone? That surely piqued my interest.

I had been working with a trainer at the U.S. Olympic Training Center. I said to the guy, "I want to lose weight but nonetheless be stronger in my sport." He told me that was impossible.

John had specifically told me, "Let's make the impossible possible. You want something to happen? Let's make it happen."

I said to the other trainer, "Okay, I'm not going to use you."

A few months later, John flew out to Colorado Springs. He wanted to gauge my strength levels. This is when I first knew that I was not working with someone who was wired the same as the rest of us.

We went to a 24 Hour Fitness outlet. "Okay," he said, by the calf-raise machine. "Get under that."

"How much weight," I asked, "should I put on?"

"I don't know," he said. "Let's see where you're at. How many reps can you do? Let's rack it and go for sixty seconds."

To "rack it" means to put all the weight possible on the machine.

Rack it? "John," I said, "I can't put four hundred sixty-five pounds on my back and do calf raises for sixty seconds. I can't do that. I can't even do half of that."

At this point, of course, I had two Olympic medals; I was a World Cup overall champion. I said, "Can *you* do that? You can do four hundred sixty-five pounds for sixty seconds? Cold?"

"Yeah," he said.

"Show me."

John hadn't done one second of warm-up. He racked the machine. He slid into it. He pushed the weight up, and for the next minute it looked like he had no weight there at all. He just bounced the mass up and down. He made it look easy.

This is where our fierce loyalty to each other truly began. With John, as I understood intuitively from the outset, loyalty isn't just a thing. Loyalty is everything.

As it is with me.

John, I was to discover, is one of the strongest guys in the world. He stands maybe five-nine. He weighs perhaps 240. His muscles, were you to touch them, feel like steel. This is a guy who tightens down bolts with his hands, and he does it so that they're too tight. He breaks his glasses and his phone with regularity. He doesn't mean to; he just does.

John has best been described as a bull in a cage that isn't big enough.

John's training can be spectacularly complex. He is a published author and sought-after professor who teaches for the International Sports Sciences Association, the organization that trains the trainers. No matter how complex, though, John's work is often remarkably elemental. John bases his training on what you can do when he gets you. Then he takes your body to a place it has never been before, physically and mentally. He puts you in position to push yourself, your body, and your mind to levels you would never have thought possible.

Training with John is raw. It's pure. It's deliberately not pretty. He wants—and thus you want—the weight machine to look bad, sound bad, smell bad. There's something about that. There's a sense of *Hey, no matter what I might have achieved, I for damn sure haven't made it yet.*

It's humbling. There are no distractions. You're in an environment you can't run from, and when you're putting on the weight, or putting it away afterward, you have to think, *Could I have done more?*

With John, the gratification is instantaneous. You do the set or the reps—or you don't. You do or die. That's my mentality, and for his part, John understood that from the beginning, too.

In the summer of 2004, I flew back east to work out for a while with John at Winning Factor. My first workout there proved the most excruciating thing I had ever experienced. We did a couple of leg workouts that day. The next day, I woke up and rolled out of bed. Literally, I had to roll. I couldn't straighten my legs. I struggled to the freezer. I grabbed some frozen peas and put them on my calves. I called John and I said, "I can't come in."

"What," he said, "do you mean?"

"I mean I can't get in the car. I am lying on the floor in the living room. I'm in serious pain. I can't straighten my legs."

John laughed at me like I had told him the most hilarious thing he had ever heard in his life.

I did finally make it into the car. I did finally make it to the gym. I did crawl on my hands and knees for two days. But I absolutely refused to give in to the workout.

John said it was then he knew that I was a different breed of cat.

That summer, John introduced me to pain thresholds way beyond anything I had known. "Let's do one-legged squats for ten minutes," he said. "Those are fifty-pound weights. You'll be holding on to those for the ten minutes."

That was just a little piece of what he had in store.

That 2004–05 season, my legs were so huge that all my jeans had to be altered. There was no way to fit into a suit because my waist was so small but my legs so big. That season, I won the World Cup overall again.

I spent the entire summer of 2005 in Pennsylvania, training with John. We hit the weights hard, and there were times that I would start to think I was getting strong. John would then slide in and make me look like some twelve-year-old who had never before seen a leg press. It wasn't just what he would do—it's how he would do it, his mentality. He would settle under 1,000 pounds on the squat rack. One mistake, and it could crush his spinal cord. But that's not what he was thinking about. He would get under that weight, and there was no question he was going to win. He was going to explode up and take that weight with him.

"More," I said. "Let's do more."

BEYOND PERFECTION

A coach would say, "Great race!"

And I would come back with something like this:
"No, I need to do more."

I have to accept that I am forever striving
for perfect. It's part of me to my core.
But I also accept now that nothing is perfect.
And it doesn't need to be perfect.
That doesn't need to detract in any way, shape, or
form from whatever it is I'm pursuing.

My personal best is good enough,
as long as I give it everything I've got.

It's too intense and too unforgiving a life if you
live trying to be a perfectionist. Perfect is, in a
very real sense, unattainable. It's a little like being
on a perpetual StairMaster—the thing never shuts
off, the stairs piling down and down, sometimes
faster, sometimes slower, but never, ever off.

Sometimes you've got to get off the machine,
hold the rails, look around, and appreciate all the
stairs you've already climbed.

CHAPTER 9

No one likes to make excuses, especially me. But it also has to be acknowledged when you're truly injured that, in fact, you're not at your best. The sore ankle I raced on in Seoul in October 2005? The one I had hurt in China the week before, at the very first World Cup of the Olympic year?

It was bad.

After all the preparation that I had put in over the summer, the gains in strength I had registered, the optimism for my prospects in Torino—it all threatened to come undone because of injury. After just that one race in China, just that fast, I was physically not anywhere near my best. The issue throughout the rest of the year, up to and through the Olympics, was whether I could get back to speed.

Essentially, from that moment on, I was racing against time—and doubt.

And denial.

I got hurt in the quarterfinals of the 500; with one lap to go, I was pushed—it's part of the sport—and that sent me flying through the air, landing on the ice on my hip and left ankle. I finished the race and advanced to the semifinals. Later, when I came out for the 1000 heats, the ankle was really bothering me. "That's enough for today," the team doctors said. "Let's get a good look at it." It appeared the ankle was severely sprained. In fact, I had torn ligaments.

I could still race—which I proved that next week in Seoul and at the next series of World Cup races in Europe in November and then again at the Olympic Trials in Marquette, Michigan, in December. I dominated the Trials and secured my spot in all three individual Olympic races—500, 1000, 1500—and the relay.

Six weeks before the Games, meanwhile, overstretching, I strained my right hamstring.

About a week before we left for Italy, the American and Canadian teams got together in Lake Placid for a series of exhibition races. There, one of the Canadians, Éric Bédard, bumped me—it was an accident— and when I went down, it was if my ankle were a rubber band being stretched way out of shape.

Again, the left ankle. The pain was intense, as if my skin couldn't even hold the parts of the ankle together. Out on the ice, I made like nothing was all that wrong. I could show no weakness, especially now, not with the Olympics two weeks away. Back in the locker room, I took off my skate and looked at the ankle. It was huge, the size of a baseball.

This, I thought, *is not good.*

I could walk. I was sure I could tough it out.

Upon arrival in Torino, in the first practice skates, my boot felt cracked, like I wasn't getting enough support. I asked the equipment guys to check my equipment. "Be super-thorough," I said. "Something's not right." They came back to say, "Apolo, we've checked everything. Your boots are fine. Your blades are fine."

The issue was not the boots or the blades. The issue was the ankle itself. I just didn't want to admit it, least of all to myself.

Time was ticking. The first races in Torino were set for the first

Sunday of the Games, two days after the opening ceremony. I now had less than a week to get this fixed—if we could engineer a fix.

It was Tuesday night in Washington State, already early Wednesday morning in Italy, when Dad called Dr. Lavine. "How soon," Dad asked, "can you get here?"

"Call you back as soon as I can figure it out," Dr. Lavine said.

"Okay," he said a little later, "here's the plan: I can get out of Seattle on the night flight Wednesday. With the time difference, that will put me into Milan Thursday night Italian time. Milan is two to three hours from Torino by car. I'll see you first thing Friday morning."

"Hurry," we all said.

Dr. Lavine, true to his word as always, showed up early Friday. He took one look at me and said, "Uh-oh."

It's normal before any Olympics for the athletes to hold a series of news conferences. In meeting the press, I had no reason to say anything about the ankle, and didn't. "Memories from 2002 are going to be special for me," I said, among other things. "I have more knowledge about what goes into an Olympic Games. Four years makes you a lot more knowledgeable. Hopefully, I go in better, smarter, stronger."

Smarter, for sure. Better and stronger—only if Dr. Lavine could work his magic. He set to work with some of his most advanced treatments, including a method called "biodynamic osteopathy," which he said would provide extraordinarily deep access into my system. "We're talking real energetics," he said, "the potency of the fluids inside your anatomy." It's not like I understood at all what he was doing, or how. I only knew that what he did worked—even if, on occasion, it made me wonder what special frequencies or vibrations *he* was attuned to, because he was definitely operating on a level of intelligence and sophistication that sometimes left the rest of us wondering, How did he know that?

Once, for instance, he had said to me, "Apolo, you're allergic to the ice." I looked at him for signs that he had been smoking something funny.

"With all due respect, doctor," I said to him, "excuse me? I spend twelve hours a day at the rink. What are you talking about?"

"Here," he said, "let me show you. This vial is filled with ice shavings. Put it in your hand. Now extend your arm all the way out. I'm going to push down on your arm. Okay?" He pushed. My arm sagged. "Now put the vial down," he said. "Put your arm out again. I'm going to push down. Ready?" My arm didn't move. It was strong and vibrant. It was like he was pushing on concrete.

"You're not pushing hard," I said, eyebrows raised in disbelief.

"Oh, yes, I am," he said. "I'll push again." He strained to move my arm. He got nowhere. Like concrete. "It's normal," he said. "Routinely, almost without exception, athletes who get injured on a surface become allergic to that surface."

He performed a treatment. "That ought to take care of that allergy," he said.

"If you don't think this is for real," he said, "here's a test for you. Use tap water instead of ice. Make it a blind test so that neither the tester nor the person holding the vial knows what's what. Then look at the results."

You can't argue with stuff when it works. So now when Dr. Lavine said he was going deep into my system and that he would be working on me upward of two hours a day, I took a look at the race schedule and the calendar, and thought, *Let's be optimistic.*

In truth, though, I was beset with distractions. There was just something about the energy in Torino that was registering as a major disconnect. And I wasn't the only one to feel it. But I felt it keenly. By all rights, Torino should have been one of the great Olympic parties in history. I mean, who doesn't love Italy? The arena where the figure skating and short-track racing would be held, called the Palavela, was featured in the movie *The Italian Job,* in which three Minis were driven onto and over the building's roof. For all that, the vibe in Torino felt not right, and that was playing itself out right in front of me.

The equipment guys had said my boots were good to go. But no matter the condition of my ankle, the feel wasn't quite right. In 2003 I had switched out of the RBC boots I had worn in Salt Lake, thinking they were too old; I'd had them rebuilt, twice, but they just felt more and more clunky. So I switched, and switched, and switched some more. I tried twenty pairs of skates. None of them felt good. In the fall of 2004, I finally found a pair of handcrafted boots I liked, made by a former skater named Bruce Kohen, who worked out of a 24-by-24 garage in Rocky Mount, Missouri. Bruce used extraordinarily high-grade materials, including carbon fiber and aerospace-grade titanium. In a way, his boots were pieces of moving art. Emblazoned on the side of each one of mine was a holographic skull. Loved the boots. Didn't know why the feel was off. Couldn't figure it out. And it was bothering me, a lot.

I'd also wrestled with an ethical dilemma of sorts. In long-track, the rule book says that you can't use a wireless earpiece. In short-track, there's no such rule. It's a gray area. It's obvious why you might want to try such a device: you don't have eyes in the back of your head. If a coach, standing by the side of the ice, can feed you info, tell you whether to go or relax, remind you even of basics that are easy to lose track of in the fury of a race (like how many laps are left), that might make for an advantage. It's like the way the crew chief in NASCAR is always on the horn to the driver. Or in professional cycling.

The devices we were thinking of using were tiny. They fit in your ear, and no one would know they were there, especially not under a helmet—or, as the case might be, a bandana and helmet. In practice, I tried it. I didn't like it. I didn't like the feel of it in my ear, and I didn't like the idea of it in general. I'd always had a very good sense of my surroundings, done fine throughout my career with my own two eyes and two ears, and this little nugget of technology separated me from that.

Plus, maybe it wasn't illegal, but we weren't sure it was, in fact, legal. And I didn't feel good about that. Maybe using it could provide an advantage. But I didn't like it.

I was going to race at the Olympics the way I had always raced.

If my ankle would let me.

"Patience," Dr. Lavine counseled.

THE OPENING CEREMONY of any Olympics, Winter or Summer, is always on a Friday night. My first heats were Sunday, two days later, in the 1500.

The opening ceremony saw athletes from North Korea and South Korea march into the stadium together for the first time at a Winter Games. Twenty-eight acrobats working on a net formed the shape of a dove. Yoko Ono read a poem that served as an introduction to a rendition by Peter Gabriel of her late husband John Lennon's "Imagine." It was cold again at these ceremonies—at least that's what I heard later. I reluctantly decided to stay in, rest, and gear up for the 1500.

There was no huge roar from the crowd when I stepped onto the ice—and why should there have been? This was Torino, not Salt Lake City. Still, there was something about that vibe; it just wasn't quite right, even if it was something you can't quite put into words.

For these Games, my helmet number, again black on yellow, was 254. Our U.S. team skin suits were mostly dark blue; the suit was trimmed in red up top and silver down below, and accented with an American flag over the left breast and the letters *USA* running vertically down the back of each suit. My bandana this day: red.

Early in my heat, I moved up toward the front of the pack.

From the time I first started racing at fourteen, I had consistently—especially in a race such as the 1500—preferred to hang toward the back in the early laps, then move up after a while toward the middle. Whether all the way in the back or in the middle of things, I nonetheless felt a sense of control. So what if there were two guys in front of me and two in back? It seemed to me as if I were the one controlling the pace. Obviously, I didn't truly have control over the guys in front of me. But it nonetheless felt to me as if I were the one around whom the race was revolving; even from the middle, I could dictate the pace, rhythm, tempo, and timing.

Now I was breaking toward the front?

If you were really paying attention, which very few were, given that this was the opening heat: Was there something wrong as well with my posture? Did my skin tone look pale, even ashen? Or was that just the lighting inside the Palavela? Such doubts that might have been stirred surely were quieted when I won the heat with ease. I went to the lead with eight laps to go, dropped back to second for a few seconds, moved back to first with four laps left, and stayed there. For the most part, my hands stayed on my back. I had advanced, and on cruise control. At least that's the way it seemed to most people watching.

The semifinal, later in the day, certainly shaped up to be as doable a grouping as I could have asked for: Fabio Carta was in the heat with me, along with Li Ye of China. Torino was Fabio's hometown, and so he would have the crowd cheering for him. All I had to do to get back to the Olympic final was finish second. In the stands, Dad sat next to Dr. Lavine, both of them taking it all in. Two and a half laps in, I went to the lead. Then I settled back. Two laps later, I was back to fourth. With seven to go, I went hard, executed an outside pass, and put myself back in front. Because of my ankle, I wanted to put myself in the safest position possible, and that reasonably seemed to be out front, ahead of the flashing skates in the pack. Li Ye, for instance, was dangerous; his skating track could be thoroughly unpredictable. This back-and-forth, though, was a complete waste of energy, and I knew that. But I was struggling, mostly with myself; I just couldn't get to that better place, physically, mentally, or technically. At the very moment I should have been at my peak, I simply wasn't.

With four laps left, Li Ye moved into first. I dropped back to second.

With a lap and a half to go, I started to set up an outside pass, to get by Li Ye. I'm not sure why it seemed so important to pass him. The top two, after all, would go on to the final, and by then he and I were clearly ahead.

Heading into the corner and the bell lap, I put my left hand down on the ice, right behind Li Ye.

Mistake. Big, big mistake.

It didn't seem like it should have been such a big mistake, but it was a mistake in the first instance—feeling the need to pass him, that is—and the karma rose up and bit me. My left hand caught the back of his left skate. It wasn't much of a touch but it was enough. I pitched forward. My right hand went down toward the ice. My left hit one of the blocks. And now I was spinning, out of my track, way out, not far enough or fast enough to hit the pads but enough to send me so far wide that I was thrown from second to fifth, with but a lap to go now.

That was the race. I ended up fourth, after a disqualification involving a Belgian skater that had nothing to do with me. I would not get the chance to defend my gold medal. I was out of the 1500.

I had made a mistake, and I was in disbelief. I looked at the small cut I had just earned on my left hand. I could not believe it was for real and that what had just happened had really taken place. Here was the most vivid evidence imaginable of what I always say: short-track is such a test of the mind. The best skater doesn't win. The fastest skater doesn't always win.

It simply did not seem real. But it was. These were the Olympics. There was no do-over. "It sucks. Straight up," I said in an interview on NBC a moment or two after leaving the ice.

Our entire team, for that matter, couldn't believe what it had just seen. We were all so undone that we forgot that I now had the B final in the 1500 yet to go. There were six skaters in the race. Five were already on the ice. I was still in the locker room. I didn't even have my skates on; one of our assistant coaches, Jimmy Jang, was cranking back on my right blade. The bend wasn't the way it should have been; instead of the blade carving toward the corner, it felt like the blade was pulling me toward the boards.

The last time I had been late to a race had been when I was in my early teens. One of the Games officials came in and put a death grip on my arm. "You have one more race," he said. Li Yan, our head coach, sprinted out toward the ice. She saw two other officials. "He's coming," she said. I started walking down the hallway toward the ice, pulling my gloves on. Meanwhile, the public address announcer started making the introductions: "In starting position number one, representing Hungary . . ."

As I got to the ice, I swung myself over the pads—only to be pulled back from behind by a clutch of yet more officials. I shrugged, walked past them by only a couple of steps, and swung myself over, just as the PA guy said, "In starting position number five, representing the United States, Apolo Anton Ohno."

The crowd cheered.

So much for the highlight of that 1500; the B final is skated only in the case of massive disqualifications and the remote possibility of a shortfall of medalists in the A final. Four skaters in the A final, the championship race, would have to be disqualified for the winner of the B final to win even a bronze medal. Of course, that didn't happen. Ahn Hyun-Soo went on to win gold, and Lee Ho-Suk got silver, after which Hyun-Soo said, "Frankly speaking, I thought that I would compete with Ohno in the final, so I'm sorry for having not faced him."

Me, too. I finished third in the B final. Mostly, I used the race to check out my equipment.

Overall, I was feeling pressure. It was strange. I was letting outside influences affect me. The most important was that I was hurt. And I was not being honest with myself about it.

———————

THE NEXT MEDALS wouldn't be awarded for six more days, that next Saturday—nearly a full week to let Dr. Lavine do his thing and, if I could, get my head straight. The only racing I would have to do would be midweek, in both the 1000 heats and the relay semifinal.

In practice, I kept tinkering with my blades. In the 1000 heat itself, my left ankle kept folding underneath me when I pushed. Plus, my hips weren't positioned where they needed to be. I felt uncomfortable and disconnected, and I looked choppy.

I won the heat nonetheless. And we made it through the relay, into the finals—after I got an adjustment, immediately before taking to the ice, to one of my skate blades.

If you didn't know better, it looked like I had turned the corner. I hadn't. I felt vulnerable, and I didn't want to admit it—didn't really know *how* to admit it. I felt that merely acknowledging that I was hurt would be a potentially devastating form of giving in to the situation, the sort of move from which I wouldn't be able to recover. It's like a fighter; he can't have any cracks in his armor. None, for sure, that he can show. I didn't want to hear that anything might really be wrong with me. I didn't want Dr. Lavine to tell me, "Look, you have a serious injury that is inhibiting the way you are skating; you need to accept that and attack it."

No, I thought. *I am not weak. My body is fine. I may have a small problem—but it's nothing.*

It's why I didn't talk about it in the media. Only once, on NBC, in one of those quickie interviews you do when you come right off the ice. After the 1000 heat, I told Andrea Joyce that the Olympic Games are a "mental battle," and said, "For me, just battling myself, battling my own mental demons, my own fears—and it was better tonight . . . definitely a right step in the positive direction."

Mentally, at some level, I had been rejecting Dr. Lavine's treatments. I told him, "I don't know exactly what it is you're doing, but it's not working. Maybe you're wasting your time? I mean, I appreciate you coming all the way over here, but I'm not getting better. I want to focus on things that make me feel good."

Dr. Lavine deserves a huge amount of credit. He is a straight shooter. He said, "I can go home anytime you want. I am here to support you, here to make you feel good. But I believe in my heart we have to be in synchronicity. We have to work together. You have to want this to work for you, so that I can help you make it work."

I looked at him and I said, "Okay, let's try this for real."

It was a little like the scene in *Rocky IV,* when Adrian goes all the way to Russia to tell Rocky he has her unconditional support. From that point on, it felt like *okay, now I believe.* And I started to get better, a lot better.

A couple of nights before the final, meanwhile, I had a dream.

I dreamed I was going to win the 1000. I dreamed it all. I saw it. Hyun-Soo, Ho-Suk, me—I saw it all play out in my head. I had won gold in the 1000 at the 2005 worlds. Now, in my dream, gold in the same event at the Olympics. This dream seemed like a signal, so powerful, so right. Maybe, after everything, this was the turnaround.

Hyun-Soo and I drew each other in the quarterfinals. Since Salt Lake, he and I had raced each other sixty-eight times. There weren't going to be any surprises; he and I both knew that. Physically, he wasn't that strong; he couldn't be, not at 117 pounds. But it sometimes seemed that his body was simply designed for short-track racing—his small upper body, longer legs, the way his hips were shaped—and, technically, he could simply be amazing, the way he could use his body weight and manipulate the angles.

Hyun-Soo and I enjoyed a mutual respect. Even with all the drama that had gone on since Salt Lake, he told NBC, "I don't have any animosity toward him."

Hyun-Soo won the quarterfinal; I took second, content to test his speed. We drew each other again in the semifinal. Actually, three of the four of us involved in the wipeout in Salt Lake were in this semifinal: Hyun-Soo, me, and Li Jiajun. Éric Bédard, the Canadian I had collided with in Lake Placid before heading over to Torino, was in this race, too.

Hyun-Soo crossed the line first, me right behind.

The final would make for the third time in this one night we'd be racing each other. Rusty had made the final, too. So had Ho-Suk. And Li Ye. All in: two Koreans, each with an Olympic medal already here in Torino; two Americans; one Chinese.

In my dream, the race played out like this: I would take the lead with about three laps to go. From there the race was mine.

The gun went off. Nine laps for gold. Li Ye grabbed the early lead. I settled into second, Hyun-Soo in third. With three and a half to go, Hyun-Soo made his move, on the inside, into first.

In my dream, this is where I made my move.

This, though, was real life. And I hesitated.

I should have passed him right back. For some reason, I hesitated.

With less than three to go, I slid in behind Hyun-Soo.

The bell sounded. Hyun-Soo and I were on the inside, him in first, me in second. Ho-Suk was making a move, well to the outside. On the far turn, Ho-Suk cut the angle and, coming out of the turn, slid by me on the inside. Now I was third.

And that's where I finished—third. Hyun-Soo won, Ho-Suk took silver.

Rusty finished fourth. Longtime friends, he and I shook hands as we skated around the ice afterward, a job well done. On the podium for the flower ceremony later, Hyun-Soo, Ho-Suk, and I posed for pictures, all of us together on the top step. No drama.

"I waited four years for this," I told Andrea Joyce. "I had to bounce back from the 1500, and I was still able to get on that podium." I smiled when I said that. Genuinely, I was happy. Now I had three Olympic medals: one gold, one silver, one bronze. And, as it turned out, at almost the exact same time that I was winning my bronze, Shani Davis was winning gold over at the long-track course, in the 1000.

But late that night, the next night, and for most of the next week, I replayed the race in my head hundreds if not thousands of times. My hesitation had cost me. Why had I hesitated?

We were staying near the arena, in an apartment complex with big marble pillars set among sprawling grounds. In one of the rooms, apparently before we Americans had arrived, someone had taken a permanent marker to one of the walls and had drawn what looked like a big bat or maybe flowers. It wasn't clear. It was gothic and weird. One night I walked in, and the room was freezing cold; the heat was working fine, and the window was not open. "This is just weird," I said. "I have to get out of here." It seemed as if the room was haunted.

I thought I might walk around the Palavela; maybe that would give me some peace. Late at night, there was nobody there. I walked in my sweats around the place; it's an eerie space, such an old building that you could almost feel spirits and ghosts.

No peace there.

Night after night, I was up, until two, three, maybe even four in the morning. The 500 was still coming up and so was the relay. Two more chances; my bronze had done little if anything to lift the mood on our team amid the belief that the 1500 and the 1000 were probably my best chances. And my own negativity was eating me up. I had been trained to acknowledge no weakness, to admit no doubt, to show no pain. And now?

Dad and Dr. Lavine told me that I had to let it all go. It was as if I was still allergic to the ice.

THE THING THAT was profoundly bedeviling me was elegantly simple. In the 1000, I hadn't given everything I could give. I was feeling the sting of regret.

In addition, I realized, I felt as if I had been dealing with so much pressure to deliver, pressure complicated by my ankle problems. *I have to win, I have to win, I have to win,* I would think. For my teammates, my coaches, fans, friends, sponsors—anyone and everyone who had poured their hearts into helping me.

That was nobody's fault but mine.

Now I had the chance to make it all right.

I had to acknowledge the appreciation I truly felt to them all for their faith. I also had to reduce the experience to what it genuinely was intended to be all along: a matter of purity and passion. And I had to go for it.

The 500 would always be something of a crapshoot. And my history in the 500 did not scream certainty. I'd had success on the World Cup circuit. But in the world championships, my best 500 finish had been a silver, and that had been in 1999, seven long years before, when I was only sixteen years old.

But so what?

I believed. I had never counted myself out, and I wasn't about to start doing so now. Maybe I didn't have the strongest start in the world, but all I needed was one great start when it counted. My ankle, thanks to Dr. Lavine, felt miles better than it had at the start of the Olympics. All I had to do was get to that final, and then anything was possible. Truly, anything was possible. If there was even a sliver of a possibility I could win that race, I was going to grab on to that and hold it with everything I had. I realized I had actually said it myself in an interview with Costas after the 1000. In trying to explain the Olympic spirit, I had said, "If you're down, you need to get back up and keep going, give your all. It's not over yet."

The quarterfinals, semifinals, and final of the 500 would go down on the same night, February 25, the day before the Games drew to a close. I got to the rink early that day. *This,* I thought, *is what it's all about. This is what I live for, moments like this.* Normally, I did a little jogging to

warm up; every other time during these Games, I had done that jogging inside the arena. *Today*, I thought, *it's outside.*

Oops. It was rainy. No matter. I jogged away and around, running
through the crowds, past the curious security guards, and thought,
*This is what I'm here for, the test, the opportunity to overcome all the dis-
tractions. It's time to stand up, man up to my own emotions, and declare,
"I am going to do this."*

Bottom of the ninth, as it were. Three balls, two strikes. Here comes
a pitch you've never seen before. *What, Apolo, do you plan to do? Swing,*
I thought to myself. *Swing for the fences.*

Maybe, I also thought, *this is how it's all meant to be.*

"Apolo will deliver," Dr. Lavine had told Dad. "He will deliver."

In my 500 heat, midweek, just the one race, I'd shown some explosiveness again. And I had enjoyed it. In my quarterfinal, I drew the best
start position, number one, on the inside. Immediately to my right, in
the number two slot, François-Louis Tremblay of Canada, the reign-
ing world champ in the 500 and a skater known for his great start.
Flou beat me to the corner; so did a Dutch skater, Wim de Deyne. They
skated one-two for the first lap and a half, then I moved past de Deyne
on the inside and, a lap after that, past Flou.

In the semi, I drew Flou again, along with Li Jiajun, himself a three-
time world 500 champ. The computer—which picked these spots by
random draw—threw me into start position number three. Li drew
one, Flou two, and at the first turn, that's how we were stacked up: Li,
Flou, me, and, in fourth, Jon Eley of Great Britain. On that very first lap,
though, I slid by Flou and into second.

With just more than two laps to go, I went wide around the turn, to
go by Jiajun on the outside. With the current world champ behind me,
second didn't feel safe.

Jiajun drifted out with me and pushed me out, almost to the pads.
Now I was fourth. Two laps to go.

One lap to go, still fourth.

Coming around the final turn, I moved back ahead of Eley and was all but dead even with Jiajun. He and I both stuck out our skate blades. Who was in second?

Flou was clearly in first.

The photo at the line was also indisputable: Jiajun's boot was a few inches ahead of mine. But wait. Jiajun had gotten tangled up with Eley heading into that final turn. Jiajun didn't quite have enough room on the inside and with a right-arm shiver had sent Jon sailing out way wide. The referees really don't like to see contact; it's what gets you disqualified.

And here it came: Jiajun was out. I was in the final, and so was Jon. I gave the camera two thumbs up and a big smile. This had to be a sign of good fortune, right?

A few minutes before the race came another. We were in the locker room. Suddenly we heard a yelping scream echo down the hallway. It was Jimmy Jang. He was sprinting, yelling, "Yes! Yes!" Jimmy burst into the locker room and looked straight at me. "You have number one on the line," he said. "You can do it! I believe! I believe!"

We were laughing and laughing. Jimmy was acting crazed. But it was so cool to see. He believed, I believed—suddenly, everyone in our little group believed. I felt so in the zone, so ready for anything and everything. I was living totally and thoroughly in the moment.

Hyun-Soo had won his semifinal, with Bédard—the 2000 500-meter world champ—second. I had watched from near the tunnel to the locker room. What I saw was that Hyun-Soo was totally on his game; he had won that race by passing on the outside. That was championship material.

Hyun-Soo was, of course, looking to sweep all three individual races in Torino. But he, like me, had never won a 500 world championship.

As we warmed up, I felt it. I had the inside start position, and I had my mojo. The computer couldn't have spit out a better start list for me if I had programmed it myself. Flou was in the two hole; Ahn, three;

Bédard, four; Eley, five. The two Canadians had probably the fastest starts in the world; they very well might box in Hyun-Soo.

If ever I was going to race the perfect race, here was the perfect opportunity.

The starter called us to the line.

Each of us dug his skates into the ice. The crowd hushed. "Ready," the voice called out over the speakers. We crouched, waiting for the gun.

Bédard broke from the line. His nickname is "the Cat." The guy probably has a better time in the 40-yard dash than a lot of football players.

In this instance, though, he was just a beat too soon.

False start.

You're allowed one false start; a second, and you're out.

We composed ourselves, got to the line, dug in. "Ready," the voice called out again.

Still no gun. Flou and I broke. But Eley hadn't gotten into the start position. This one was a penalty on Jon.

A third time now to the line.

The tension was absurd.

I was yawning, doing everything I could to relax; my heart felt like a jackhammer.

Be calm.

There's a dot under the ice just behind the start line; that dot is there so you know where your lane is. I got to my dot and extended my right arm out toward Flou, a perfectly legal move, just making sure that he and I both knew the reach of my territory. I also thought, *The thing to do here is to time this start precisely, like it's a 100-meter dash in the finals of the Summer Olympics.* If everyone else might have been thinking about the false starts, I was thinking about the *best* start.

Time to take a chance.

"Ready," again. A beat, if that. I leaned.

And I was off.

With the gun. I timed it perfectly.

The race wasn't yet a second old, and already I was half a body length ahead of everyone else. I simply could not have timed it any better. Dad said later it was as if I had been connected to the gun itself.

At the turn, I was indeed first. And just as I had thought it would play out, the two Canadians were second and third, Hyun-Soo fourth. Half a lap in, I snuck the quickest of looks behind me. I could see I was a full body length ahead of Flou. Hyun-Soo was in fifth.

A lap and a half in, three to go—me, Flou, Bédard. I didn't know quite where Hyun-Soo was, but clearly, he couldn't be any better than fourth. And fourth, with three laps to go, two guys to pass just to get to me, was a lot to make up.

Two laps to go, and I was in control of the rhythm, the tempo, and my destiny. I had to keep moving, and at high speed, but not so fast that I created space behind me for someone to move into. For the two Canadians, for Hyun-Soo, it was a little like being in a Ferrari on the interstate with a big semitruck directly in front going 65 miles per hour, and two eighteen-wheelers on either side, each of them doing 65, too. They surely wanted to go faster. But there was nowhere to go.

One lap to go. Behind me, as I knew he would, Hyun-Soo was going way wide, aiming to cut the corner. Flou was waiting for me to make a mistake. The Cat was waiting for Flou to make a mistake or—better yet for him—for me to falter.

No way. There were twelve, maybe fifteen seconds left in the race, and I absolutely turned on the jets. I went all out. Every bit of training I had ever done in my life—the time was now to bring it, and I brought it. Around the final turn, I made sure to keep to the inside. Not a chance anyone was going to slither through there. *You want to get by me? Try the outside.* But there wasn't enough time left in the race for that.

I flashed across the line, clearly first, and yelled, not a word, really, just a sound, "Waaah!" I threw my hands up in the air, a look of redemption, relief, gratification, joy, happiness—all of it, all mixed up, all together—across my face. It was a clean race. I had won fair and square. I had come back, beaten the odds and the obstacles. I was the 2006 Olympic 500 champion.

It was electric. It was perfect—or, at that instant, given everything, it surely seemed as close to perfect as perfect could be.

Perhaps others hadn't believed I could win this race, of all races, but I had believed in myself. And here was living proof of what faith and belief, hard work and discipline, courage and tenacity could get you: a wire-to-wire, undisputed, unchallenged, emphatic, no-question-about-it victory.

My second gold and fourth Olympic medal in my career, in what should have been the wildest of races, an event I had turned into a classic display of tactics and strategy and will.

The scream I let loose as I had crossed the line had been so loud that Dad heard it up in the stands. My momentum carried me around the ice, to the American coaching box. Li Yan and I exchanged a huge, huge hug. I skated away and gave the crowd two big fist pumps. Then I put my head almost to my knees and clenched my fists in triumph, then skated over to the corner of the stands where some fans were holding American flags, and waved.

Hyun-Soo came over and shook my hand. What a great display of sportsmanship.

At the end, Hyun-Soo had just gotten past Bédard for the bronze. Flou took silver.

Someone threw me an American flag, and I skated around the ice with it. Flou came over, and he and I shook hands, too.

I circled back to the coaches' box. Here were Derrick Campbell, a Canadian who over the past several years had been instrumental in my staying in Colorado Springs; and Paul Marchese, a great equipment guy; and others. Hugs all around, every one of them in tears. All of them felt they had won, too.

Shani was in the stands, watching. I looked up and found him, and shot him a tongue-out, ha-ha, I-did-it-just-like-you smile.

I put my guards on my skates, tapped congrats with Eley, and started off the ice. I got to sit for just a moment. Then it was time to move on. I took a few steps and there, above me in an orange shirt, a cream-colored jacket, and some super-bad sunglasses, leaning over the Plexiglas railing, was Dad.

I reached up and grabbed Dad's hand, and I shouted, "I did it!"

NO TIME TO relax. No time to savor the 500 fully. We had the relay still to go.

The perfect ending for me at these Games would be a relay medal. Canada had won the relay in Salt Lake; the Koreans had won the prior three world championship relays. Those two were obviously the favorites, but, as we had learned ourselves in 2002 when Rusty fell, the relay was impervious to predictability or probability. And this relay was more complicated than usual because there were five teams instead of four, twenty skaters rather than sixteen. Korea, Canada, China, Italy, and the United States.

On our American team, Rusty and I were back for one last relay together, along with J. P. Kepka and Alex Izykowski.

We held the early lead. But about ten laps in, the Canadians passed us. A couple of laps later, we slipped to third, behind the Koreans. With eighteen laps to go, Hyun-Soo flew around the outside to the lead. The Koreans and the Canadians then opened it up on the rest of the field. The Chinese spun out. It was us and the Italians for third. The Italians moved ahead, but just for a moment. Seven laps to go and the Canadians grabbed the lead. And we slipped to fourth.

On the final laps, Hyun-Soo edged past Mathieu Turcotte. The crowd was going crazy. But not for the Korean gold or the Canadian silver. They were cheering for the Italians. The final exchange: Rusty to me, and I dug deep, executing an inside pass, past Nicola Rodigari, to move us up to third.

This most satisfying bronze was just the second relay medal for American men in Olympic history, our first since silver in 1994. We had all put in so much pain, shed so many tears for our sport, each other, ourselves.

Hyun-Soo had his third gold medal in Torino. I had a third 2006 medal and the fifth of my Olympic career, as many—several reporters pointed out to me later—as Eric Heiden.

At the relay ceremony, we posed for pictures: the Canadians, us, the Koreans, all together, smiles all around. And at the ceremony for the 500, Hyun-Soo and I shared an embrace. Certainly that made for closure to the drama. Hyun-Soo said so: "What the Korean people were upset about is Kim lost his medal. I was certainly sad with them. But I believe these things are understandable in these types of competitions."

For my part, in the afterglow, I profoundly felt the essence of the Olympic spirit. "The whole experience has been very, very touching to my heart," I told some reporters. "This whole Olympic experience is amazing."

They wanted to know, naturally enough, whether I would be returning for another Olympics. I laughed. "I've got to figure out what the next part of my journey is going to be," I said. "I'm just enjoying the moment right now."

After the relay, meanwhile, someone had produced pizza. A lot of pizza.

We were in Italy. It was good pizza.

FEAR

———

Fear kills your potential to be who you are
and who you can become.

The trick is to acknowledge it—and then let it go.

Blocking out fear never works. You're just closing
the door. You know it's still behind the door,
lurking. But if you open the door and greet it,
you've made an appropriate acquaintance
with that emotion: Hi, I know you're there, but,
no, you can't come in right now. Later!

Once, Dad and I were talking about spirits and
ghosts. We were on a long plane trip. This was a
deep conversation, just he and I; everyone else in
the cabin was sleeping. I asked him, "Dad, what
would you do if a ghost was in the house and you
were all alone? If it was talking to you,
what would you say? Would you be scared?"

In his Japanese accent, Dad said, "Scared?
No way. I would tell him, 'Hey, listen, ghost,
I'm a very busy guy! You have to go away.
I have to sleep. Go bother someone else.'"

I laughed so hard I was in tears.

CHAPTER 10

The phone rang. It was my manager, Lee, calling from his office in Beverly Hills.

"Apolo!" he said.

Lee grew up in New Jersey. He has a little bit of that accent. He said, "Apolo! How are you?"

"Hi, Lee. How's everything?"

"Listen," he said. "I got something for you here. I've got an opportunity."

"Lee, what is it?"

"Don't say another word. Just listen. Don't say anything. I've got this show. Now hear me out."

He said that a couple more times. I just listened. The man said to hear him out; I was hearing him out.

"Hear me out: *Dancing with the Stars*. Apolo Ohno."

"What? What the hell are you talking about?"

Frankly, I wasn't even sure I knew what *Dancing with the Stars* was. Emmitt Smith. The football player. Hadn't he been on that show? Cleverly, I said, "Didn't Emmitt Smith do that show?"

"Hear me out," Lee said. "Listen. Are you near a computer? Check out the website." He gave me the link.

"Okay, Lee, I will. I'll check it out."

I went to put the phone down.

"Lee," I said after checking out the website, "this isn't happening."

He and I said our good-byes.

I thought for a second, then picked the phone right up again. "Dad," I said, "I've got this opportunity."

I called John. As usual, he was direct and to the point. He said, "Are you serious?"

I called some others I trusted. They said, "Are you kidding? That show is so cheesy." I said right back, "Cheesy is just a start. Have you seen what I'd have to wear? Do you see what kind of dancing I'd have to do?"

And now here came the jokes: *Okay, maybe you know how to move— but you only know how to turn left.*

It took some convincing, particularly from Dad, who again pointed out that opportunities presenting themselves ought to be taken seriously indeed. Look, for instance, at all that had happened since the door to the training center in Lake Placid had opened for me so many years before. What if this was, in its way, another door? A door to my future after skating, perhaps the kick start to a blossoming entertainment career? Even if this was . . . a reality show?! Even if it involved . . . dancing?!

What did I know, aside from break-dancing in the halls back in middle school, about dancing?

My friends were calling me now. "Apolo, if you're going to be on that show, you have to win."

I had to win?

Then again, who was to say I couldn't learn how to dance like a master? If I put my mind to it, if I gave this 100 percent, anything was possible.

Even dancing.

Check that—*especially* dancing. Life, as I once put it in an interview with the *New York Times*, was something like an antique Japanese dresser, wasn't it? I could have a large drawer for skating and the Olympics, and other drawers for dancing and acting; I could have a drawer here for fashion, another over there for nutrition, another for business, another for philanthropy and projects with kids; I could even have empty drawers waiting to be filled up.

The more I thought about it, the more I was intrigued. *Dancing with the Stars* would allow me to show what I was really like—no helmet, no bandana—to millions of people who might know little if anything about me. Also, it would show me what goes on behind the scenes at a huge production-oriented show.

If I could apply the same mentality toward *DWTS* that I had toward my sport, who knew what might happen? It might even make me a better skater—assuming I wanted to gear up again for another Olympics, in 2010 in Vancouver.

Now, *that* was a big question mark.

After Torino, I had been living out of a suitcase. Mostly, I had been in Southern California, exploring possibilities in the entertainment industry. But those weeks also saw a whirlwind of television appearances, promotional opportunities—even an invitation to a formal dinner at the White House with President Bush and then prime minister of Japan, Junichiro Koizumi.

I had been featured on the front of the Wheaties box, thrown out the first pitch at a Seattle Mariners game, chatted with the likes of Jay Leno and Ellen DeGeneres, and been on the "Nickelodeon Kids' Choice Awards."

In Colorado Springs, at the Paralympic Military Summit, I was left in awe after meeting a number of veterans who had been wounded in the war in Iraq. We didn't do anything spectacular that afternoon; we didn't have to. We just sat around a big table, nibbled on some red velvet cake, talked about where we were from and about the kinds of cars we all liked. (Me: a 1964 Lincoln Continental.) These were soldiers who had lost arms or legs. But they had their dignity. And they kept saying how lucky they were to be alive. After I had left, one of the soldiers, Luke Murphy, a twenty-five-year-old army sergeant whose one leg was held together by screws and rings, told a reporter who had been there, "I just wanted to meet a gold medalist."

With due respect, the honor was mine.

Back in Washington, DC, I put on in-line skates to zip around a fountain on Capitol Hill. I'd been asked if I would help promote a federal government initiative aimed at encouraging middle school kids to be more interested in math, and of course said sure. How did that equal math? I was the 500-meter Olympic champion; one lap around the fountain was 460 feet; how many times did I have to skate around the fountain to equal 500 meters?

(The answer: three and a half.)

Vancouver? It seemed so far away. Maybe I ought to go as a goodwill ambassador, to represent the United States and short-track, to do something beyond winning medals, aim to reach more hearts.

I loved the Olympic Games. I loved being an Olympian. But did I still love doing what I do, every single day, even on my worst days?

I had given myself a long, long break after Torino; I didn't start training seriously again until late in 2006. A few months later, in February 2007, I won my eighth national title, placing first in every event. The 2007 short-track worlds were in back in Italy, in Milan, the second week of March. The *DWTS* production schedule meant I would have to practice my dancing while I was competing in Milan.

Maybe it could all be worked out. I decided I was in.

I picked up the phone.

"Lee," I said.

"Apolo."

"Lee, I'll do it. I'll do *Dancing with the Stars*. But I have to win."

Pause.

"Well, okay," Lee said. "But you know I can't really control that?"

"Seriously," I said. "I cannot not win. You don't understand. My friends will never let me live it down."

Another pause, this time from me.

I said, "They might never let me live this down, anyway."

THE *DWTS* PRODUCERS paired me up with the beautiful and blond Julianne Hough. That 2007 season was *DWTS*'s fourth; this would be Julianne's first turn on the show. She was just eighteen, wouldn't turn nineteen until that summer. But she was already a seasoned dance pro and a star in the making.

All four of Julianne's grandparents were dancers; her parents met while on a ballroom dancing team in college in Idaho. Julianne was from Utah, one of five children, four girls. She began dancing competitively at age nine and had then been sent to London, with her brother, to study. When she was fifteen, she became the youngest dancer, and only American, to be named both Junior World Latin Champion and International Latin Youth Champion at the Blackpool Dance Festival.

Julianne could also sing. That would be the next chapter in her career. *DWTS*, the way she saw it, could be her launchpad.

I had no idea what I was in for. I could not possibly comprehend what lay ahead. You dance for a couple of minutes: how hard could it be?

Julianne and an entire *DWTS* crew came to Italy. She was there to practice; they were there to film us.

She and I hit it off immediately. Good thing. It's one of the reasons she was willing to be so patient.

To begin, I had to sneak out of the hotel late at night to practice this dance stuff. My coaches didn't want me leaving the hotel at all. Understandably, they wanted my focus to be on my skating.

Julianne was staying at the sort of grand hotel that graces a place like Milan. It had a ballroom. The hotel also had a dance studio. "Meet you there at ten at night," I'd say to her.

In Milan, I won four medals, gold in the 1500, bronze in the 1000, the 3000, and the relay. Overall, I was the bronze medalist, behind Hyun-Soo and Charles Hamelin of Canada.

Julianne, meanwhile, was quizzical. She would ask, "What about the dancing? Apolo, are you going to take this seriously?"

We got back from Milan about a week before taping the first show. In theory, the way the show works is that you get four weeks before that first show to practice, to get used to your partner, to learn the dance itself, or even just how to dance.

That didn't happen for me.

The day I got back from Italy, back in Los Angeles, the producers arranged a photo shoot for all the dancers and cast on the show. Now it's down to business. Clyde Drexler, the NBA star, is here. So is Paulina Porizkova, and she's a supermodel; Shandi Finnessey is Miss USA 2004. John Ratzenberger and Ian Ziering are actors; Billy Ray Cyrus, an actor, country singer, and famous dad; Laila Ali, the daughter of boxing legend Muhammad Ali and a boxer herself; Heather Mills, an animal-rights activist, among other causes, who, oh, had been married to Paul McCartney; Leeza Gibbons, a TV host; Joey Fatone had been in the boy band 'N Sync.

And then there's me.

Everyone is talking about their dances; Ian and Laila and some of the others are saying they already have that first dance down and they're on to the second dance. I thought to myself, rapidly now: *Are you kidding? Julianne and I haven't even done the first dance yet. What the hell have I gotten myself into? I am going to embarrass myself before the entire United States of America. I am going to get kicked off this show.*

I am, I thought, *so damn scared.*

"Okay, Julianne," I said, "let's hit it hard."

That first dance was a cha-cha. We practiced. Julianne was the teacher; I was the student.

Before the first show, I had the dance down—more or less. I wasn't comfortable. But I could swear I had it down, had the mechanics and the steps memorized.

Julianne dressed to impress that first week, in a short red miniskirt dress with matching red gloves that reached above her elbows. Me—a black long-sleeve shirt, black pants, and a red bandana.

The way the show works is that you get a heads-up about a minute before you're supposed to go onstage: "Apolo, Julianne, sixty seconds, sixty seconds to camera."

Okay, okay. I'm getting ready. Feeling not bad. Getting set. All of a sudden—boom. *Oh, my God.* I blanked out. I didn't remember the dance. I didn't remember a thing. I was having a complete mental blackout.

"Julianne," I said. "Julianne."

"What?"

"We have to practice. I don't remember a single thing. What are we dancing to? I don't remember the music. I don't remember a thing."

Now it's thirty seconds till go-time.

I never, ever had experienced this before a race. I had never blacked out. But this little dancing show—I was so nervous, so scared. I was dead-bang terrified. There were 25 million to 30 million people about to watch me dance, live, on national television.

Be calm.

Okay. I am supposed to do the cha-cha. The song is "Let's Hear It for the Boy." I think that's the song.

Hey, thanks, producers! "Let's Hear It for the Boy," by Deniece Williams? Way to make me feel like a real man. That's totally uplifting—makes me feel so very confident. Like, like I'm a sixteen-year-old again. Of course, the producers had picked it for me because I was so young, twenty-four, and Julianne was even younger.

"Apolo, Julianne—you're on."

We stood at the top of a three-stair landing. As the announcer introduced us, I stood there with my arms crossed. Fortunately, Julianne had the first steps. She slithered down the stairs and grabbed me by the shirt, and I, just as I was supposed to, followed along. All I had to do for the next few moments was look, well, sultry. Until, about a half minute into the song, I was to take over the lead. Which I did. After that, for the next minute, it was muscle memory.

The dance ended with me on my left knee, Julianne across my right thigh on her back.

No one got eliminated that first week. Nonetheless, it was impossible to avoid the feeling that we had survived. Somehow, we had survived.

Not only that, when the scores from the cha-cha were added to the totals from the other dance of the night, a foxtrot, we actually were near the top of the pack, tied for third.

At the Training Center in Colorado Springs, they had organized a viewing party for the first night. They'd called it "A Night at the Apolo." A reporter from the local newspaper, the *Gazette,* showed up to take it all in. "Around here, we're used to seeing people do their sports very well," said Eli Bremer, who competed in modern pentathlon. "He looked good to me. He's going to win."

After that first show, the Wynn Las Vegas Race and Sports Book said Laila, at 4–1, and Joey, at 5–1, were the odds-on favorites to win the show. I was a 15–1 choice, ahead of only Heather, Paulina, and John—for entertainment purposes only.

Though the show was of course itself entertainment, it was amazing nonetheless how it had become such a cultural touchstone. The *New York Times* devoted nearly eight hundred words to that first show, much of the column about Heather and her artificial leg.

. . . The deeper appeal of Dancing with the Stars *is simpler. Dancing, particularly ballroom dancing, is a lost art that everyone has a vestigial feel for in his or her toes. The competition taps into that yearning and weaves around it a melodrama of perseverance, defeat and triumph over adversity—or low expectations.*

After Ms. Mills's performance, Bruno Tonioli, a judge, told her, "You have more guts than Rambo." Actually, what she really demonstrated is that Americans will always love a Rocky.

Tim Dahlberg of the Associated Press, a sports columnist who had covered some of my Olympic races, wrote, "Someone needs to hold Emmitt Smith accountable for all this. It was he, after all, who showed America that real men can really dance."

A bunch of us had gone on *Good Morning America* to talk about the show. "I mean, I feel like I have rhythm," I said. "I think I can dance. And speed skating has a lot to do with tempo and timing."

The judges told me that first night that I had speed and flair. But I got dinged, appropriately enough, as well.

We were still catching our breath from the dance when Bruno Tonioli said to me, "You are a joy to watch. It's like watching *Happy Feet*," the animated toe-tapping penguin movie, "all over again.

"It's really—your potential," he went on to say, "is probably the highest potential of all the people I've seen tonight. Obviously, obviously— there is a lot of work to do, because there [were] a lot of technical mistakes. It's not for lack of trying. But your hands, your feet; you know you really have to focus on the technique side of it.

"The performance is there," he said. "More rehearsals . . ."

Another of the judges, Carrie Ann Inaba, said, "Your hip action is amazing. I must say your footwork is great. I don't think you missed one step. But—the thing that's a little strange is your hips—the way, when you're not doing the movements, when you're walking, they kind of get turned in, and I think it's the athlete in you. So watch that and get a little more graceful there. And watch when you turn that you don't lead with your shoulders."

The third judge, Len Goodman, said, "Well, my concern is not that cha-cha-cha, because I thought it was excellent. My concern is next week, when you dance the quickstep, because for me your posture isn't right. You've got this stooped-over look. You've got to get yourself working straight through your neck and get that lovely ballroom look for next week."

What had I gotten myself into?

"This is unlike anything I've ever dreamed about, and it's a lot more than I had anticipated," I said as we came off the stage.

Afterward, truthfully, I didn't remember a thing about it. I was still in something of a blackout zone. To see my performance, to remember the judges' comments, I had to go watch it on YouTube. All I remembered was getting the scores.

After week two, and that quickstep, which we performed to "Two Hearts" by Phil Collins, Julianne looking radiant in a salmon-colored gown, me in tails and a salmon-hued tie, the critics started paying attention to me and to Julianne just a bit. We were long shots. But maybe we might need to be taken seriously.

"You're going to stay for weeks, and weeks," Len said in his critique, with Carrie Ann calling us "the surprise of the season to me—it's so not expected for you to be this good this early." Bruno went so far as to call us a "dancing tonic," exclaiming, "That's what America needs!" He also said, "You've inspired every kid in the country to take this on and make it look cool, fresh, young, exciting—what more do you want?"

A note on the *Entertainment Weekly* website said, "Apolo Anton Ohno definitely stepped it up this week—footworkwise, his routine was very complicated, and he and Julianne were almost alarmingly in sync. And since they're so young, they look a bit like that power dance couple who are way better than everyone else at their high school's talent show, sort of a Benji and Heidi from *So You Think You*

Can Dance kind of thing, half sexy, half incestuous, only not annoying. I dig. For now."

Week three saw us dance the jive to Chuck Berry's "You Never Can Tell," Julianne channeling Uma Thurman, me John Travolta, she in skinny jeans and a white halter top under a platinum-blond wig, me in a tight black suit, white shirt, skinny black tie, my hair tied back in a ponytail. It was corny. It was camp. But it was fun.

Paulina was the first to go. Then Shandi.

Meanwhile, despite our early successes and the encouraging comments, the truth was I had still been keeping myself at an emotional distance. This was still, pretty much, that little dance show. To Julianne's enormous credit, she would not relent. She kept saying, "Apolo, you have to be more animated. This show is about animation, about magnifying your personality. It's the only way it reads on camera."

As an athlete, I had spent so many years performing without regard to any of that. When I skated, I wasn't obligated to smile for any camera. I didn't have to showcase anything, didn't have to spotlight the real me. If I chose, frankly, I could look mean, not perky. Plus, on the ice, I knew exactly what I was doing. I was in my element; I had spent thousands and thousands of hours in preparation, and so by the time I actually stepped into the rink, it was extraordinarily familiar and comfortable, even in its way comforting. Not this. On top of which, on the ice, I for certain did not have to look pretty. On this show, I was trotted out in clothing that was so tight it was ultratight, in shirts that barely could be classified as shirts—the V in a V-neck can go down only so far, after all. The guys who design these costumes are major talents, but let's face it, you wouldn't catch me walking through the Beverly Center in any of them.

All in all the whole thing felt—uncomfortable.

And the dancing itself—the dancing includes arm movements that are profoundly elegant but, when you're learning them and then when you watch them later, don't seem, well, manly. When you extend your fingertips, when you're reaching out in a certain way to connote a particular emotion, it may well be, it certainly should be, fluid—but it's a very different move from any sort of move I had known before.

Dancing was a different sort of sport. And make no mistake: it was athletic. It was so demanding, in fact, that Vincent Pastore, who was perhaps best known for his role as the gangster Salvatore "Big Pussy" Bonpensiero on *The Sopranos*, had taken himself out of season four after just one week of rehearsal. That's what brought John Ratzenberger—Cliff from *Cheers*—in, on short notice.

"I didn't realize just how physically demanding it would be for me," Pastore had said in a statement.

I could handle the physical side of it. My challenge was elsewhere. Julianne knew that, of course. She kept trying. "Apolo," she would say, "you have to show confidence. If you can do that, people are going to enjoy you, and us, and it."

Julianne would see the real me—the way I was when we were hanging out or just goofing around—and she would say, "This is the personality you have to show when we're in the studio. You have to allow yourself to let people see you."

Traditionally, I had been guarded in terms of emotional access. The nature of being in the spotlight amid the Olympics had naturally made me just that much more cautious. Now, here was a very wise eighteen-year-old who knew what I stood to gain, professionally and personally, by opening up.

Bluntly, it wasn't as if I had much choice. This wasn't a small dinner party for a few close friends. This was about the show itself, being on national television in prime time, and about getting ready for each week's show, the twelve to fifteen hours per day of being under constant watch by video crews there to record seemingly everything we did or even might do.

In high definition.

The camera barely turned off. Practice. Interviews. Rehearsal.

Camera blocking for the coming show. The show itself. Every day of the week. For weeks and weeks.

The show goes live on Monday. That day alone is enough to wear you out for the entire week. You're in the CBS studio from ten in the morning until eight or nine at night. There's what's called "dry rehearsal": a run-through but in street clothes. Then dress rehearsal in costume. Then the show. Then afterward, the entire group—dancers and crew—would go out together.

On Tuesday, it's back to the studio, again at ten in the morning, to gear up and then do the results show. That night, assuming, of course, that you didn't get kicked out, you get your dance for the following week, as well as the music; you are told the dance and get to pick the song from a list. That night you have a choice: either dinner and relaxing with friends or getting to work on the dance.

Wednesday, Thursday, Friday, Saturday—that's when you learn and, you hope, perfect the dance.

Over the weekend, it's back to the studio to block for the camera crews and to do preproduction interviews that get woven into the show.

Amid all of this, you're also doing radio interviews, sometimes starting as early as five in the morning Pacific time, as well as television and other media. As a dance couple, each of you has to try to build up the buzz around you; a huge component of the show, of course, is audience participation.

To that mix, I added an extra ingredient. On top of everything, I was trying to stay in skate shape. John Schaeffer came out to LA; after dance practice, it was off to the gym with him, sometimes at midnight.

There's an invincibility factor that many men have, or we like to think we have, in sports or in business. It's that poker face. The show-no-emotion thing. Being very guarded. You see it in teenage boys, too. It can all be traced to one simple proposition: we don't want to make a mistake. To that end, we don't want to show any cracks or weaknesses.

That's how I thought I could handle all of this.

This might have been just this little dancing show, but with Julianne's direction, it dawned on me that dismissing it in that manner was another proposition entirely: denial. I didn't want to show anyone I was tired or, worse, I could be beaten.

What this show and what Julianne Hough were teaching me was fundamental: If you fall on your face, does it matter? You get back up. It's okay.

This was one of the essentials of showbiz: on the show, if you made a mistake, it was not only okay to show that you made that mistake, the very best thing to do was to own it. You had to say, "I'm going to perform, going to entertain these people, and if everyone in the crowd figures out that I made a mistake, they're going to be thinking, *Oh, he made a mistake—so what?* If you act like, *Oh, I was supposed to do that, the crowd is on your side.*"

It was taking all the energy that's wrapped up in fear, saying hello to that fear, and then letting it go.

In a different arena, I knew how to do that.

In this context, the only way to do that was to take the show seriously. It's what I had to do. I would give the show the respect I showed my sport. And when the dancing run came to its end, whenever that would be, I would be able to say, *no regrets.*

At the same time, serious did not—could not—mean uptight. I would allow myself to open up, show some emotion. I understood now with clarity: when you are on TV in HD, you can't hide. I am who I am. If I fall down, so be it. My dad is still here; my friends are still my friends. There are people out there whose legs don't work right, whose eyes don't work, whose hands don't work. Why get frustrated about a little mistake I might make?

I had here an opportunity to be a part of a great show. So what if some people called it corny? American families like to watch the show, the same families who like to watch the Olympics. They see in the show a sense of purity and wholesomeness. You learn to dance, you face your fears, you grow as a person. The show lets everyone watching see you outside of the "celebrity" status that's put on you, a tag that's bogus, anyway.

It was like a switch. I started to enjoy the show. Really, thoroughly enjoy it.

Week four saw us do a waltz to Simply Red's "If You Don't Know Me by Now." It got the second-best score of the week, all the more remarkable because the waltz demands a portrait of maturity and intimacy—and we were not only the youngest on the show but also more like brother and sister than a romantic couple. If I looked more emotionally accessible, maybe it was because, genuinely, I was. Or maybe I just seemed more free and easy because of an old show trick. The sleeves of my shirt had been sewn into the jacket; underneath my jacket, I'd gone sleeveless.

Week five brought the samba.

In practice, Julianne told me, "We had better get frickin' tens on this. I'm sick of being in second and third." She also said, "You need to start using your face, using those facial expressions, and be sexy."

"Be sexy?"

"Be sexy. Be the tiger," she said, adding, "Rowr!"

Julianne also said, "I like to win."

Showtime. Julianne appeared in a tiger-striped leotard. My matching costume included a brown shirt and a dark brown bandana. As the red light went on, I thought, *Okay, let's really give this a ride*—and gave the camera a healthy, animalistic growl, accented with a slash of my right paw.

"Up to this point," I said on the air, "we have been known as Mr. and Mrs. Cute Couple. No longer. Now we're going to be known as Mr. and Mrs. Hot Sexy Samba." For emphasis, I gave the camera a big wink. Might as well be that tiger. Be sexy.

The music came from Reel 2 Real, "I Like to Move It." We were on it.

Toward the end of the dance, I gave Julianne a little come-here motion, making like I really wanted her. The crowd gave us a standing ovation. The judges then gave us what Julianne wanted: frickin' tens, across the board.

"Perfection," Carrie said. "That's it. Perfection. That was—perfect."

Afterward, I was asked on camera to show my best samba face. "Samba face?" I replied. "How about samba hips?"

There have been many, many times in my life, far too many to count, when I have envisioned myself as a warrior. The warrior always has a shield and a sword. On this show, I could not have that. I had to let down both and go further still: I had to take off my armor. To practice something for three or four days and then perform it in front of millions of people, and then have all the people in the studio get on their feet and applaud for you—that feeling was amazing.

Week six, and the rumba. The rumba is sexy, romantic. Julianne's brother, Derek, who is also a professional dancer, came to give me some advice: "If I can dance the rumba with my sister, so can you, Apolo."

The soundtrack for the week was Gwen Stefani's "Cool." We went out there and made it hot. Us and a chair. We danced on and around it, and ended the dance all cuddled up on it.

Dad was on hand for this week's show. He cut my hair before we went on and noticed how I seemed so at ease, how I had such a big smile. My father has a great sense of humor. After the show, he told *People* magazine, knowing full well he would be quoted, "I hope he teaches me so I can go on a cruise ship."

A twenty-eight from the judges for the rumba, tied for the week's best. A "choreographed poem," Bruno said.

Week seven, with the field thinning out, those of us remaining were asked to do a double dance, in our case, a foxtrot and a mambo. This week was where the stronger dancers would begin to separate from the pack. To make things that much more intriguing, we did some of our rehearsing back in Seattle, where I had the privilege of being inducted into the Asian Hall of Fame; Dad and I shared a big hug there that night, and he said he was so proud.

Julianne cut no slack because the schedule was compressed. One time in practice that week, she said, "Do you think that's the best you can do?" She didn't say it to be mean, she was asking sincerely. Another time, she reminded me, "You've got to give me your all, every single time."

The audience was on its feet after the foxtrot and the last sounds of Dinah Shore's "Steppin' Out with My Baby." Nonetheless, Len wasn't pleased. He looked past Julianne, radiant in a soft blue dress, and directly at me and declared, "You're a good dancer. So whatever dance comes on, you're going to do a good routine and a good performance. But from you I don't want good. I want great. And there was no great there."

John was among those in the audience that night. Listening to Len, he shook his head in disbelief.

For the foxtrot, I had been in a suit that called to mind a riverboat gambler. For the mambo, it was back to an open-neck shirt, no jacket. Julianne switched from the soft blue long dress to a flouncy bright red number. This was, after all, a Latin dance. The music, suitably enough: Gloria Estefan and Miami Sound Machine's "Dr. Beat."

Again, though, Len was not moved. "I don't want to repeat myself," he said, and then did: "I've got to say. It was a very, very good performance. You always come out and you dance really good. But, again, I can't call that great."

Even Carrie Ann was reserved: "It was a little off."

Fortunately, we weren't sent off. On to week eight.

"Len's comments sucked," Julianne said later. The cameras were rolling, of course. "Sometimes," I said, "you have to get knocked down to come back even stronger." For both of us, this next week amounted to a challenge. To meet that challenge—was there anything sweeter?

Our two dances for week eight were the tango and the paso doble. The choreography that Julianne put together was challenging. But to meet that challenge would not leave even a single doubt in any mind: we were going to be in that final.

For the tango, I was dressed in a black tux and a wine-colored shirt with a black tie; Julianne was in a black backless number. "Jessie's Girl," the Rick Springfield hit, rocked the house. We danced with authority.

Again, Len didn't like it. It lacked passion, he said to a cascade of boos. It was far too hectic, a cacophony of noise and movement, he said. He gave us an eight. Carrie Ann and Bruno gave us ten apiece.

The paso doble demands that the man appear very aggressive, very masculine, as if he were a matador in the ring. I had to project abject control hinting at anger that made it abundantly plain I was dominant. There simply could be no doubt: I was in charge. I had to control the dance; I had to move Julianne around. Of all the dances in the course of the show, this one would most require me to step out of my comfort zone. The art of this particular dance, though, required me to take on a very different role. To make this dance work, I had to dance with an attitude that was something like severity.

This, it turned out, was my moment.

I was dressed in black pants and a black jacket; the jacket was emblazoned on the back with a huge yellow bull's head; my shirt matched the color of that bull. Julianne had on a long black skirt, trimmed in yellow. In the first two seconds of the dance, she turned to me, and I ripped off her skirt. On purpose, of course.

As she knelt to my side, in her black-and-yellow leotard, I twirled her skirt over me as if it were a cape. Several seconds later, I put the fabric in front her eyes and beckoned her to rise. She did, and I fixed the skirt back around her waist.

From there on, it was electric. Dario G's "Carnival de Paris" blared out as I moved Julianne this way and that. The dance ended with her on the floor, beneath me, my right hand poised over her, as if holding a lance.

The paso doble was the first time in the show that I thought to myself, *I am doing this right. Not a little bit right. Dead-on right.*

I put out both hands to Julianne and helped her up. The dance was over. It was back to being respectful. Maybe even gallant.

"That is a proper dance!" Len exulted. Ten points.

"That," Bruno all but shouted, "is a champion looking at the finishing line and going for the kill!" Ten.

Carrie Ann said, "I could tell, Apolo, you were in it to win. I had chills the whole time. That was fabulous!" Ten.

"I definitely think," Julianne said afterward, "that you reached a new level."

For the semifinals, we reprised the quickstep and the cha-cha. The quickstep earned us another perfect score, the cha-cha a twenty-nine.

"The Apolo Express is on for a magic ride, and you've taken America with you!" Bruno said. The man has a way with a phrase.

So does Len. The cha-cha, he said, was "gyration and raunch."

Even so, we were into the finals. And—raunchy or not (not!), I thought that was a great cha-cha.

Shani Davis was in the audience for those semifinals, along with Rusty, Dave Creswell, and some other good friends: Mark Fretta; Justin Mentell, a former short-tracker; and track cyclist Giddeon Massie. And Dad.

Justin was always bound for Hollywood, an actor and an artist even when he was a skater. Just his movements, his gestures, the way he spoke, the way he talked about the things we talked about when we were teenagers—it was clear he was bound for bigger things, and ultimately he landed a role in the cast of *Boston Legal.* After the Salt Lake Games, as I had more and more reason to be in Los Angeles, Justin would inevitably pick me up at the airport or arrange to meet me for a meal on Sunset Boulevard—maybe Greenblatt's Deli, Mel's

Diner, something like that. Justin didn't have family in Los Angeles. Of course, neither did I. That's what we were for each other when I was there. So it was great to have him, and the others, there that night.

Dad cut my hair again, too. He said I needed a sleeker look. He said I ought to make my neck look longer for the final round.

They went around before the final show and asked each of us to reflect on the season. "Winning this competition is what I signed up to do," I said. "I'm not scared of anybody."

The judges picked a rumba for us to do. "No chair this time," Julianne said.

Then a freestyle dance.

Then one to please the judges: an encore of the paso doble.

For the rumba, I wore a white shirt, black tie, and black suspenders; Julianne was in a cream-colored camisole, gauzy wrap top, and hot pants. The music was lush—"Midnight Train to Georgia," the Gladys Knight and the Pips standard. As the dance started, she ran across the floor to me. From there we danced together with soulfulness, teasing each other, blending into each other's arms, as Bruno said afterward.

Len demurred, saying we were too fast, too hectic. "They made love on the dance floor!" Bruno shouted. "I can understand people liking it," Len conceded.

"You did great," Julianne told me.

Twenty-eight out of thirty.

For the freestyle, out came black tops, shiny white track pants, his-and-her white bandanas, and a boom box. A minute in, I rolled onto the floor and did some break-dancing; after that we pulled the bandanas over our eyes and went for it blind for a few moments; at the end, I went back onto the floor and Julianne executed a somersault over me. Up I popped, and onto my shoulders she went.

Ten, ten, ten. All of Len's nice words were drowned out by the shrieking fans. Carrie Ann insisted on giving us each a hug.

The paso doble, I told Julianne in practice that week, was going to be our last dance together—at least on the show. "Let's leave the dance floor," I said, "with no regrets."

"No regrets," Julianne said. And she added: "A ten, ten, ten."

We pulled out the black-and-yellow costumes one final time. As good as the week eight routine had been, this one was better. The cheering inside the studio carried on and on.

"Like a real athlete, you keep coming back," Len said. "There wasn't one step there that I could fault."

"You are such a team," Carrie Ann said.

"You put a fresh spin on everything you do. It's great to watch you," Bruno said.

Ten, ten, ten it was.

A little while later, we were named champions. Julianne jumped into my arms. Dad applauded and beamed.

Joey Fatone and Kym Johnson took second, Laila Ali and Maksim Chmerkovskiy third.

"Thank you, Julianne," I said.

"I'm so proud of you," she said, adding a few moments later as we held high the mirror-ball trophy, "Happy birthday!" That Tuesday in late May was my twenty-fifth birthday.

What a gift.

Not so much the winning—though of course that was great.

The experience. That was the gift.

The entire experience of being on this little dance show—it proved totally transforming. If you put your mind to something, if you give 100 percent, if you sacrifice, and if you dedicate yourself, anything is truly possible.

———————

AFTER THE SHOW ended, we went on a short *Dancing with the Stars* road tour. Great fun and a great lesson in the reach and power of the show.

At one point, a very nice lady who had been eyeing me approached. "Hello," she said. Then, in rapid-fire fashion: "You're that dancer. I saw you on *Dancing with the Stars*. You were fantastic. I'm visiting my son. I'm from Florida."

"Where," I said with a big smile, "are you from?"

"Tampa. You were magnificent. Are you still going to dance?"

"I don't know," I said.

She paused and seemed confused.

"Ma'am," I said, "have you heard of the Olympics?"

WHY SET LIMITS?

Once, Dad and I were talking about film—that is, me maybe having a role in a movie. I said I was a little bit afraid of my skills. He said, "Apolo, in life you can't put a ceiling over your head. The only ceiling you have is in your house. That's it."

What he was saying is that just because you have a certain set of talents that you know about doesn't mean that maybe you don't have others, too. Don't disengage yourself from an opportunity because you're scared or you don't think you can do it.

You can be anybody you want to be.

I have gained such inspiration through my dad's words. His words—they're so organic, just a dad speaking with a son, trying to instill values, thoughts, perspective, and this mind-set that anything truly is possible.

Think about it: Who wants to live with a ceiling over your head? You're just going to bump your head.

CHAPTER 11

The nice lady from Tampa was just one of the untold numbers of people who saw me as a dancer, not as the skater guy.

Was I still the skater guy?

Did I want to commit myself to another Olympic Games?

I had a decision to make. No right way, no wrong way. Just different paths.

In the summer of 2007, after *Dancing with the Stars,* so many opportunities presented themselves, so many things I could do to advance my interests outside my sport, so many possibilities that were available to me in the entertainment and Hollywood scenes. Frankly, they were enticing.

After 2006 and Torino, and what seemed like a perfect race, did I have more to accomplish in short-track? I had won everything I had set out to win. I was at a very good place in my career. I could feel content with what I had done on the ice. Was there more?

In conference calls with reporters, I would typically be reminded that I had five Olympic medals, the same number Eric Heiden had, that he and I were tied for second-most in U.S. Winter Olympics history behind long-track speed skater, Bonnie Blair, with six. If I stayed in the game, in Vancouver I could become the sole survivor.

Oh, I thought, *that would be cool.* I had always put Heiden in his own category. Blair, too. You have to respect what they did, and I certainly do. It was an interesting idea that I might break their records. But it was not anything near enough of a motivator to keep going. I had not taken up short-track to break any records. That's not why I skated.

So why, I would ask myself, *do I want to keep skating? Why would I, should I, keep skating?* All the memories of me on the podium, getting medals, crossing the line first—I never thought about those things when I was taking time away, in the summer of 2007, from the sport. The only things I would think about were the times I was truly at my lowest, mentally and physically, reminders of the moments when it would be snowing in Colorado and no one else wanted to go outside, the training alone, the sacrifices I had made. That's what I missed. That's what I enjoyed.

Those times of self-trial and self-triumph. Both.

Obviously, I thought, *there's a part of me that skates because I want to be the best and I want to win.* But I was getting older, and winning itself might be that much harder. That was a real consideration. From a pure results standpoint, I had to acknowledge the risk that I might not dominate short-track speed skating as I once had. I was twenty-five; by the winter of 2010, I would be twenty-seven, and three more seasons into the sport. Other guys were coming onto the scene who were the teens I once was, and as Monica Seles, the tennis star, would later put it in her book, in words that resonated deeply with me, "Teenagers are fueled by a naïve invincibility that can lead to tremendous achievements—it just goes to show how much power the mind has. . . . Before you know it, a new generation just like you will be rising up, but they'll be faster and stronger. You'll have everything to lose, and they'll have everything to gain."

Some of my friends were saying to me, "Listen, man, if you stop now, you go out on top." They would say, "Everyone knows about the guy who couldn't stay away. Do you want to be that guy?" Michael Jordan—he made that comeback with the Washington Wizards after all those great years with the Chicago Bulls, and was he the same Michael Jordan we remembered? Muhammad Ali, the greatest of all time—did anybody want to see Ali the way he was late in his career? "People want to remember you, Apolo, as a champion."

It mattered—of course it mattered—that I might come back and not do well. That was not an unreasonable fear. But that was just fear talking. I did not have to listen to fear talking. Instead, I could focus on what I wanted. And on who I wanted to be.

If I was going to carry on through Vancouver, it wasn't going to be for financial reasons, not for fame, not for popularity. It had to be because, solely and simply, I loved the sport.

This, at its essence, was it.

I loved the sport when I was a teenager and I'd had to decide on the rocky shoreline of western Washington whether I was going to be all in, and I loved it still. I especially loved the purity of it. In perhaps no other aspect of our world can you go head-to-head with your own demons, battle fear and insecurity, and say, "Today is the day I am going to perform"—and, no matter the result, get instant feedback, an exhilaration and clarity that come with knowing you have truly given all of yourself. That purity was something worth staking your life on. I loved, too, the journey aspect of it. There's a famous saying that the journey is the destination. For me, that's what my sport was about—and, in particular, the things I learned about myself, the challenges I faced.

The short-track team the United States would send to Vancouver would be a young team: Up-and-comers like J. R. Celski and Simon Cho would still be only teenagers in February 2010. I hoped I could help lead the younger guys. That would be an honor.

The thoughts kept coming. The 2010 Olympics would be in Vancouver, which was like a second home to me. If there was anywhere else in the world I would want to live, it's Vancouver; I have friends there, the Games would have a local flavor for me, and I would have a ton of local support.

My first Olympic experience was in Salt Lake in 2002. Now I was maybe nearing the end of my Olympic time, and I was moving to Salt Lake to train. U.S. Speedskating, the federation that oversees all aspects of the sport in the United States, had moved its base there, and so after ten years at the Training Center in Colorado Springs, I was buying a house in the Salt Lake area and setting up in Utah. If the federation hadn't moved, I surely would have remained in Colorado, but given the realities and my longtime commitment to the national team, being in Salt Lake just made sense.

It all made for a circle I could close: Salt Lake to Vancouver back through Salt Lake.

Should I keep going for a third Olympic Games? The lights all seemed green.

I knew I was meant to skate. At my core, I believed there had to be a reason I was still skating. There had to be a reason I was still healthy, a reason I was here at this juncture. By renewing my own commitment to skating, could I perhaps do more to help change people's lives? If I had inspired some number of people with what I had done before, could I do more? Had I done all that I could to help bring about changes in the way we as Americans approached fitness and health?

There's another saying: be the change you wish to see in the world.

I did my sport because I lived and died with it. I believed in it with my heart. I believed, too, in the Olympic spirit. Olympic symbolism was in my blood, my father's blood. I wanted to embody that spirit— what that means, the constant struggle. The philosophy of winning is not determined by getting on the podium. It's much, much bigger than that. That's what the Olympics are about. And I could be the ambassador to carry that, to show athletes and the world.

Of all the turns I could never have expected, *Dancing with the Stars* had helped give me that sort of perspective. It allowed me to see talents I didn't know I had. It showed me that I could take on any challenge. The show carried me back to my sport with a fresh attitude and new confidence.

Dancer, skater guy—together, bound for Vancouver.

I was in.

———————

THE FIRST WORLD championships after my run on *Dancing with the Stars* took place in March 2008, in Korea, in a remote eastern coastal city, Gangneung.

I skated with renewed commitment, with relaxed confidence, and without fear. It showed. For the first time in my career, I won the overall title at the worlds.

I won even though I was skating on Korean ice and against the very best Korean skaters, an event that had never happened before and might never happen again. When the Koreans are on home ice, they rarely let up; it is plain they do not want to lose.

Even so, I won.

Lee Ho-Suk came in second. Another Korean, Song Kyung-Taek, took third. Another, Lee Seung-Hoon, finished fourth.

I won the overall title even though I was disqualified in my first race, the 1500, ruled out for pushing Seung-Hoon on the next-to-last turn. Then I won the 500, got second in the 1000 and third in the 3000, and the points fell my way.

At those worlds, the Koreans knew a secret. I knew it, too. Very, very few others, however, were in on the secret.

I knew their ways.

A year and a half before, I had been training with Korea's best, in Korea, invited to train there at the Mokdong rink near Seoul, the center of Korean skating. The invitation certainly put to rest the notion of any ill will left over from 2002.

When I told Dad I had been invited, at first he was hesitant. "You're going to go over there and you're going to have to show humility," he said. "To show face, you might have to lose to twelve- or thirteen-year-olds. Maybe this isn't a good idea."

Then he thought about it a little more. "Apolo," he said, "this is an opportunity. For you to reach your next level, you have to see them in their own environment. The less you know about an opponent, the more mysterious he can seem; the more you wonder. This is an opportunity to see the Koreans in their own light, to see them for what they do. It is a rare glimpse into their world."

The year before, I had been met at the Seoul airport by riot police. This time, the airport was still—by chance, somebody famous was arriving there at the same time I was, and so I was barely noticed.

From the beginning, I thought that being invited to train with the Korean team was not just an opportunity, it was also a distinct honor. I stayed in Seoul for about a month; without exception, every single person I encountered could not have been more gracious and welcoming. For that month, I lived the life of a Korean short-track speed skater. I ate Korean food, and only Korean food. Practice at Mokdong began early in the morning; it would have been a grave insult to be late, and so we were always early. The first few days, I stayed with Chae Ji-Hoon, who won gold in the 500 and silver in the 1000 in Lillehammer in 1994. Then one of the skaters' families said, "Please let us host Apolo," and they opened their house, and their arms, to me.

The scene at Mokdong never failed to amaze me. As I took it all in, it finally made sense why the Koreans were so good. They simply breed success. The depth is amazing; they have one hundred talents the likes of Ahn Hyun-Soo. They have coaches who know their stuff, and the coaches work with those talents 24/7.

I saw girls who did faster times than boys in the United States in the 1500 and the 3000. I saw dozens if not hundreds of kids at practice, doing drills, every single day—with no complaints about being so regimented. None. Not one, not ever.

I saw a six-year-old girl working on what's called a "turn belt" off the ice, a rubber belt you can use to pull against while in the skating position. She was doing this particular drill better than anyone I had ever seen, and she was just six. It was at that precise instant that I thought, *Wow, the Koreans know exactly what they are doing.*

My first day at Mokdong, not long after I arrived and got onto the ice, the coaches ordered us to do a drill called a seven-lapper. It's just what it sounds like: seven laps, a common test to see where you stand. Just one problem: I had not skated since Torino. I literally had not been on the ice since the Olympics, and that had been eight, going on nine months beforehand. This would be like Lance Armstrong starting his comeback by going over to Europe and being told on day one that practice meant time trials up the Alps. It was borderline insane.

Of course, I had been put in the top group, along with Lee Ho-Suk and all the other best skaters. There was no point in making a show out of what I was thinking: *I haven't been on skates in months. Plus, I've just gotten off the plane and I'm still feeling the jet lag.* There was nothing to do but to do seven-lappers.

I kept up every single set.

When I told the Korean coaches afterward that I hadn't been on skates since Torino, they didn't believe me. They actually took the step of calling Jimmy Jang, the assistant U.S. coach in Torino who had howled with such delight when I'd gotten the number one lane draw in the 500, to confirm that I was telling them the truth.

"It's true," he said.

At Mokdong, every day after ice training we would all sit down in a classroom and talk short-track. In the front of the room, naturally enough, was a chalkboard; on the chalkboard were magnets; each and every day, the magnets would be moved around amid a discussion of team skating.

I could not believe it.

The rules specifically say team skating is not okay.

Finally, I couldn't stand it any longer. "Coach," I said during one of these sessions, "this is illegal."

"Oh," he said, "we know. We have to do it."

I just laughed—a wry laugh. They were doing this right in front of me.

Back on the ice, the Koreans would then practice team-skating strategies with me. To be precise, they would practice *on* me. As I was going around, I would think, *Is this really happening?* It was, and it was an incredible experience. I became great friends with a good many people there. And I learned a lot—about their national culture, about the culture specific to the short-track program, about how the Koreans train. It gave me great insight in training and technique, and also got me thinking about another matter entirely.

My weight.

I raced in Torino at the same 165 pounds I weighed in Salt Lake City. The sport was changing, and 165 clearly wasn't going to keep working, even if while I was at Mokdong I didn't have a fully formed plan about what to do about it.

I could handle the world-class regimentation at Mokdong because, even though I hadn't been on skates, I had been working out with John Schaeffer. I excelled at the 2008 worlds because, through everything, even the doubts I'd had about whether to keep going, I worked out with John.

Dancing is obviously great exercise. But John demanded more. On the *DWTS* road show, for instance, after checking into whatever hotel we were at for the night, John would order up a little fun: eighteen flights of steps, over and over again.

That was John's idea of good fun. To make it more fun, he would instruct that the stairs be run in this sequence: every step, then every other, then every third, then every fourth. We would keep this up for at least ninety minutes, at high intensity, with little to no rest.

Being on the road was so distracting and otherwise demanding that, despite the stair work and other routines, I actually developed a nice little layer of fat around my waistline. This amused John to no end, and he would tease me about the donut around my middle. When the tour ended, John took me back to Pennsylvania for three weeks of intense training, three workouts per day. In the morning, he had me doing interval runs on the treadmill; in the afternoon, ninety minutes of sprinting up the steep local mountains; and in the evening, weight training.

I started at around 10 percent body fat. I left twenty-one days later at about 6.5 percent.

To get ready for the 2008 worlds, John squeezed what he estimated was a full year's worth of training into three months. He was not the least bit surprised when I came away with the overall gold.

The week after those 2008 worlds in Korea, we moved to Harbin, China, for the world team championships. We won.

The team worlds feature heats in the 500 and the 1000, with one entry per nation; one 3000, with two entries per country; and a relay. The winner in each heat gets five points for his or her country; second gets you three; third, one. Points in the relay are doubled. These team worlds came down to the relay. The Canadians led in the race with one lap to go; I made a pass that moved us from third to first and gave us the win, in the race and the event itself. The last time a U.S. team had even won a medal at the world team championships had been in 1995, thirteen long years before, a bronze.

As that 2008 season came to a close, I felt clear and clean, like I was starting fresh. It was all so simple. I was training hard, living a life that felt in balance, loving skating.

It's why the frustrations of the 2009 season seemed so endless and so maddening.

Then again, things wouldn't be so interesting, even exciting, if they were easy. To carry the struggle forward, sometimes that struggle is not only genuine but unforeseeable.

I DID NOT win a single race the entire 2009 season. To top it off, my performance at the 2009 world championships was horrible. I finished fifth overall. I really started to doubt myself. I not only started to hear—I started to listen to—all the chitchat, all the chatter, inside the rink and out, from the media, from certain writers, from people who thought they knew anything and everything: *Apolo is past his prime. He should have ended on that perfect note in 2006. Maybe he doesn't have it anymore.*

I kept thinking, *I just don't feel good on the ice. My skates don't feel good*—short-track lingo to mean not the boots themselves, because they were fine, but the pressure with which you push off, the angles in which your foot, ankle, knee, and hip line up. Some days you're lined up just right, and you push directly on the ice and it feels better than good; it feels like total synchronicity, just amazing. It's as if you were doing tai chi, the full range of motion, and the energy transfer goes from being held in the hand to total release.

I didn't feel that sensation once the entire season.

Every single day on the ice felt worse and worse. It was a downward spiral. I couldn't win. Not even in practice. Worse, I couldn't win mentally. I felt I was doing every single thing right; thought I was dedicating myself. But no.

These weeks and months were very rough. In times of stress, your body produces a hormone called cortisol. For anyone, and particularly for an athlete, high cortisol levels are bad; you don't burn fat the right way, you don't rest properly, and more. My cortisol levels seemed through the roof. I couldn't bring them down. I felt stressed out of my mind. I felt myself becoming somebody I didn't want to be on the ice—not skating with control, but skating with a feeling of desperation—and I didn't feel I could change the situation. Even my racing strategy started to change. Since I was fourteen, my style had typically been to go from the back, and now I found myself racing a lot more from the front.

The 2009 worlds were held in Vienna, at an arena called Ferry Dusika, a cycling velodrome converted for the week to short-track. During the last race of the competition, a 3000, I was skating badly; physically, technically, strategically, it was all bad. Overall at these worlds, I would finish fifth. With a few laps to go in that 3000, I looked up and shouted to Jimmy over in the coaches' box, "What the hell am I doing?" He looked at me. I looked back at him. He looked confused. I looked confused. For the next three laps, we just looked at each other. We didn't know what to say.

I got off the ice, went to the locker room, and proceeded to lose it. I punched the wall as hard as I could, gave that gray wall a hard right, punched a huge hole in it.

I leaned over the sink, not in tears but feeling lost, my head in my hands. *What*, I thought, *am I doing?*

The last time I had reached out to hit anything or anyone had been when I was a kid, in Federal Way, when it was normal to get into fights. I fought a lot of big kids back then and never lost.

That seemed almost like a different lifetime ago. So what was I doing, hitting a wall like that?

Standing at that sink, I felt so not in control.

Human emotion is an amazing thing. You can be so passionate

about something, and it shows. I was completely passionate about my sport; I loved it, breathed it, wanted to die in my sport, wanted to die in the Olympic spirit. That day in that bathroom, when I punched that wall and freaked out, it triggered something in my head: *Look, man, you are not being you.* And then: *Why did you do this?*

Are you really that desperate to win—to win a race? Why? Why? Why?

At that sink I also realized that I had reached another fork in the road. This was a moment very much like when I was fifteen and Dad dropped me off at the cabin; I had to make a choice about the direction I wanted my life to go.

The rest of the American team was in the locker room; they had heard me take it out on the wall and were now, each of them, part of a scene none had ever imagined. They were scared and questioning. *Isn't Apolo supposed to be the team leader here?* To be honest, I was questioning myself. I was mad I had thrown a punch—at a wall, of all things. I was fortunate I hadn't hurt my hand. And I was embarrassed. A champion must be in control no matter the outcome or result. That's the true bottom line: if you are a champion on the ice, you have to be a champion off the ice as well.

My first step was to do the right thing. I apologized to every single member of the American team.

My next step came on the flights home: Vienna to Amsterdam, Amsterdam to Minneapolis, Minneapolis to Salt Lake. I didn't sleep for even a second.

The apologies were right, they were necessary, they were appropriate, but I was still very upset at myself. I wasn't who I wanted to be, wasn't the person I thought I was. I felt I was losing grasp of the core values in my life, the ones I hold close to my heart, the ones that define who and what an Olympic champion should be like.

On the flights home, I thought, *Okay, in preparation for these next Olympics in Vancouver, you have listened to certain coaches and certain training programs. Maybe, though, all the answers aren't to be found with those coaches or within those programs. Maybe the answer isn't, for instance, with the Korean team.*

All of us tend to look outward. But so many times the answer to whatever it is that may be at issue is within. We just have to listen.

I just hadn't listened to myself the entire season, hadn't tapped into the inner core of who I was as a person.

It's almost like shock therapy. In this instance, it took my fist to go through that wall to shock me into seeing the truth.

The calendar said the time was right, if that's what I wanted, to take a short vacation. This was now an Olympic year, so an extended break wouldn't do. But a week or two somewhere warm—maybe Maui or Jamaica? Perhaps the Turks and Caicos? These were all places that well-meaning friends had been suggesting. "Go somewhere warm, relax, get your head right," they counseled.

Inside, though, I heard a different voice: *The lazy vacation can wait. Now is not the time to be lazy. Now is the time to confront your self-conflict and the destructive inner dialogue, to go head-to-head with it and defeat it.*

The worlds were in March; I wasn't due to see the U.S. team again until June. The thing to do, I thought, was to get myself back to Colorado Springs, back into the Training Center for a couple of months. Write a training and nutrition plan and don't deviate. Bring the skate tapes, the bike, in-line skates, running shoes, hiking shoes, swim trunks. And bring that weight vest. Get ready for a lot of trips to the Incline.

Back in Salt Lake, I went through my plan with my close friend Ian Baranski, who was living at the house as part of his comeback plan for 2010; I told him in detail how much working out I wanted to do, and why. Altogether, I was thinking three workouts a day, six days a week. "Apolo," he said, "here's my first impression: this is nuts. You cannot work out twenty-six hours per day."

It wasn't nuts. There was a method to the madness.

I loved to look at where the sport had been and where it appeared to be going. This was, in its way, like analyzing the stock market, the way I had done in school long before. There are patterns to everything if you just bother to look. As a starting point, I now weighed 159, give or take. The trend on the ice was obviously toward smaller, leaner, lighter. In 2002 the sport was all about speed; in 2006, a sustained pace. In 2010, I figured, I would need to have it all.

I would need a very high top-end speed as well as great endurance. That way, I could attack multiple times if need be during a race. That way, simply put, I would be the fastest guy on the ice.

Ian and I met when we were both teenagers. We were thrown together as roommates on a short-track trip to Red Deer, Alberta, in Canada. At that meet, before we raced, we would hang out together in the bleachers, eating Cadbury chocolate eggs. The U.S. Speedskating Federation was even then so strapped for cash that it put the two of us up at night in the same hotel room. Two teenagers from opposite sides of the country, in the same hotel room—how was this going to work?

Apparently, we figured it out without any great trauma. We have been great friends ever since.

Ian is intelligent, logical, and loyal. He makes a great devil's advocate, a very sound source of reason; he asks a lot of intriguing questions that I might not necessarily want to hear but that really need to be asked. Close friends do that for you: they say the very things you don't want to hear.

"Apolo," he said, "I understand what you're trying to do. But does this make sense? You can't ride or run and lift that many hours in the day and give yourself enough time to recover."

Besides the three workouts Monday through Saturday, I was also thinking that on Sunday, my off day, I would go for a long, easy three-hour bike ride.

"Apolo," he said, "you are scheduling workouts for every day that you should be doing at max once or twice a week. You are planning to do in one week what anyone else would do in two and a half."

"Right," I said.

"It's insane," he said. Then he added with a smile, "Brilliant insane."

A week or so after the end of the worlds in Vienna, I was a couple of days away from leaving for Colorado Springs; we were puttering around the house, and I was still getting my stuff together in Salt Lake. Then came the weather report predicting a massive storm later that day. This was early March. Spring was a distant thought. A huge storm could shut down Wyoming for days. "I gotta go," I said. "Otherwise, I'm going to lose a week. I can't lose a week. I can't be trapped in Salt Lake or in Cheyenne or somewhere. I have to get to Colorado Springs, now!"

Ian looked up from the couch to say, "Why don't you just wait a little bit? You can do your runs here."

"I gotta go, I gotta go, I gotta go!" I shouted as I ran around the house, throwing stuff in the car.

I beat the storm. My Training Center family was thrilled to have me back. They put me up in room 238, immediately under dorm mom Sherry Von Riesen; she promised she'd be quiet. In the cafeteria, Mama Flower set about spoiling me all over again.

As I made the rounds at the Training Center, after saying hi to everybody, I immediately apologized. I said, "I know I'm here, but you guys aren't going to see much of me. I have a crazy, crazy training schedule. That's how it's going to be for the next eight to ten weeks."

"Have at it, Apolo," they said. "Let us know how we can help."

I called my father and told him I was back at the Training Center. "I'm going to spend some time here, Dad. I need some solitude."

"Great," he said. My father trusted me; he knew that when I said I needed to do something, I needed to do it, and when I said I was all in, it was all in. And I wasn't looking back.

I called John, back in Reading, and told him I would be out in the

Springs for a bit, told him my goals and what I was doing. I called
Jimmy Jang, too. And Jae Su Chun, our new head coach. Jae Su had a
master's degree in speed skating from the University of Seoul; he was
one of the smartest, best coaches in the world. Jimmy is incredibly
passionate, with a great eye for technique. Together they made a great
combination.

"Have at it, Apolo," everyone said. "Let us know if you need anything."

My primary mission was to regain my confidence. I had to find my
mojo. I didn't want to find it by having a coach, even ones as brilliant
as Jae Su and Jimmy, tell me I had it. I wanted it to come to me.

The entire experience for me that summer was mental. I have
always said that for people to make a big change in their lives, it comes
from a psychological change, and the easiest way for me to do that
was to make a physical change—to lose weight while gaining muscle,
strength, stamina, and endurance.

The concept was simple and blunt. I had 30 or more pounds on
most of the other top skaters. I couldn't make up that difference in
the weight room, though I had tried. The ice can hold only so much
body weight before it breaks. I was known as a skater who created a
tremendous amount of pressure on the ice. If this were basketball and
I could break the glass with a monster dunk because of all the pressure
and strength I brought, that might make me a legend; in speed skating,
though, broken ice would only slow me down.

So I had to lose weight. I told Ian before leaving for Colorado, "I want
to be at one forty-seven this year." He looked at me and said, "Dude,
you have not been under one fifty since you were fourteen."

Too true.

I build muscle very easily; I hold muscle very easily. It's how my
body works. It's how I am built. That makes it difficult for me to
burn fat.

I was hardly fat. My body fat percentage was almost surely under

10. The problem was physiology. Let's say I dropped my body fat level another single percentage point. That would be maybe a pound. I would still have more than ten to go. How to lose that much weight— meaning that much muscle—without getting weaker?

As I looked at the Koreans, the Chinese, even some of the Canadians, it was clear to me how their body types were very different from mine. Anatomically, these guys were built to speed skate, from the way the pelvis would tilt forward to the way the back was already rounded. They had a built-in advantage. So while I was stripping away muscle, I had to increase endurance and hit the weight room hard for strength, power, and explosiveness on the ice.

The overall structure looked like this:

Riding and running every day.

The Incline two or three times per week.

A jump circuit, done with the weight vest, developed by Heiden and by Derek Parra, the long-track speed skater who won gold and silver at the Salt Lake Games. The vest is filled with 35 or 40 pounds. The circuit requires, among other things, some elevated benches and is done at the rink or a suitable park. It can last up to three and a half hours and is typically done in training maybe once a week. I was doing it twice. When others do the jump circuit, they don't also head to the weight room to lift as well. I was still lifting.

Some in-line skating.

The sauna.

Also, the steam room.

It's very difficult to host your own training camp. You don't have anyone pushing you. But that's exactly what I wanted. I wanted to be there alone. I wanted to bike alone. I wanted to run alone. That's when I would start creating dialogue with myself about some of my insecurities—about my performance, about not training enough, about a lack of confidence.

At the same time, being by yourself can also make you train harder.

It makes you train more. A lot of days, I would get up very early, and I would be gone on the bike, a sturdy blue Cannondale I had bought nine years before, riding out from the Training Center west to U.S. Highway 24 and up into the Pike National Forest and the mountains. Those first few weeks, it wasn't uncommon for snow to fall. Way up high in the mountains, there's no shoulder on the road; it wasn't all that safe. There were other times when my iPod would stop working. So here was the picture: snow, no tunes, nobody else out for miles because the weather was so bad, two and a half hours to get back to civilization, and I was out there alone, climbing up the mountain on a bicycle.

I knew when I got back from that kind of a ride that there wasn't—there couldn't be—anyone else in the world who was putting in that much time and effort. That is what gives you confidence.

If you were to take the guy lining up to me on the ice and ask him how hard he works, double or triple that, and that would be me. That gives you confidence.

On these long bike rides, I took my cell phone with me for safety. But for the most part, I didn't talk to anybody at any length throughout all those weeks in Colorado Springs.

It was lonely.

But lonely in a good way. It allowed me to reset my mind, to really go deep into my heart and soul and ask myself questions, to remember that champions are made when nobody else is looking. When you're training by yourself, there's an undeniable temptation to let up, even if it's just a little. It's easier to get off the bike, or decrease the pedaling frequency, or run for forty-five minutes instead of the hour and a quarter you had set out to go. I made sure to train just as hard as or harder than ever; that builds so much more confidence and reflects your character so much more.

That June, Shani showed up to do a little training. A bunch of us went out on our bikes. After a little bit, Shani said to me, "What the hell have you been doing?"

"I have always been strong on the bike."

"Not that strong," Shani said.

It was true: off the ice I was crushing all comers. I felt like a different person; Jimmy and Jae Su said I looked like a different person.

Every day, I was feeling better and better. Overall, I knew I was on the right track.

In mid-June, we started ice training. Ugh—I still didn't feel good on the ice. It was no big secret why; I hadn't been doing any speed work yet. I was sluggish and slow on the ice because I was so committed to base training and cross-training. On top of which, I found myself battling equipment problems. Nothing new there.

Now, though, came something of a dilemma.

The Olympic Trials were coming up in Marquette, Michigan, in September—incredibly early in the racing year, designed that way because it was thought that having the lineup picked five months ahead of the Games would contribute in a big way to team building. The others in position to make the Olympic team were focusing on the Trials and on the World Cup season just beyond. Instead of a focus on endurance-related base training, they were already doing speed work. That didn't make good sense to me. The point was to peak in February in Vancouver—not in September in Michigan.

Jimmy and Jae Su were, understandably, nervous. The Trials are unforgiving; you make the team or you don't. There's no coach's discretion. It wouldn't matter if, for instance, I came down with a cold the week I was in Marquette; there's no pass onto the U.S. Olympic team in short-track for years of good service.

Shani took me aside one day. "Listen, man," he said. "Trials are coming up. You need to start focusing more on the ice."

"I appreciate it," I told him. "But I believe I'm doing what I have to do. And I am willing to take that risk."

MATURITY

When you're younger, you just hammer.
You're naïve, in a sense. You don't know. You don't
know what it's like to fail. You have no Olympic
medals. You have nothing to lose.

It's why the people who can stay on top for so
long can be so interesting. They're the ones who
have to change, the ones who are being viewed,
watched, scrutinized, analyzed.

I never think about the end. It's not about
that. You get sidetracked if and when you start
worrying about it. If you're always thinking about
winning and crossing the line first,
you're distracted from the actual process.

CHAPTER 12

What the U.S. program should do is hold the short-track Olympic Trials in December, immediately before the Christmas holidays. Then everyone who makes the team would be told, "Congrats—and now go home and celebrate the season with your family and friends; we'll see you again immediately after that."

That way, everyone would come to the pre-Games training camp refreshed, happy, and ready to train for an Olympics just six weeks away.

Instead, it was off to Marquette in September. I hadn't skated a race of any consequence in September in years. But I knew my body. It would not work to peak in September. I had a plan, and I couldn't deviate from the plan—summer was the time for base work. Two weeks before the Trials, I was still doing three-hour bike rides. I showed up in Marquette and was still going for hour-long runs.

"This is getting dangerous," Jimmy and Jae Su said.

I struggled at the Trials. The time trials kicked them off—I finished second in the nine-lapper, fourth in the four-lap. I mean, I rarely lose time trials.

At the Trials, I chose to skate in the same RBC boots I had used at the 2002 Games. They were ten years old, and they had been rebuilt three times. I thought they might give me something I was missing.

They did not.

To qualify, I needed to make the top two at every one of the three individual distances. Until the last night of the meet, the best I managed were seconds; then I broke through to win both the 500 and the 1000.

So, after everything, my strategy worked—barely.

In a 500 semifinal, J.R. hit the boards coming out of a turn. His right blade cut into his left thigh near his knee. It was obvious immediately it was bad. He said later that he could see the bone. Another skater, Walter Rusk, who hadn't qualified to compete, jumped out of the stands and rushed to J.R.'s side; he used his own sweatshirt to apply pressure to try to stop the blood that was spilling onto the ice. They took J.R. off to the hospital for surgery. He ended up with roughly sixty stitches. The cut was six inches long. Luckily, the blade missed his femoral artery by maybe an inch. For him—and for us as a team, because J.R. had a great 2009 season and at the Trials finished second behind me in the overall points count—it was now a race against time. Could he get better by Vancouver?

For me, the question was even more personal. J.R. is from Federal Way, Washington. He had taken up short-track after watching me on television at the 2002 Games, an echo of the very thing that had led me to the sport in 1994. The team that got together to help J.R. in his Olympic push included three doctors. One of them: Heiden.

THE FIRST TWO World Cups of the season followed the Trials in short order, the first in China, the next in Korea. I didn't want to show too much, didn't want to give even a hint to close watchers of my endurance levels.

I needn't have worried about showing anything. I got so sick in

China. It was so bad, I wrote on Twitter, that I was "shaking, literally" before one of the races in China. A later Twitter post said, "Ughh. Need medicine! Maybe some Korean kimchi will help? Feels like a squirrel is running around in my body."

Ughh.

Early November brought the next two World Cup events in Montreal and then the next week in Marquette.

Off with the ten-year-old boots. Back to the ones with the holograms on them, the ones I won on in Torino and then again in 2008. Time to stick with those boots, time to focus, time to concentrate. No time to keep being distracted by this kind of thing.

I need to compete well in these two World Cups, I thought, *or it's just not going to happen.* And in Montreal, I kind of got my spark back, my flow, my mojo. I took second in the 500 but, more important, felt that indescribable feeling you sometimes get when you're in the zone. I hadn't felt that for nearly eighteen months, and here it was.

Bring on Marquette.

Ughh.

In Marquette, I came down with swine flu. Bring on the vitamins and the herbs. And bring on the sauna. A friend found one I could use at an apartment complex. There was no shut-off switch; the thermostat was broken. I don't know how hot it was in there. I don't know how long I stayed in. I do know that when it came time to skate in Marquette, it didn't matter how fast anybody else was going to skate. Unless something weird happened, I was going to win.

I almost never feel like that. There's no guarantee of anything in short-track for being the fastest guy. But I knew it going in: It was going to be a really good day of racing.

I took second in the 1500 and won the 1000. We took second in the relay.

In the 1000, two Koreans finished second and fourth, Lee Jung-Su and Sung Si-Bak, with François Hamelin of Canada third. This was the best I had felt since before Salt Lake City, a feeling that was validated in conversations around the rink, when I was told any number of times: "We haven't see you skate like that in years."

To me, Marquette was proof: I was back.

But I needed more. I could do better. I hadn't yet done everything I could do to prepare, not by a long shot.

John had come to Marquette to watch. "Let's do it," I said to him. "Come out to my house in Salt Lake, move in with me. I want to hire you from now through the Olympics."

———————

THE PLAN ALL along had been to have John oversee some of my training in Salt Lake.

Now, though, I saw the possibilities, and saw them without hesitation. He and I could do what no one else in short-track had ever done before. We could create the short-track version of a fight camp. Before a championship bout, that's what a fighter does with his trainer. They head out to the middle of nowhere, sometimes even up to the mountains, and with no one around to bother or notice, they get ready, physically, mentally, and even spiritually. We could do it at my house in Salt Lake. It had everything; I had made the basement into a fully functioning gym, with stationary bikes, a treadmill, weight racks, and even—especially—a sauna, where the thermometer read up to 270, and I cranked it up higher.

There was some measure of risk. Traditionally, John hadn't worked with me that late in the season. It would be unbelievably intense. Once we started, there would be no turning back. It would be do or die.

But the possibility of bringing a fight-camp regimentation and a fight-camp mentality to short-track was too amazing not to try. If we didn't do it, we would for sure regret not seizing the opportunity. And if we did do it—no matter my performance in Vancouver—I would have zero regrets about how I had gotten ready for the Games.

If these were to be my final days of Olympic training, the lasting memories from the training part of my journey to Vancouver, my last chance to be who I wanted to be—how could I fully maximize all of that? When the Games in Vancouver came to a close, if fate held that I would go home with no medals of any sort, could I nonetheless feel satisfied because I had given it everything I had?

This was the way.

"Um," John said at first, "I can't do that."

"What? John, I've talked this over with my dad, with Ian, with Fretta, with Giddeon. Everyone agrees."

"Apolo, I have twenty other clients, athletes I work with."

"John," I said, "this is a once-in-a-lifetime thing. It's a fight camp for short-track."

The more we talked and the more John thought about it, the more the idea grew on him. He knew everything we had done to train together in prior years; this would be more challenging, by several degrees, than anything that had come before, for me and for him. He would have to cut 12 to 18 pounds from an already lean athlete and still manipulate enough calories so that I could recover from some of the most intense training that any world-class athlete would ever endure. There could be no margin for error. My conditioning, weight program, nutrition—it would all be in his hands. He would have to structure a program through which he would control everything I did. Training, eating, rest, studying the competition, downtime, re-covery, sleep—he would be dictating my life twenty-four hours a day, seven days a week, and not just for weeks but for months.

He would be the teacher, with me as the pupil, and I would have to do what he said. I would have to sublimate my personality, my sense of what was right, to him and to his ideas. This would be an exercise in many things, but perhaps most of all, it would be an exercise in trust.

"Nothing to it but to do it," he said.

WHEN JOHN MOVED in, our first night together seemed like something out of a movie. A fight film. We were in the basement. It was late at night. Ian was watching something on the big screen.

"You're going to go through hell," John told me. That got Ian's attention.

"You're going to go through hell, but you know I am going to be with you," John said. "You not only are going to go through hell, you *have* to go through hell. This is going to be worse than any nightmare you've ever dreamed of.

"There will be times," he said, "when I'm going to tell you to keep going. And you're going to say, 'No, I can't.'

"And there are going to be times when I say, 'You can only eat this little bit,' and you're going to say, 'I want more.'

"There are going to be times when I will say to you, 'That is not your best effort.' And you are going to come back to me and say, 'It's my best.' It's not. You're going to have to give me more. You're going to have to pick it up.

"This is going to be hell. But at the end, I know you're going to be the one standing.

"You know what you've got to do."

I did, but not really. Truthfully, I had no concept of the full scope of what I was getting myself into.

"Your pain threshold," he said, "we're going to take you way past what you think it is.

"Understand one thing. Your mind has total control of your body. What you want to get out of your body starts with your mind."

John had typed up a page of notes on mental preparation. He had made dozens of copies. Now he posted them everywhere in the house—at every doorway, on the refrigerator, on the door to my office, on my bedroom door, in the bathroom. These affirmations would work not only consciously but subconsciously, in the way that you get hungry for popcorn at the movies.

This is what the page said:

THE POWER OF POSITIVE THOUGHT AND ATTITUDE

THOUGHT = IF YOU TRULY BELIEVE, IT WILL HAPPEN!

ATTITUDE = POSITIVE ATTITUDE WILL ALLOW YOU TO
PERFORM MAXIMALLY, BOTH
PHYSICALLY AND MENTALLY.

THE POWER OF NEGATIVE THOUGHT AND ATTITUDE

NEGATIVE THOUGHT = WILL DESTROY ALL DREAMS.

NEGATIVE ATTITUDE = WILL RESTRICT PERFORMANCE,
BOTH PHYSICALLY AND MENTALLY.

MENTAL CONDITIONING IS AS KEY AS YOUR PHYSICAL FOR SUCCESS

YOU WILL BLOCK ALL NEGATIVE THOUGHT!!

YOU WILL REPLACE ALL NEGATIVE AT ONCE WITH
POSITIVE THOUGHT AND ATTITUDE.

YOU WILL VISUALIZE SUCCESS EVERY NIGHT
THROUGH THE GAMES.

YOU WILL BELIEVE YOU CAN DESTROY ANY
OTHER SKATER IN THE WORLD.

REGARDLESS OF WHAT YOU THINK OF THEIR SKILL!

REGARDLESS OF ICE CONDITIONS!

REGARDLESS OF THE FEEL OF YOUR SKATES!

WHETHER YOU TRULY BELIEVE SOMETHING OR NOT, YOU ARE RIGHT!

YOU ARE THE BEST IN THE WORLD. DO NOT LET
YOUR MIND DESTROY THAT REALITY.

IT IS WHAT IT IS!

MENTAL WILL DO ONE OF TWO THINGS: HELP YOU OVERCOME OR DEFEAT YOU

In addition, John had a little slogan that he put right in front of me that summed it all up:

> *To accomplish your goal, you have to be willing to sacrifice beyond what others are willing to sacrifice; you have to be willing to train at levels others are not willing to train at; you have to be willing to accept accomplishing goals that others never reach.*

John's vision, as it played out, was rooted in a classic training principle called GAS, or general adaptation syndrome, which says that a high-volume training session must be followed by low or no intensity for the body to adapt. In the simplest terms, a coach's job is to monitor the teardown and the buildup of his or her athlete. If the athlete can handle more volume, you step on the gas. If it's the opposite, you back off.

In practice—and this for me is where, as the Mr. T character in *Rocky III* put it so aptly, I was going to feel pain—his vision held five distinct aspects:

- **Weights and interval training.** Ice training was always the first priority, he would make clear. Thus, in the work he and I were doing, I could expect tweaks from day to day, even workout to workout, to ensure as much recovery as possible for work on the ice. John had such a good eye, such a thorough understanding of all eleven of the body's major organ systems, that he knew when to push and when to back off. For instance, when he would have me doing interval runs on the treadmill, he would look for what he would call "foot drop"—that is, the ball of my foot getting lazy from step to step. For him, that was a nuanced indicator of my fatigue. When I was running right, it would all flow. When I was too tired to do it right, he would see that he might need to dial back the tempo just a bit.

- **Nutrition.** John not only planned out what I ate but cooked most of it himself and made sure I ate whatever it was at a particular time each and every day. If it was nine thirty in the morning, it was time for a snack. The two most important nutrition times, he would say time and again, are pre- and post-activity. That's where you're feeding the activity and the recovery. You neglect that, and you don't have a chance of taking out onto the field what you should.

- **Focus.** This is the one John worried about most. Everyone gets distracted, he would say to me; you cannot afford to get distracted. "So," he said, "when we lift weights at the team facility here in town, we're going to go in when no one else is around; that way, you're not going to be talking to this person or that one, and I'm going to get one hundred percent focus. Believe me, given the amount of weight you're going to be lifting, it has to be one hundred percent." Also, he said, "When you're training at this level, to be the best you can be, you have to shut down the outside world as much as possible. So here's the deal. You have to turn off your cell phone and laptop at six every evening. Plus, no leaving the house on weekends. There's no point in running the risk, even if it might seem remote, of getting in a car crash."

- **Mental prep.** "At least one hour every evening," he said, "you need to be reviewing tapes of prior competitions as well as daily practice tapes." He scheduled it for six to seven in the evening Sunday through Friday, Saturday off.

- **Recovery.** "Enough really is enough, and you, Apolo, are a constant overachiever," John liked to say. "You like to think that more is better. That's not the way it works." Recovery is essential, and on three levels: micro-recovery, between sets and sessions on a given day; macro-recovery, meaning day by day and week by week; and meso-recovery—that is, the process of tapering off what I was doing as February drew near so I would peak for the Olympics.

John would laugh a wry laugh sometimes when it came to how little attention I had paid to the concept of recovery. He would tell me, "You don't really know how good you can be because you have never skated at one hundred percent. Even when you won, that wasn't the best you could be because you have what might be called 'chronic training syndrome.' You'd do three-a-days and then think, *I had better go run,* or *I'd better go climb.*

"No," he said. "You also need to rest.

"Big picture, here is the way this thing is going to work: Team training in the morning and afternoon. But after that morning session, you're going to do another workout with me. Then you're going to go back to the rink and do the afternoon session with the team. After that, you're going to do another workout with me, either at the team's facilities or back here at the house. Then we're going to address the recovery issues.

"Specifically, here is what your days are going to be like:

"You're going to wake up between five thirty and six.

"You have to eat breakfast. You're going to have one egg, scrambled; half an apple with a little bit of honey; and an oatmeal mix I'm going to make that has coconut oil for fats, applesauce for medium-index carbs, and some other stuff. I'm going to make batches of this stuff and put it in the refrigerator; you're going to take a couple of spoonfuls of the mix.

"From seven to eleven you're at the rink.

"At nine thirty, you need to take out the snack I'm going to pack and eat it. The snack is most days going to be one hard boiled egg wrapped in romaine lettuce with a dab of chili sauce. That will give you a little sodium and a little sugar; the lettuce will give you a little bit of enzyme.

"At eleven thirty, you're going eat the same egg snack unless I change it up—maybe a small piece of salmon with seaweed along with a little bit of pasta. We'll see.

"When you get home, you have to eat two or three tablespoons of the mix.

"Then we're going to do ninety minutes of workout here. That'll take us to two thirty in the afternoon.

"You'll eat a couple more spoonfuls of the mix.

"Get yourself back to the rink and along the way eat another of the egg snacks. On the way, take your vitamins and minerals.

"Jump onto the ice and skate from three to five.

"At five, eat another egg snack.

"Then, depending on the week, we're going to do weights or a jump workout or run. You're going to do a lot of running on the treadmill.

"You'll eat dinner. You're going to eat mostly salmon. Not very much. The piece of salmon I'm going to put on your plate is going to be about as big as if you quartered a lemon and put three of the peels together. I'll probably stir-fry a green vegetable of some sort with the salmon, most likely in coconut oil, maybe with a little butter if I think I need to pick up your fat content.

"Now, the computer and the cell phone are off. Got it?

"At the same time you're doing the mental prep, weeknights between six and seven, use the recovery-stimulation ball you already have downstairs in your home gym. At least two times per week, between seven and eight in the evening, you should do the sauna and have massage therapy. At least two—you can go up to four—times each week. I would like your massage guy to focus on the erector muscles in the back, on the hip flexors, and then on the abductors and adductors; that really ought to help your hip movement and flexibility.

"After that, one final egg snack.

"Then go to sleep.

"We'll get up the next morning and do it all over again.

"Timing is everything. If I want you to do a particular exercise at a particular time of day, we have a five-minute window; that's when I want you in there. That prepares you for what comes after that and for the evening, and if you know what you're doing in the evening, you know what you're doing the next day."

After so many years together, I knew well his fundamental philosophy about such things. John relates the drive of hard training to cruising along a road when, all of a sudden, you come across a brick wall stretching across the pavement. You have two choices. You can drive through the wall. Or you can stop and hit the brakes, then drive around the bricks. John's approach is never to take a step backward. He'll take a lateral step—more recovery between sets, for instance— but never goes backward. His view is that if he goes backward, he has screwed up as a trainer.

"Oh," John said. "Maybe once a week, Saturday or Sunday night, we're going to have a big bowl of brown rice pasta with some chicken, carrots, onions, celery, peppers, and kale. It'll be a treat. You'll see."

Every person beats at a certain pace. John and I were undertaking a plan that would have me come to Vancouver with a different beat and thus almost as a different person—which would play out not just physically but technically and strategically. A part of that would be the fun of showing up and having the other coaches and skaters do a double take. All the videotapes of me at prior World Cups, the certain impressions of who I was and what sort of rhythm and tempo they could expect—that would all be useless, because I would be somebody else. It would be like showing up to race somebody who had always competed in a Honda Accord; now he was in a Ferrari or a Lamborghini. What the hell? How did that happen?

The first thing to do was to get me stronger. Strength would equal power and, in turn, explosiveness and thus, on the ice, speed.

"There's a weakness in your core," John said. "We're going after that. We need a more dynamic response. Here's what you're going to do: you're going to hang from the bar; bring your legs up to a forty-five-degree angle. Now you're going to do leg lifts, but not just straight up.

You're going to do them at three or four different angles—left, right, center, side-to-side. Then one leg to a side, then the other. You have to keep constant tension on your abs." When we started, I could barely do one set. By the time we were finished, I could do them all day long.

"Let's see where you are with your legs," John said. "Let's see a one-legged back squat; in that one, you hold the bar behind your neck or across your upper back, with your legs split, one leg in front and the other behind you, as if it were a static lunge."

I started at 275 pounds. Only four weeks in, I could already do 415.

On the leg press, I started off on one leg at about 500 pounds; as the weeks went along, I got to the 800s.

We would load so much weight that it felt sometimes as if it was going to crush me. John knew it wouldn't. I just had to master it.

After first making me bigger, the second part of John's master plan was to make me smaller—that is, smaller but without compromising the gains in strength I had made. "Have faith," John said. "I know what I'm doing."

This was one of the hardest parts—just staying focused and knowing there would be light at the end of the tunnel, even if you don't know quite how long the tunnel is, even if you almost can't see the light. You just have to have the faith to keep going. In the middle of a process, it's natural to have questions and doubts, especially when you're going through excruciating physical pain. I would lie down in bed at night and I'd be so hungry. In the car that was me, the gas tank was empty. I was running on fumes. I was getting barely enough protein to sustain my workouts and barely enough carbs. Every day I would get on the ice, and I'd be more tired than anyone else would; I would nonetheless feel I ought to be dominating, because that's what I had always done. My tempo, rhythm, timing—they were all off because I was so tired and beat up.

Sometimes the Saturday night pasta treat would be preceded by a Friday night pasta treat, too. Either way, I would gorge myself like a prisoner tasting freedom. Within an hour, I was starving again.

Ian would order pizzas on the weekend. I couldn't be around the smell. I went down to the basement to escape.

At one point, John actually said I was allowed to have a piece of pizza every now and then. I didn't. This was me against me. I wanted to go to the Games and say, *Look what you did—nobody else could say they did that, only you.*

I had to exhaust everything. That's what I felt I had to do to be at my best. It was that zero-regrets mentality.

In the sauna, for instance, with the thermometer rising past 270, it was as if I had put myself in a Crock-Pot. It could sometimes feel as if my skin literally was cooking. But it wasn't. And this was about will. I wanted to conquer myself.

The voice inside my head would go: *This is too damn hot. This does not feel good.* I would answer: *How long can I keep at it?*

I wanted to stay in as long as I could.

As a device, I would count one thousand drips from my nose. When you want to get out of the sauna, even one more second can feel like an eternity. Instead of getting out, though, I would wipe the sweat off my arms, my face, my nose, and shift to a dry spot in the sauna. Then I would start to count. One, two, three, four, five. All the way to one thousand.

I came, too, to another concept: If somebody was outside the sauna door and had a gun, and you knew that if you got out in the next fifteen minutes that gun was going to your head—wouldn't you stay? Even if you were saying to yourself, *I want to get out. I can't be in here anymore. I can't do it.*

I guarantee you, if you were put in that sort of life-and-death situation, you would stay in that damn sauna. You would not get out.

Or this:

Someone says, "I'll give you one hundred million dollars. The only thing is, we're going to watch you twenty-four hours every day. If at the end of three months, six months, whatever—if at the end of it, we think and you think that you have given one hundred ten percent on every one of those days, the one hundred million is yours. Straight up. Cash money. All yours."

Who wouldn't want $100 million? That's easy.

Except: What's the difference between earning $100 million that way and simply giving 100 percent no matter what? Why should money motivate you to do that?

Later at night, while my stomach rumbled, as I lay there in the dark on my bed, I would ask myself, *Did you do everything possible today to be the best you could be*? More often than not, I would say, *No, I didn't do every single thing.*

That didn't defeat me. It made me hungrier—in every sense. This was the pursuit of excellence, of self-empowerment, of self-achievement.

And right or wrong, this is what I felt I needed to go through to feel good about going to the Games.

"Have faith," John said.

And all of a sudden, just as he promised, we turned the corner. My size started to drop for real. "Oh, my God," I'd hear at the rink, "you are getting so lean." My muscles acquired unbelievable definition and striation.

Something else happened, too, that was completely unexpected. I used to say I could never have an eight-pack. When I was seventeen or eighteen, I had a flat stomach, but I was never ripped up. Now I could look down, see not just a six-pack but eight, and say, "Whoa, I can lay bricks with these things." As a man, that is a cool feeling.

In the third segment of John's plan, the idea was to take the strength I had built and convert that to power, through workouts—some moderate, others heavy—that relied on dynamic explosive movements.

On the leg press machine, we did weights that were heavier than anything I had ever done before, and we were doing them explosively. Ultimately, I leg pressed 1,980 pounds. That's just twenty shy of a ton. Pressing 1,980 pounds is like pressing a killer whale or maybe a buffalo.

This was another sign that John's plan was really working. I was smaller and yet stronger—much stronger than I had ever been before.

I needed those kinds of signs for assurance, because I was still doing six to seven hours each day on the ice. Plus, in the first instance to spark and then to maintain the weight loss, I was doing some of the most intense, insane treadmill intervals anyone has ever performed. In all, with John watching every step carefully, I logged 850 to 900 miles on that treadmill.

That total is outrageous. But it only hints at how hard it was.

Again, these treadmill runs were my third or fourth workout of the particular day. These were not casual little jogs. These were long. John would order up, say, a twelve-mile run. They were also speed workouts. Within the twelve miles, I would be ordered to run some number of sprints. The sprints would have to be run at a very specific cadence, to increase my leg speed while making me light on my feet, John figuring these qualities would translate directly to the ice.

John might say, "Let's start this run at level seven for one minute." That meant a pace of seven miles per hour. "We'll follow that with a level ten. Then twelve. Thirteen. Eight. Fourteen. Ten. Fifteen. Eleven." And so on.

Ian would often ride the stationary bike next to the treadmill, both for his own training and for moral support. John was watching and taking notes. I was allowed to listen to music. So through my headphones came the blasts of hip-hop, R&B, reggae, house music, anything to keep me going: Drake, Rihanna, Flo Rida, Collie Buddz, the Black Eyed Peas, The-Dream, Snoop Dogg, Mobb Deep, Usher, Akon, Timbaland, Jason Derulo, Lil Wayne, Johnny Monsoon, Above & Beyond.

These runs would usually last for ninety minutes. After sixty, I would put on a hooded sweatshirt and gloves to sweat some more. I had already cranked up the heat in the basement to 78 degrees.

The first time I had ever done a treadmill session with John, many years before, he said, "Okay, we're going to put the level at twelve and we're going to do it for a minute."

I said, "John, I can't run that hard for a minute straight—that's my sprint pace." After several weeks, twelve got to be easy. So I knew what I was in for, more or less.

Dad had no idea. He and I were speaking once by phone and he asked, "How's training with John?"

I said, "Insane—you have to come see it." So he did, making the first of what came to be regular visits down from Seattle to watch us at work in my basement in Salt Lake. Dad had been through so many World Cup races and world championships, through two Winter Olympics; but he hadn't been through anything like this, and nothing in our experience together had prepared him for how demanding this was. It was killing him, I could tell, to watch me either get eaten alive or make it. I was getting so skinny he could see my ribs, and it seemed to him like my stomach and back were almost touching. John would order me to crank up the treadmill to fifteen or even sixteen, and I would be breathing hard and then harder, and it would seem to Dad that I was near collapse or about to black out.

I couldn't have pushed myself any harder. I was at the point, after all, where I was running on three or four hard-boiled eggs and a couple scoops of oatmeal; I had already burned 6,000 or 7,000 calories on the day and taken in maybe a quarter of that.

Mentally, there were days I felt I would crack. But that was totally necessary. "I can't do it," I would say.

"Yes, you can," John would reply. "Give me more."

"You can do it, Apolo," Ian would say, looking over from the bike. "Believe it. You can do it."

I loved those moments. I lived for them—even though it hurt so bad. It was excruciating. My head felt like it was about to explode. My heart, too. My lungs were burning. It's in those moments that your body says, *Stop.* Your mind says, *Stop, it hurts too much, you can't handle this.* The natural human instinct is to stop. If you don't, if you take it to the farthest extreme, your mind ramps it up: *Hey, if you don't stop, you're going to pass out. Or die.*

But I knew that if my body were truly done, I would just collapse there and then on the treadmill. I had to use my mental game. If what I said to John was, "John, I need to slow it down," inside that made me that much more aggressive, and I could start to attack the treadmill with even more tenacity. I got so passionate I almost got angry at the treadmill. I was not going to let it conquer me.

Same for the weights I was being asked to lift. Those weights didn't conquer me, that treadmill didn't own me. I felt the surge of inner confidence that comes from blood, sweat, and tears. As the Games drew near, there were days when I could truthfully answer yes to the question that came to me in bed, every night. Had I done everything in my power to be the best I could be? Performance, effort, preparation— today was a day, I could say, when I was at my max.

Now, I would say to myself before easing off to sleep, *Let's do it again, tomorrow and beyond, in Vancouver.*

THE ESSENCE OF THE OLYMPIC SPIRIT

There's a sense of purity that we don't see as often anymore, a glimpse into a life that is dedicated, with a central purpose—and that is to love a particular sport and to compete within it.

The Olympic Games were my spark—to come to the Games prepared, to represent my country the best I could. And every single time I have been treated so well by the Olympic Games.
They have given me so much insight. And I have been blessed and lucky enough to be my best.
To go out there and give my all, that's all I ask for. Whether I'm disqualified, or I come first, second, or third, it's not really up to me.
I carry my struggle further.

At an Olympics, we come together on one stage. We come together to compete in fair play and with goodwill.

You see people from countries all over the world, in one place, together—a unity of ethnicities and languages. It's what we look for. It's what we all really want. It's what we want to see.

And it really is cool.

CHAPTER 13

The very first practice we held in Vancouver, about a week before the opening ceremony, went pretty much exactly the way I had envisioned it. It was all I could have hoped for.

The Koreans watched us skate. Afterward, a number of them came up to Simon Cho on our team, who speaks fluent Korean. They said to Simon, "Ohno looks really powerful, and his technique looks better than ever. He looks so lean. Also, he looks really scary—in an intimidating way. What happened?"

Four years before, in Torino, I was the one searching for a secret weapon. This time, I had it. I had wanted the Koreans to prepare for me as if I were the skater they had seen months before in Marquette. Now I was someone totally different.

Two weeks before leaving for Vancouver, just as John had planned it all along, my performance on the ice started to tick.

Dad had managed to come to Salt Lake every three weeks or so. On one of his visits, on two yellow Post-it notes that he put up in the kitchen, he wrote "147" in Japanese, the weight I had told Ian was my target. Dad wrote one of the notes in *kanji*, in characters; he wrote the other in *hiragana*, the set of phonetic symbols that's used to render the language.

Weightwise, John had said at the outset he figured I'd get down to 145, give or take. Before I left for the Games, I was indeed at 145. And I was stronger and faster and had way better endurance than I ever had at 159 or 165. By the end of the Games, I was at 141, with a body fat percentage right around 2.

My skin was clear. My eyes were clear. I felt clean and strong.

The American coaches met with some reporters about a week before the Games. Jimmy said, "I've been with him for seven years, and this is his best and perfect condition. He is very skinny and powerful."

Skinny, powerful, and happy. Even before setting off for the Games, I felt genuinely happy. I was relaxed. I was confident. I was at peace with myself. I felt the most calm I have ever felt before a competition, almost a sense of serenity. I was alive and present in my life, every minute of every day.

I felt powerfully the gift of life itself. The Games started February 10; at the beginning of the month, I had gotten a call from Shani. "Hey," he said, "I've got some really bad news: Justin died last night. A car crash, in Wisconsin." We both were quiet for a long moment, then Shani let out a long sigh and said, "I'm never going to hear his voice on the phone again, or his laugh."

Justin had a crazy, contagious laugh. Now it was gone. Life is not fair. You wonder why—why someone is taken like that, at such a young age, only twenty-seven. There was no sense to it.

Justin Mentell, a former short-tracker who had chased his Hollywood dream and lived it, was passionate about what he did, and I loved that. Now I had the most vivid of reminders: I needed to bring all my passion to the experience of these Olympics.

I felt keenly, too, the honor of representing the United States. At the Salt Lake City airport, I was running a little bit late for my flight; I didn't want to check my skates as baggage—if that bag were to go missing, I was done—and so I walked up to the security line carrying them, only to think, *Uh-oh, am I going to be allowed to carry blades nearly eighteen inches long onto an airplane?*

The TSA people were totally cool. As I walked through security, with my skates, I was applauded and cheered. If that sort of support doesn't move you, something is seriously wrong.

Upon arrival in Vancouver, I marveled at the mysteries of time, of endurance, of will. Here I was, coming full circle, twenty-seven years old, back where the journey had started so many years before. Bryce Holbech, one of the local guys who had seemed so much older when I was the kid from the States making my first impressions in Vancouver, was working for the local organizing committee. Éric Bédard, the Cat, was now coaching the German team. The British, Japanese, Chinese, Polish, Dutch, French coaches—I had skated against each of these guys. Ahn Hyun-Soo was struggling with a knee injury and wasn't even on the Korean team. Steve Bradbury would be working the Vancouver Games from press row, doing color commentary for an Australian broadcaster; Andy Gabel, who had served as president of U.S. Speedskating, was doing color work for NBC.

I was still going.

It didn't matter to me that there might be skeptics. Skeptics came with the territory. *Sports Illustrated* predicted I would win a bronze in the 500, a silver in the 1000, and nothing in the 1500; the magazine also predicted we would come up empty in the relay. But there were those who knew the odds were significantly better than that.

"I say, 'Try to enjoy your Olympics,'" Jimmy also told reporters after that first skate at the Olympic venue, the Pacific Coliseum. "But my goal is four gold for him."

The press was all over the numbers game. In Olympic history, six skaters had won five short-track medals; the other five were retired, among them Gagnon and Li Jiajun. And, of course, Heiden and I were tied with five medals; one more, and I would be tied with Blair.

In all the weeks I was running on that treadmill in Salt Lake City, the Heiden and Blair medal count had never come up. One day, though, pounding away, I said to Ian, there next to me on the stationary bike, "I could medal at every distance at the Games—that's pretty crazy even to think about."

Just as he had done in Salt Lake, John had mapped out, down to the minute, a day-by-day schedule for Vancouver. He was there with me, along with Dad and Ian; a few other friends came and went as the Games went along. We had rented a couple of condominiums outside the Olympic Village, the goal being to share the experience with family and friends. U.S. Speedskating had also rented a house that was within walking distance of the arena; we called it the safe house, and because it was convenient, that's where I slept most of the time. On one of the chalkboards, Fretta wrote a note that harked back over the years, a reminder that it was good to dream big dreams, the way they did before Roger Bannister made history in the mile: "Nobody has run under four minutes. I'm going to be the first man to ever run under four. Try to keep up."

In Vancouver, that was the mentality.

———

OUR VANCOUVER UNIFORMS were blue-on-blue, the arms and legs of the skin suits navy blue around a light-blue top, the top adorned with a small American flag, the *USA* on the back this time in red. The helmet wraps were also blue on blue, dark on light, a departure from the usual black numbers and yellow background. The bandana I grabbed—blue.

I was so skinny the suit sagged on me.

The Vancouver organizers knew a good thing when they had one.

They scheduled the 1500 for the very first full day of the Games, the day after the opening ceremony—which, to comply with Jae Su's order to rest up, I had watched at the condo with Dad, Ian, and John.

The races that Saturday didn't get under way until later in the day. I killed time with an easy jog on the treadmill, just enough to break a sweat. I sat by the window and took in some sun.

At the arena later, Dad and John sat in the stands next to each other for the one-night marathon that is the Olympic 1500: heats, semis, final. They had always gotten along; now they had become exceedingly good friends, each one thoroughly respecting the other. Dad had a notebook and a pen at the ready, as always; John was nervous enough that he kept wrapping and twisting an umbrella wrist loop around his hand.

In the warm-ups, you could hear the shouts from the stands as they saw me under helmet number 256: "Hey, Chunky!"

It was great to be home.

My heat was the fifth of six.

For some reason, my hamstrings were a little sore. Not terrible—just a little sore. John had no idea; I hadn't told him. Plus, before that race, I felt some nerves; that was natural. But I also felt supreme confidence. My technique was solid and smooth, my pushes longer, everything so much more fluid. I was at my peak and rested.

The idea in the heat was just to test everyone's physical capabilities, how strong they were or might be as the night went on, to see what kind of track they wanted to skate. Pieter Gysel, for instance, had carried the flag for Belgium the night before in the opening ceremony. How was he feeling?

With three laps to go, I was in fifth, my hands on my back, just cruising. Time to send a message.

With two laps left, I went to the outside, and then around everyone in front of me, all four guys, and first.

With a full lap to go, I put my hands back behind me and coasted home, nearly a full second ahead of Gysel, who finished second.

Message delivered: I was that fit.

As I waved to the crowd, I felt as if I could do the race all over again, if need be. I was relaxed, in command, in control.

The semifinal was expanded to seven racers instead of the usual six; that meant more bodies and more potential for a problem. The race matched me up with, among others, Charles Hamelin of Canada and Lee Jung-Su of South Korea. Jung-Su had won the 1500 at the Marquette World Cup; I had taken second in that race. Jung-Su weighed all of 132; at least that's what the Koreans said he weighed on the start list. He was all of twenty years old. Charles had gotten fourth in the 1500 in Torino. He had been a monster in the buildup to Vancouver, ranked in the top three in the 500, the 1000, the 1500, and the relay, winner at the Montreal World Cup of the 500 and this distance, the 1500. He liked to skate from the front, and that would get the crowd going, to see a Canadian in the lead; I knew I would have to be very clean with any pass around him.

While Charles could expect the fans to be rocking behind him, he also knew full well—we all did—that he was in an unusual position. History weighed heavily on this race. Canada had played host to the Olympics twice before—the Summer Games in Montreal in 1976, the Winter Games in Calgary in 1988—and in neither of those Olympics did a Canadian win a gold medal. The entire country was giddy with anticipation, waiting to anoint the first-ever Canadian gold medalist. Would it be Charles?

For me, this semifinal wasn't about winning. It was solely about positioning. Top two—that's all that mattered, advancing to the final.

Circling the ice before stepping to the line, I gave it my usual yawn, as much physiological as psychological, mentally gearing up and relaxing at the same time. At the line, I adjusted my gloves, the white one on my right hand, a soft golf glove, on my left the black glove with the gold tips on the fingers—solid gold, the tips that would touch the ice on the tightest turns.

Bang!

Bang! Again, not even a second later.

A false start.

Jung-Su, who had the inside start position, had broken for the corner just a beat too early.

We lined up again.

Bang! A clean start, and, as I expected, Charles made a quick move for the front. After two and a half laps, he was out in front, Jung-Su third; I was sixth. A lap later, Jung-Su surged out to the lead. With nine to go, I moved up to third, behind Charles. Jung-Su was setting a fast pace; I felt it. Plus, with seven skaters in the race, with only two qualifying, it didn't pay to stay back for too long. For the next several laps, Charles and Jung-Su jostled for position. I drafted just behind, hands back, not just looking but feeling calm. This was just as I had seen it beforehand.

With a lap and a half to go, I tried to go outside. No room.

On the turn into the bell lap, Charles went just a bit too wide. I slid inside. As Jung-Su and I rounded the far turn, we nudged each other; a step or two later, he put his hands up in an echo of the gesture I had made in Salt Lake. One big difference: I hadn't blocked him, or anyone, and he had to know that. I was already by Jung-Su, if ever so slightly, when we made contact; besides, the contact was slight.

The theatrics were obviously merely a ploy to try to get me taken out. In a peculiar way, it was a mark of respect.

Jung-Su went back into the lead down the backstretch. He flashed across the line first, me second, Charles third. I pumped my fist as I crossed; I knew I was going to be in the final. There wouldn't be any disqualification.

Charles knew it, too—knew he was not destined to become Canada's first gold medalist. Both his hands rested on his knees as we bled off the speed of the final laps, his body language spelling out disappointment.

A moment or two later came the official word. Jung-Su and I were through. The times came up, too, showing that Jung-Su had set an Olympic record, 2:10.949. He was fast, no doubt about it.

A little bit later, we lined up for the final. Jung-Su had confidence; I could feel it in his energy.

Two other Koreans had made the final: Lee Ho-Suk, who had won three medals in Torino—gold in the relay and silver in both the 1000 and this race—and Sung Si-Bak, who for the past couple of seasons had been steady in the 1500.

J.R. was in the final, too. To his enormous credit, he had made it all the way back from the horrible accident at the Trials in Marquette.

Gysel, the Belgian, didn't have enough; he had faded to fourth in his semifinal.

One Canadian had made the final after all, Olivier Jean. And Liang Wenhao of China.

Again, seven bodies in the race. And this race was stacked. Any one of the Koreans could win. Olivier could win. Me. J.R.

Probably not the Chinese guy.

"Good luck," I said to J.R.

Clearly, the Koreans were going to skate the way they had been taught. I knew it, they knew it, everyone knew it. Were they going to be called for anything against the rules? No way. I knew it, they knew it, everyone knew it.

We got a clean start. Instead of dropping way back, I moved up early toward the front. Better there than behind a wall of Koreans.

The Koreans, as I knew they would, responded. Three and a half in, with Olivier in front, Si-Bak sat second, Jung-Su third. I skated by on the inside, back to the lead. Nine to go. Then again with six and a half to go. With five to go, still in the lead, I snuck a look back, over my right shoulder. Jung-Su was second, Si-Bak third, J.R. fourth.

Jimmy and I had talked about it before the race. "Be careful of Si-Bak," he said. "Si-Bak might grab at you."

With four to go, Jung-Su set up a pass on the outside. No problem if he wanted the lead, I figured. I could draft off him.

Except that he bumped me going around the far turn. Both of us put our hands down for balance.

That opened up a lane on the inside for Si-Bak. He sped to the front. I was still second.

Two to go: Si-Bak in front, me just behind, the other two Koreans— Jung-Su and Ho-Suk—over my right shoulder, on the outside.

I swung wide, then cut back to the inside to pass. The setup was perfect. The race was mine. I could see it. I was going to flash by Si-Bak, and this would be all but over. At that point, no one would catch me.

Just one thing: Jimmy's prediction.

As I moved to go by him, Si-Bak totally wrapped his arm around my leg and my arm. I had to put down my left hand to stay up. I lost my speed. Jung-Su sailed past.

Now there was only one lap to go, not much time left to make a move. Worse, I was fighting the laws of physics, trying to recover the speed I had lost. Jung-Su was in the lead, Si-Bak second. I was third.

Not for long.

On the far turn, Ho-Suk came around the outside. Now I was fourth, with a wall of Koreans in my way.

Heading into the final turn, Jung-Su was lined up for the win, Si-Bak the silver.

Ho-Suk had another idea. He moved up on the inside and tried to cut the corner.

Bad idea—a move of pure desperation.

Ho-Suk couldn't hold his edge.

He slid out and took Si-Bak with him. Down they both went, crashing out of the race and into the pads.

The mayhem was behind Jung-Su. He crossed the line first, clapped his hands, and let out a yell. With the other two Koreans out, I instantly had a clear path to the finish, with J.R. a body length behind. We crossed second and third. Incredible, but no. This was my sport. It wasn't over until it was over, and even then it might not be over.

Would there be a disqualification?

Someone threw me an American flag; J.R. came over, and we slapped hands in congratulations. The crowd was deafening. J.R. was ecstatic, clapping his hands in joy while he skated around and around. A few months before, he had been lying on the ice in his own blood; now he was an Olympic medalist. I picked him up in a bear hug and lifted him off the ice.

"Whoo!" That was me screaming with joy, waving the flag.

It took a long few moments while the race was reviewed. Now they posted the results: Jung-Su, me, J.R.

Jung-Su was not going to be disqualified.

But Ho-Suk was.

I kept staring at the scoreboard, making sure I was still in second.

There it was—I was still in second.

Afterward, it was hard to find just the right words. I was thrilled for the sixth medal, and both Heiden and Blair couldn't have been more gracious. She said, "It's wonderful for the sport, it's wonderful for speed skating."

I was also thrilled that the silver had made me the winningest short-tracker in Olympic history. But that's not why I was out there racing. I was out there way, way more because of my love for my sport. I was out there because I wanted to make my country proud and to compete hard. My goal had been to walk away from every race in Vancouver—win, lose, or draw—with no regrets. After this 1500, I had no regrets.

And after this 1500, it was clear I had my mojo back. Three more races to go.

IN A NEWS conference after the 1500, Jung-Su said I was "too aggressive." He told a Korean news agency, "Ohno didn't deserve to stand on the same medal platform as me. I was so enraged that it was hard for me to contain myself during the victory ceremony."

Just like that, it was déjà vu all over again.

In Korea, I was back to being the athlete they loved to hate the most. I shrugged it off. I couldn't control any of that, so there was no point thinking about it. "Nothing new—same ol' obstacles and challenges—I live for this!!!" I posted at one point to my Twitter feed.

At the condo, we weren't dwelling for even one second on what might be going on in Korea. Neither, though, were we engaging in wild celebrations of the silver. John had a schedule; the schedule didn't call for parties or celebrations.

John had mapped out whether I had ice time in the mornings, was doing weights, was due for a run, had afternoon ice time, and, naturally, when I had to be at the arena to race. He was indisputably precise. The 1000 heats, for instance, were due to begin at 5:27 in the afternoon on the coming Wednesday, it said on the master schedule.

I followed John's rules. I ate John's food. Every single thing I had in Salt Lake City in terms of food was identical in Vancouver. Some of the ingredients we had shipped beforehand, from Salt Lake to Seattle, to Dad, who then drove them up; the rest we bought at the local outpost of Whole Foods. We wanted to leave nothing to chance. How to maximize possibilities? Let's just duplicate here what worked in Salt Lake.

I didn't watch much of the rest of the Olympics on television, though I knew the American team was getting on a roll. If I was watching TV, it was maybe Anthony Bourdain's cooking show. I love the Travel Channel. I would watch the news and check the stock market.

I needed to keep my mind free and clear until it was time to really turn it on.

Which, according to John's schedule, was that next Saturday; we had moved through the 1000 heats and the relay semifinals that Wednesday pretty easily.

That Saturday, as I did on every race day, I got to the arena two hours before the on-ice warm-ups, iPod sound in my ears. On race days, I don't want music with words. Just beat and rhythm. I got my stuff settled and laid out, found a calm spot, and relaxed. An hour before getting on the ice, I got dressed and started the process of getting loose. On-ice warmups last for fifteen minutes. I used the time mostly to feel the temperature, the hardness, and the texture of the ice itself. Then the final stage in the routine: I sharpened and polished my blades. After that—it was go-time.

Stepping out onto the ice is always extraordinary, especially so at an Olympics: I feel the heat from the lights. I sense the body heat around me. I hear the buzz of the crowd. That buzz is a pretty incredible feeling—to know that most of these people genuinely want you to do well. Internally, I'm just smiling. It all makes me want to dig deeper, gives me more desire to do better, to deliver results.

In the 1000 quarterfinals, Charles Hamelin and I were back together, along with Tyson Heung of Germany and Nicolas Bean of Italy. As usual, Charles raced from the front. Tyson hung with him until the gun lap, when I blew by him on the outside, then settled into second and let Charles take it home.

The semifinal, we both knew, would be a lot tougher.

As it happened, Charles and I got each other again in the semi, along with Si-Bak and Han Jialiang of China. Again, two would advance. This race is perhaps—perhaps—where I peaked physically at the Vancouver Olympics. Everybody has a unique rhythm they beat to; it's called your set point. The reason John had put me through the treadmill runs at such a high cadence was to change mine. The proof was this kind of race.

Charles was the world record holder at the distance. Si-Bak had won a World Cup 1000. We stepped to the line. We dug in.

Bang!

Bang!

Si-Bak false-started.

Back to the line. Now it was abundantly clear that Charles would go hard from the start. Si-Bak couldn't afford another false start; that would bring him a disqualification.

I yawned as we were ordered again to the start.

Bang! And off Charles went. I drifted to the back and let the first few laps play out, not wanting to risk any contact; after all, Si-Bak was in the race.

With seven laps to go, Si-Bak skated in front of Jialiang; that took Jialiang out of his rhythm, and he dropped back.

With just one lap to go, I made my move. I attacked, ferociously. Charles and Si-Bak, just ahead, had the inside line. I went way, way wide, cut in on the backside of the far turn, and passed them both, then dug hard for the turn and the line.

I crossed first, Charles second, ahead of Si-Bak by six-thousandths of a second. Si-Bak was out.

I pumped my fist as I crossed and tried to suppress a smile. I wasn't even breathing hard.

In the stands, Dad, John, and Ian were jumping up and down and hugging each other. Four years before in Torino, I had hesitated. There was no hesitation here. I saw my chance; I went for it; I gave it my all.

Maybe I would win a medal in the final; maybe I wouldn't. It mattered and it didn't. Every single coach who had witnessed that move, who had seen that race, came up to me afterward and said, "You are the absolute best skater in the world. Hands down, you are the best."

Later, Dad said to me, "You showed such confidence."

John said, quietly, "Way to show your stuff."

———————

BONNIE BLAIR WAS in the audience that night.

The stands were dotted with red, white, and blue signs that read, "USA 4 AAO," and "Oh No." The atmosphere in the arena, the energy as we came to the line, the crowd hushing, was fantastic.

Five skaters. Three medals.

Two Koreans, Jung-Su and Ho-Suk. Two Canadians, the brothers, Charles and François Hamelin. Me.

François—we all call him Frank—had been advanced to the finals after J.R. had been disqualified for causing Frank to crash in their heat.

On the ice, I could literally feel the others' energy. The Koreans were in this together. So were the Canadians; if need be, the Canadians would sacrifice Frank for Charles. Charles's girlfriend, Marianne St-Gelais, was in the stands, rooting him on. She had already won silver in the women's 500.

It was all good. I didn't think Charles could win. That is, he could—it was a possibility. But I had shown in both the 1500 and the rounds of the 1000 where things stood.

Ho-Suk was starving, hungry to win. You knew from the 1500 that he would do anything.

Jung-Su radiated confidence. He had already won one gold medal.

I drew the inside start position. I yawned, a series of yawns, one after another; I felt clear and focused, calm and strong.

A deep breath as the official announced, "Go to the start." Into the crouch as he said, "Ready."

Bang—a clean start, and we were off, Charles breaking to the front, just as I had figured he would, Frank right behind him, just as I had figured as well. I settled into third.

Charles and Frank went out hard. The pace was legitimate, the lap times right around 9 seconds. Even so, I felt completely in control of the race, sitting there in third, sandwiched between the Canadians and the Koreans, Ho-Suk fourth, Jung-Su fifth.

With four laps to go, I moved up on the inside on the backstretch, into second, picking off Frank and setting up to move by Charles.

The race was mine.

And then, in the blink of an instant, it wasn't.

Coming around the turn, I slipped.

The slip threw me off my rhythm, disrupted my timing. Both Koreans passed by. As we swung into the next turn, with less than three to go, I was dead last.

Really, I should have fallen. All my weight was on my left leg, and I was leaning over the ice at a crazy, crazy angle. If I had gone down, I probably would have taken out both Koreans.

For a lot of reasons, I was very lucky just to have kept my balance.

For sure, in these situations you don't have time to articulate what it is you're thinking. But you know you're thinking it, even if the words themselves have to wait until later.

I had a choice:

I could give up.

Or I could crank it up.

After passing me, the Koreans took aim on the Canadians.

With a lap and a half to go, Ho-Suk and then Jung-Su went by both brothers.

Jung-Su then set up wide to swing inside Ho-Suk on the backstretch; Jung-Su rocketed by. Jung-Su was going to get his second gold.

The race, for me, was now for third.

First, I had to get by Frank.

Then, with a half lap to go, Charles.

Charles had to know I was coming. Again.

I got him on the final turn, with an outside pass.

The television cameras were right on me as I unlaced my skates backstage. I said, "It was a good race. Just one little mistake—I slipped. That's how crazy this sport is—one mistake."

It wasn't until a lot later, when I could watch a replay of the race in slo-mo, that I could see why I slipped. Frank, who'd had his right hand on my hip, had given me a shove. I hadn't slipped because of anything I had done. I'd gotten a little push.

When this sort of thing happens in a final, there's no recourse. There's nothing to do about it. It happened, it was over, and I had rallied to finish third.

The seventh medal made for history, followed by the awkwardness of being asked afterward if I considered myself the greatest American Winter Olympic athlete of all time. "That's a hard question," I said. "How do I answer that? I don't put labels on myself. My goal was to come and put my heart and soul into the Olympic Games, and I've done that."

More awkwardness: "Apolo, can you try to find the right words to describe how you feel at this moment?" "I really can't, especially in a sport as crazy as this," I said, adding a moment later, "I have been blessed."

Bradbury, up in the TV booth, said of the seventh medal, "I think it arguably places him as the greatest short-track athlete in history."

Bonnie issued an incredibly gracious statement that said she was "very happy" for me. She said, "It's a great feat for him, U.S. Speedskating, and the United States of America. We hope that more kids will see his accomplishments and want to try our great sport that has been so good to us and taught us so much about what it takes to be successful in life."

On the podium, I put my arm around Jung-Su as we posed for photos. And Ho-Suk tried to calm the waters. He said, "I wouldn't say that anything that happened in 2002 still mattered today. That was then and this is now. That's not any reason for us to defeat Apolo. We will focus on the present and try to beat Apolo."

I didn't win gold in the 1000 in Vancouver. I won bronze. For anyone who might doubt that third could feel great, this race was proof. This was one of my best races, ever. When all seemed lost, I thought, *No, that is not going to happen. I am in this all the way to the end. I am going to fight.*

Those who knew, knew.

Marc Gagnon was so moved watching what had gone down, he sent me an email with this subject line: "WOWWWWWWW." The email went on to say:

That is the only word I can think of. Apolo, I know you probably wanted to win that 1000m, but I have to admit that I have admired some skaters in the past, including you, but in that 1000m, it was the first time I was impressed by a skater. People just keep talking to me about how disappointing it was for our guys, and the only answer I had was, yeah, but have you seen Apolo??? WOW. After almost going down, and I know how painful to a leg it can be to go that low and work to keep yourself on your skate, be sent back in 5th, and then come back like that . . . it was incredible. 1 more lap and you had the Korean too. I had to write 'cause I can't think of anything else right now. I have been really, really impressed.

And now, enjoy a really well-deserved title of being the greatest skater ever, and surpassing Bonnie Blair. And you are not done. Who knows what will happen in the 500 and the relay.

Keep it up man . . .

To get that kind of note from an athlete I had always respected—wow, indeed.

Later, John delivered his verdict. "All things considered," he said, "that was maybe your best race."

————

THE NIGHT AFTER the 1000, Bob Costas asked me on the air, straight out: "It would be nice to end with a gold, wouldn't it?"

I paused for just a moment, then said, "It would be very nice. I'm not going to lie. I'm here because I want to win. I'm here because I love competing. We have two of the most crazy races left in short-track. One, the 500-meter, is a pure sprint. The other is the 5000-meter, four-man relay; there are going to be five teams in that relay final.

"I'm excited. It's going to be fun."

It was fun.

It was fun because America was tuned in to short-track speed skating, and that was great for all of us on the team. The NBC email in-boxes were flooded with inquiries, many of which had to do with the same thing: "Why is Apolo yawning so much before he races?"

I wasn't tired. I was getting plenty of sleep, I kept saying. Everything was good all around. There was even a sauna at the safe house—although it wasn't hot enough.

Yawning relaxes me. Do you watch Discovery, the Nature Channel? That yawning is what lions do. I like that. I want to be a lion.

It was fun, too, because every day at the Olympic Games felt like a celebration. When I won a medal, it felt like we were all winning collectively—all Americans. It wasn't just for me; it was for everyone. That made it feel incredibly special.

The full circle I had envisioned when I was deciding whether to keep going through Vancouver had seemingly come to fruition. Every day I woke up knowing I had made the right decision; every day, I hoped I was motivating others to find the passion in their lives.

Between races, I had time to reflect, quiet time. John made sure of it.

The master schedule said I was due back at Pacific Coliseum for the 500 heats on the second Wednesday of the Games, and those heats would again begin at 5:27 in the afternoon.

I had told Costas the 500 was crazy; the first seconds of my heat proved it. Two seconds after the gun went off to start the race, Aidar Bekzhanov of Kazakhstan, starting from the inside lane, fell forward onto the ice. He was just seventeen and had the bad luck to execute a classic belly flop.

I had been put on the outside in this heat, the number four hole. I barely got by Aidar. It was now a three-man race, and I was third.

I didn't have any doubt that I would qualify—two went through—but there had been a rules change. Times now mattered. The faster you went in the heat, the better start position you got in the quarter, and so on; the fastest guy from the various semifinal races would get the inside lane in the final.

I finished first in the heat, Olivier Jean of Canada second.

"Well . . . another epic day in this journey," I posted later that night on Twitter. "Glad to be able 2 share it with all of you. Without struggle—there is no satisfaction."

The 500 quarterfinals, semis, and final were all scheduled for Friday, two days later, along with the relay final. That Thursday, I felt particularly reflective. If these were my last Olympics, I was truly nearing the end. "Was my last training in these Olympics," my Twitter feed read. "1 more day! Yes!!!! I'm in the zone. Call me Mr. 25/8."

I added later, "For those who don't know: 25/8 = pushing forward—25 hours a day, 8 days a week. This is not the end, rather, another chapter. I love it!"

On Friday afternoon, before leaving the safe house for the walk over to Pacific Coliseum, I filed one more Twitter post: "It's time. Heart of a lion. I will give my all—heart, mind & spirit today. This is what it's about! All the way until the end! No regrets."

My heat time had given me the inside start position in the quarterfinal. Jon Eley of Britain was in the race, along with Tyson Heung of Germany and Thibaut Fauconnet of France.

The 500 is crazy.

On the second lap, Thibaut went down, taking Tyson with him. I had to execute a balletlike pirouette to stay clear. Thank you for the dance lessons, Julianne!

Jon and I were the only ones upright. So no question we were going on to the semifinal. But because of the mayhem, our times were slow. So apparently, that's how it was going to be. It was going to be a struggle making every single round.

Struggle was okay with me.

In the semi, I lined up on the outside. To my left were two of the Koreans, Ho-Suk and Kwak Yoon-Gy; Yoon-Gy had been the silver medalist in the 500 and the 1000 at the 2009 worlds. Between them was François-Louis Tremblay. Flou, second behind me in the 500 in Torino, had set an Olympic record in the 500 in his heat here in Vancouver; that had lasted until the quarters, when Charles had gone even faster.

Charles and Si-Bak were in the other semi.

I had enough to deal with in mine. The field was stacked.

The 500 is crazy.

I got a good start—enough to get me to third into the first turn, behind Flou and Ho-Suk. We stayed that way until the next-to-last lap. Coming out of the far turn, Ho-Suk tripped on his own skates or lost his concentration—or something. He rose up out of the skating position, jerked to his left, made like a scarecrow, hovered on his left skate, got turned around backward in a squat—and then fell down, a sprawling mess on the inside of the track.

The entire sequence took all of about a second. It played out immediately in front of me.

You never know when in a race a crash might happen. Part of the response has to be to trust your instinct. But if you've visualized the race beforehand, thought about how to handle surprises, calculated different scenarios, it makes handling them that much more doable.

I leaned to the outside and zipped by as Ho-Suk tumbled, his skates pointing up and out, toward Yoon-Gy and me.

Ho-Suk's momentum carried him halfway down the ice. He slammed into the pads as the three of us ripped into the turn, Flou in front, me just behind, Yoon-Gy in third.

On the last lap, I passed Flou on the backstretch, on the inside. It was easy; to my surprise, Flou seemed somewhat gassed.

I looked up into the stands and smiled. Dad was sitting between John and Ian; John was smacking Dad in the shoulder with delight and hugging him, and Ian was fist pumping like crazy.

Four for four: I had made every Olympic final at these Games. Four years after Torino, I was getting another chance at gold in the 500. A dozen or so years after learning to skate, here I was, back in Vancouver, in an Olympic final, my last individual race of the 2010 Games. Talk about your full circle.

To put it another way, the stars surely seemed aligned.

But, you know, the 500 is crazy.

We lined up for the final about twenty minutes after my semi. The dynamic of the race made for all kinds of subplots. Charles had earned the inside start position. Si-Bak was in the number two hole. I was third, Flou on the outside. The Canadian men had yet to earn even one medal in Vancouver. The 2010 World Cup standings showed that Charles was number one in the world in the 500, Flou second. Si-Bak was third. Me—I was ranked ninth.

The other three guys typically got great starts in the 500.

Including mine, the last three golds in the Olympic 500 had been won by the guy starting in lane one. Nothing to do about any of that now. I was in the race. Lane three it was.

And at the first turn, I was fourth, behind Charles, Si-Bak, and Flou.

We stayed that way as we came across the line a first time, a second, a third. Two laps to go, and I was still fourth.

On the backstretch of that next-to-last lap, Si-Bak passed Charles on the inside.

We crossed the line for the final lap: Si-Bak, Charles, Flou, me. The noise in the building was insane.

On the very last turn, I made my move, on the inside.

The next thing I knew, Flou was going down, Si-Bak was going down, Charles was stumbling, trying to keep his balance—shades of the 1000 in Salt Lake.

Charles and I crossed the line, Charles just ahead of me, twisted almost—but not quite—backward.

Charles was the winner, no question. Was I going to win silver—or did the referees have something else in mind?

No question I had put my hand out on that last pass. No question I had run up on Flou, and my hand had touched his hip. But I hadn't pushed him; my hand was up to protect myself. Flou had just slipped; he had put his left hand down and lost his balance. Si-Bak had gone down all by himself, his left hand catching Charles's right skate; that's why Charles was left stumbling.

Was putting my hand out enough to earn a disqualification?

If Flou hadn't gone down, would it be different?

What else might be in play? Of course, we were in Canada. The head referee, a good ref, Mike Verreault, was Canadian. The Canadians were waiting to win something, anything, in men's short-track. The crowd was in full roar. Did any or all of that matter?

An official walked over to the Korean coaches and said a few words. They started celebrating. Jae Su shook his head in disagreement. Jimmy sighed.

I was disqualified.

Charles was obviously the gold medalist. The refs bumped Si-Bak to second, Flou to third. They had obviously seen something I hadn't.

I disagreed with the call. But I made sure to congratulate all three of the other guys. And I walked off the ice with a smile. You have to be like that. You can't dwell on what happened. You can't live even a moment stewing in bitterness. It's why everyone on my team had helped me prepare the way we had; regardless of what happened in the races, we had won before I ever stepped to the line.

Some things in life are simply out of your control, no matter how much you might think otherwise. Sure, I thought I had an eighth medal. But at that instant in my life, I had done everything possible to prepare, had put myself in position to win, and, most important, was the best I could be. Win, lose, or draw—in the big picture, it didn't matter.

It's short-track. It can be so subjective. I just should have been faster.

Plus, we had a relay left to go.

IF YOU DON'T know the relay, if you were just watching it for the first time, it's easy to look out over the ice and see so many bodies and wonder, *What in the world is going on out there?*

This particular relay would be even more cluttered and confusing, with five teams and twenty skaters instead of four and sixteen: Canada, China, France, Korea, and us, the Americans.

Out there on that ice, we know what's going on. With that many skaters, the ice always gets really, really chewed up, especially by the end of the race. There's a lot of traffic. You can't afford to get caught in the back; positioning is critical.

I always like to say that the relay is a little like an NBA game: you just kind of show up in time for the fourth quarter and see whether it's tied or not. In the relay, you watch the last four laps. That's sometimes all that really matters.

In Torino, we had won bronze in the relay. In Vancouver, though, I was the only one left from that Torino team still racing. In fact, two of the other three guys on the Torino relay—Rusty and Alex Izykowski—were sitting in the stands in the row immediately behind Dad, John, and Ian.

This Vancouver relay team was young—J.R., Travis Jayner, Jordan Malone, and me. Simon Cho had raced in the semi. Our guys had a lot of heart. I believed in our enormous potential. The Koreans and the Canadians would be tough. But as the football saying goes, on any given Sunday, anything can happen. Even on a Friday night in Vancouver.

For most of the race, we found ourselves at or near the back. About halfway through, the French started lagging; we went around several more laps in fourth place. With about a dozen to go, the Canadians, who had been going back and forth at the front with the Chinese, started pushing the pace. The Chinese dropped back to third, leaving the Koreans in second and us still in fourth.

There was something wrong with my right skate. I couldn't lean on the blade the way I wanted. Another equipment issue—now?

With eight laps to go—nearly disaster. We missed an exchange. Somehow we avoided a fall.

Four laps to go, and J.R. narrowed the gap, putting us in striking position. I took over with two laps left, and just after the exchange, I squeezed ahead of the Koreans. Now we were third, behind Canada and China.

On the final turn, one more moment of mayhem. To my right, on the outside, the Chinese skater, Han Jialiang, slipped. On the inside, I was fighting for position, trying to get by Yoon-Gy. The Canadians, Flou pulling anchor duty, crossed first. It was a photo finish for second and third: Yoon-Gy got his right skate across about five-hundredths of a second in front of my left skate.

The Chinese were roughly a tenth of a second behind. Forty-five laps, and that was the difference between a medal and fourth place: just over a tenth of a second.

"Your sport," Costas said to me later, "is insane."

"Insane," I agreed with a big smile. "The most unpredictable sport out there."

I slapped hands and exchanged hugs with J.R., Travis, Jordan, and Simon. I trained with these guys year-round. They poured their heart and soul into this sport, too. I wanted to be able to share a medal with these guys, and we delivered. I waved to the crowd, skated over to the coaches' box, leaned over, and hugged Jimmy, who was ecstatic. I skated over to congratulate the Canadians and the Koreans. I held up all five fingers of my left hand, three on the right. Eight—I had eight Olympic medals.

The relay medal was also the thirty-fourth medal for the United States in Vancouver, tying the all-time U.S. best Winter Games medal performance, set in Salt Lake. The final weekend would bring three more, lifting the U.S. total to a record thirty-seven. All ten of us on the U.S. short-track team went home with a medal—testament to Jae Su, to Jimmy, to Laurent, and to the others who had worked so hard to put us in position to shine.

Before leaving Vancouver, Dad and I were invited to NBC Sports & Olympics chairman Dick Ebersol's office in the broadcasting center.

"I want to show you something," Dick said.

He popped a DVD into the player and sat down between us, Dad to Dick's right, me on his left. On one of the several screens in his office came up one of the features NBC had shot of Dad and me, of the journey we had undertaken.

My father—he lived that journey with me. He felt my pain, lived my struggle. Nobody else was willing to do it. Nobody else had that mind-set.

My father led me to see the way: when you want something badly enough, you've got to be willing to do those things nobody else is willing to do. Body, mind, and soul, you can't hold back, you don't hold back.

My father had risked everything to come to the United States. When he landed, he had some cameras around his neck and an immense faith in the value of hard work. He learned the language; he found his craft and passion; and then, amazingly, he was not just my father but the number one supporter in my life. My father lived dedication and sacrifice.

When I was a little boy, my dad would wonder, were we going to make it?

And now, here we were, in Dick Ebersol's office in Vancouver.

The images flashed across the screen, the first few of me as a boy, then me as a man, of Dad and me together.

Dick said to Dad, "This is what the Games are about."

I looked over at my father. He had tears in his eyes.

CELEBRITY

I always try to sign autographs or pose for photos. If I am doing an appearance, and it's three hours long, I want the first person I meet and the last person I meet to see the same me.

You do get some funny situations, though.

We were jogging in Beverly Hills. A car screeched to a stop in the middle of the street. A guy jumped out. A split second later, the rest of his family jumped out, too. The guy asked, "Can I take a picture?"

The same thing happened in Seattle.

In New York, on Wall Street, I heard somebody yelling, "Apolo!" The yelling was insistent; the guy just would not stop. I thought, *Uh-oh.* It turned out the guy yelling had on a really, really nice suit. He came up to me and said, "You kicked ass." Then he shook my hand and walked away.

EPILOGUE

I have a vision," Dad told the *New York Times* in a story that ran just before the Vancouver opening ceremony. "Apolo will entertain the world with an unbelievable performance. The battle," he said, "is just getting started."

It is, indeed. And even as I look ahead to what's next, I want to make it clear I don't regret any of what has come before. The experiences I have gone through, each and every one of them, have truly shaped me and given me insight into all the many things in life to appreciate. For instance, if it weren't for those struggles when I was younger, those times when I butted heads with my father, I don't think our relationship would be as strong today as it is. Also, growing up in Federal Way, I had a lot of friends whom I had a lot of fun with; though we have gone in many different directions since, those moments helped shape me, too. I accept that. That is the point of this book. Regardless of what has happened in my life, I have no regrets.

I could be leading a very different life. The Apolo Ohno I perhaps seemed destined to be in middle school is far away from who I am today. But as my father helped me see, the important thing is to try to do the right thing at the time. The decisions you make, the actions you take—they accumulate over time, they shape you, they give you direction.

Over the years, I made one decision after another. I learned from my mistakes. I kept on swinging. Now, with the confidence I built early on from having to grow up so fast, with the experience I've gained from my Olympic pursuits and more, I stand ready to tackle any and all challenges. And I will do so with zero regrets.

Before leaving Vancouver, Dad and I and some of the people who have been there both for us and with us along the way got together for a great dinner. "There's no greater satisfaction in the world than knowing you were all you could ever be," I said when it came my turn to talk. "That to me means more than any medal. It has been a life lesson, an ongoing one. I'm learning every day. Luckily, I'm surrounded by wonderful people to teach me about life, you know, what its meanings are—how sports and life are sometimes very related."

So what's next? Many things. Probably not just one thing.

The nutrition industry, getting people to be healthier—that's a passion of mine.

The television and film industries have always been interesting to me.

Reaching out to young people—of course.

Skating? Another Winter Games? Bonnie Blair didn't retire until she was thirty-one. The next Winter Olympics will be in Russia, in a town called Sochi, in 2014, when I will be—thirty-one.

John says he won't believe I'm done until my medals are in a display case and that case is up on the wall. Until then, he says, all bets are off.

The medals are not up in a case.

Jimmy Jang left Vancouver convinced I wasn't done, telling an Associated Press reporter, "If he's not lost his confidence, he will come back. No problem."

I'll make that decision when the time is right. In the meantime, eight is a good number—a great number, a lucky number for me, meaningful to me on so many different levels.

It's the yin and the yang.

It's infinity.

The possibilities are endless.

In pursuit of zero regrets.

ACKNOWLEDGMENTS

Each of us is on a journey. No matter what it is each of us might be reaching for, no matter where each of us might be going, there's an essential truth about that journey—you can't get there by yourself.

Many, many people have helped me see my dreams become real. I would like to pay tribute here to just a few, mindful that I simply can't name everyone and that I so appreciate the support—indeed, the love—everyone has shown to me through the years and along my way.

Maria Kelly has shown me a different approach to life, a philosophical and thoughtful process in which we ask of life what it may bring. Maria has been a strong force in my father's life as well as mine; she would provide advice and ask questions that would require my father to rethink how he was raising me and how to better himself. She is the most intelligent, inspiring, strong woman I have ever met. She has helped me see how to approach life itself outside of sport. Maria gives me the inspiration to reach for what I cannot, to leave no stones unturned in my preparation for life.

John Schaeffer has lived one hundred lives. A man so strong and powerful, he is in many ways a remarkable human being. The epitome of a true optimist, a man who never backs down from the impossible, and who will not give in to fear or to doubt, John has shown me the true possibility inherent in mind over matter. Through him I have learned that creating a physical body so strong requires a mind that is even stronger. His mantra exists in my life in every aspect and for that I am grateful. I would take a bullet for John and he would do the same for me. We are, in a sense, warriors, bound by our pure love of sport and the pursuit of Olympic excellence. John has touched the lives of many and given me the knowledge to do so, to help others through health and nutrition. One life, one world, one chance, your choice . . . winning factor.

Beyond John and Maria, I'd like to acknowledge the special contributions made by, among others: Ted Wells, Jimmy Jang, Jae Su Chun, Brent Hamula, Jack Mortell, Ian Baranski, Shani Davis, and my 2002, 2006, and 2010 Olympic teammates.

And, too: Eric St. Pierre, Mike Fratto, Kim Kirkland, Sherry Von Riesen, Dokmai Nowicki, and my family and friends at the U.S. Olympic Committee and its Colorado Springs training center.

And: Mark Fretta, Giddeon Massie, Doug Jowdy, David Creswell, Pat Maxwell, Pat Wentland, Larry Diagnault, Stephen Gough, Li Yan, Derrick Cambell, Nick Metskas, Chris Schoer, Dr. Lawrence Lavine, Sov Ouk.

And: Alan Abrahamson made this book possible, along with the invaluable help of Judith Curr, Peter Borland, Nick Simonds, Alysha Bullock, Patty Romanowski, Philip Bashe, Jim Thiel, Jeanne Lee, Paul Olsewski, and David Brown. The groundwork was laid by Jan Miller, Lee Kernis, Devon Durand, Peter Carlisle, and Drew Johnson. Thanks to all of you.

And: Alaska Airlines and all my sponsors. Thanks!

Finally, and of course, Dad.